THE AMERICAN SCIENCE
OF POLITICS

THE AMERICAN
SCIENCE OF POLITICS

Its Origins and
Conditions

by

BERNARD CRICK

University of California Press

BERKELEY AND LOS ANGELES

1959

First published in 1959
by University of California Press
Berkeley and Los Angeles
California
Printed in Great Britain
© *copyright 1959 by B. Crick*

PREFACE

THIS BOOK is concerned with the idea of a science of politics as an episode and as a tendency in American political thought and intellectual history. It seeks to explain the special plausibility to American students of politics of the view that politics can be understood (and perhaps practised) by 'the method of the natural sciences'.

Here, then, is a critical history of an idea in a particular country, not of a discipline or profession. I do not pretend to give a history of American political science as a discipline, although because the idea has been, and may still be, the dominant one among the uniquely large body of American political scientists, many of the conditions for the remarkable growth both of the particular idea and of the wider discipline are the same. I am well aware that the hope to create an artificial science of politics upon natural principles is not uniquely or originally American. But nowhere has the idea achieved such power, vitality and great institutional and academic expression as in the United States during the last fifty years.

I should be candid and say that my interest in this topic first arose from a dissatisfaction with what I took to be the traditional methods of English political studies. I was at least sympathetic to the style of thought of the late T. E. Weldon's *Vocabulary of Politics*, except that I had more hopes than he that a scientific theory of politics could replace his scientific scepticism as to the possibility of a political philosophy. So I soon found myself immersed in the works of a school of American writers sometimes known, between the wars, as the 'Chicago School'—those associated first with the late Professor Charles E. Merriam and then with his finest pupil, Professor Harold D. Lasswell.

But in studying their writings I soon found the nature of my problem changing. As 'scientific' I found them in fact more prone to narrow than to explain the field that I had conventionally thought of as 'political'. Of course, a science, they all said, must first perfect its own methods before significant results could be expected. But there were, throughout their works, some strong assertions of political doctrine, seemingly inexplicable according to their own criteria of truth and method. The habitual confidence of their espousal of 'democracy', indeed the mere fact of their congregation in the United

States, began to seem more important to me than their formal claim to be scientific. It was when I tried to discover the quality of this 'Americanness', apparently so different from the autocratic implications of the Enlightenment and the Comtean science of politics in France, that a shift, indeed a turning, began to take place in my own thought—that is to say, in my perception of what problems were important. For the methodology of these books seemed of little help in understanding their own obvious and intense democratic moralism: (the presuppositions outweighed the propositions.)

It was then like waking up on the other side of the mirror to see the whole school more as an expression of American political thought than of science. Their meaning became clear only when studied in the whole context of the American liberal tradition. Thus what I now offer is an interpretation of American political culture that seeks to show why in recent years political theory in the United States has commonly taken the form of belief in a political *science*. Though there have been many reports on the state of American political science in recent years—indeed at times there have seemed more such reports than books about actual politics—yet none of them, to my mind, are satisfactory, since they all consider the study of politics in relation to the idea of science, rarely, if ever, in relation to *the* tradition of American political thought.

I began this study hopefully and have, I trust, always striven to be objective, though certainly not neutral in relation to certain disputes, sometimes taken to be purely 'professional', but which are, in fact, of a much wider significance for American self-understanding, and ultimately involve the character and capacity of American political leadership in relation to the outside world. I know of no technique that can ensure objectivity, though I have discovered in these researches several posthumous ways of creating the appearance of it. Re-reading what I have written, I find that some passages have become not other than polemical. But if they are so, it is because in my study and experience of America I have gained a sense of an American political tradition that I have come to admire deeply—almost to envy—but have found it to be, at the least, somewhat obscured by many of the writers I have studied. When Gunnar Myrdal—surely echoing De Tocqueville?—said that 'America is . . . conservative . . . . But the principles conserved are liberal', he provided a clue both to the appeal and to the paradox of American thought, a paradox that can allow me to say both that the idea of a science of politics has become in our age distinctively American, and also that it is nevertheless a discord to a deeper harmony of American thought, a harmony uniquely difficult to maintain, but when sounded rightly more worthy of repetition than any—as one day I hope to show.

Preface

A final prefatory word, half of apology: a copiousness of quotation is necessary for two reasons. Firstly, because I wish to examine the precise assertions of particular writers. And secondly, because I wish to guard myself in maintaining an unpopular thesis against some scepticism or forgetfulness that some men—who are dear to many American political scientists today as their early teachers and encouragers—said quite what they did say. The proof of the pudding is truly in the eating. But if we then suspect our taste, we will want to know what was in it and how both the cook and the recipe came to be. If I am rude about the cooking of some of my late hosts, it is only because, in the gregariousness of social being, I have eaten better native dishes elsewhere in the United States. I do not even claim to describe all the recipes in the past, still less the many dishes simmering this moment. The character of what I seek to describe was, with some exceptions, well established before the Second World War. And I also avoid what some think to be the special issues that arise in the studies of Public Administration and International Relations.

The present work is—the admission is due—a slightly shortened and revised version of a doctoral dissertation accepted by the University of London in 1956. Of books published since that time I think that there is only real need to mention Heinz Eulau, Samuel J. Eldersveld, Morris Janowitz, editors, *Political Behavior: A Reader in Theory and Research* (Glencoe, Ill., 1956) as a particularly interesting discussion or example of the doctrine whose power and origins I seek to explain; and also Roland Young, editor, *Approaches to the Study of Politics* (Evanston, Ill., 1958), a symposium of unusual variety.

My debts to my American mentors and friends are very great, especially to Professors William Elliott, Carl Friedrich and Louis Hartz of Harvard, and Norman Jacobsen, Peter Odegard and Dwight Waldo of the University of California at Berkeley, where the Division of the Social Sciences of the Rockefeller Foundation enabled me to spend a year writing. These prefatory remarks, as well as the variety of forceful viewpoints held by these gentlemen, make it obvious that none of them can be held responsible for the uses and abuses that I made of their advice. Also my good friends Gordon Lewis, of the University of Puerto Rico, and Melvin Richter, of Hunter College, New York, have both encouraged and restrained me more than they may recognize, but less, I fear, than they might have wished.

BERNARD CRICK

London School of Economics
3rd September 1958

Locke sank into a swoon;
The Garden died;
God took the spinning-jenny
Out of his side.

W. B. YEATS

CONTENTS

PART THREE: CONSEQUENCES

PART FOUR: INCONCLUSIONS

INTRODUCTION

Americans respect technology and science: political scientists envy authority that can be based on experiment, not argument.

HAROLD LASSWELL

THE STUDY OF politics in the United States today is something in size, content and method unique in Western intellectual history. Professor Pendleton Herring has told the American Political Science Association that: 'Political Science as a subject of systematic enquiry started with Aristotle but as a profession it has won its greatest recognition in the United States and within our generation. One fact is clear: no other country in the world has so large, so well trained, so competent a profession dedicated to the teaching and analysis of government. . . .' And he adds: 'This profession is now part of our national strength.' [1] And not merely has the size of 'the profession' grown so much since Aristotle's day,[2] but a distinctively modern belief has come to be shared by many of its members. In a recent and a judicious stocktaking Professor Dwight Waldo wrote:

The most consistent and significant trend in American political science for more than two generations has been toward 'science', and this trend is the one most easily distinguished today. So far as can be discerned its force is not spent, but rather, while always challenged—and divided within itself—it is still growing in momentum and penetration.

By 'science' is meant what are understood by students of politics to be the conceptions and techniques of the physical and biological sciences.[3]

Whether or not the main force of the movement is spent, certainly the idea of a science of politics has dominated the imagination of American students of politics in this century. Thirty years ago we

[1] 'On the Study of Government' (Presidential Address to the American Political Science Association, Sept. 10th, 1953), *American Political Science Review* [hereafter referred to as *APSR*], XLVII (Dec. 1953) 961. Professor Herring is Chairman of the Social Science Research Council.
[2] An idea of the vast size can be gained from the tables in Professor W. A. Robson's *The University Teaching of Political Science* (UNESCO, Paris: 1954), see pp. 147–8. Probably about one-fifth of all students take one or more courses in political science in any one year, in a country where nearly 30 per cent of the population between 18 and 21 are enrolled in some form of Higher Education; and the number of teachers of Political Science is around 5,000.
[3] *Political Science in the United States of America* (UNESCO, Paris: 1956), p. 20.

may find James T. Shotwell writing: 'The only safety for democracy
. . . [is to] apply scientific methods to the management of society as
we have been learning to apply them in the natural world. . . . We
are in the political sciences where the natural sciences were two
hundred years ago.' [1] And the same kind of claim is still being made
today: 'Many of the problems now besetting the world arise from
the fact that physicists and engineers know how to combine theory
and fact more efficiently than do political scientists and political
policymakers.' [2]

There is, of course, a uniqueness to American political science even
apart from its methodology and its political theory of scientific progress. The discipline in general owes both its origins and its unique
size primarily to the idea that there was need in American society for
the direct teaching of the principles and the techniques of *citizenship*.[3] But though some tension is visible between the two commitments, yet we will seek to show that the idea of a science of politics
has actually thriven on the belief that there is a true, clear and
obvious concept of American citizenship that can be thus taught in
schools and universities; certainly the vast majority of American
teachers of politics feel no incongruity between these two activities.[4]

The importance of the 'science of politics school' in American
political science is vividly apparent in the huge UNESCO volume,
Contemporary Political Science.[5] Professor Lasswell has referred to
this mammoth as showing 'the relative uniqueness of American
political science'.[6] While only eleven out of forty-eight contributors
from twenty-two countries were American (a fair, even a modest,
proportion in relation to the relative numbers of teachers), the whole
venture was, however, distinctively American. A discipline is known
by the dilemmas that it keeps. The Editor submitted these questions
to the contributors, questions prepared by Professor William Ebenstein of Princeton:

1. What is now the value of traditional approaches, such as the juridical
historical and philosophical? How far can they still be used in political
science, and in what particular fields most usefully?

---

[1] *Intelligence and Politics* (New York: 1921), pp. 21, 26–7.
[2] William A. Glazer, 'The Types and Uses of Political Theory', *Social Research*
(Autumn 1955), 292.
[3] An illuminating article on this is C. J. Friedrich's 'Political Science in the United
States in Wartime', *APSR*, XLI (Oct. 1947), 978 ff.
[4] Cf. *Goals for Political Science*, Report of the Committee for the Advancement of
Teaching, American Political Science Association (New York: 1951).
[5] . . . A Survey of Methods, Research and Teaching (Paris: 1950).
[6] A passing remark in his contribution to R. Christie and Marie Jahoda (eds.),
Studies in the Scope and Method of 'The Authoritarian Personality' (Chicago: 1954),
p. 212.

2. In what respects has psychology (psychiatry, social psychology and psycho-analysis) influenced the study of the political process?

3. To what extent can the research methods and data supplied by sociology and anthropology be utilized for a more penetrating understanding of political phenomena? This question is based on the assumption—the validity of which bears on theoretical analysis as much as on practical policy—that the key to a political civilization, system or institution lies in the non-political factors which give it life and meaning.

4. What are the specific materials of a scientific study of politics (personal observation; participation in political . . . bodies; diaries and memoirs, etc.)?

5. For what kind of investigation is the quantitative method applicable (public opinion polls, election statistics, etc.)?

6. To what extent is it possible to achieve qualitative measurement . . . ?

7. To what extent has the technique of group research, organized and carried out in common, contributed to the development of political science in your country? . . . the technique of group research is destined to play a more and more important role in the development of the social sciences, and we invite you to comment on the possibility of using it in political science in general, or in the field of study in which you are most interested.[1]

As these somewhat rhetorical questions show, the volume was an attempt to teach the other nations a new technique, immediately of research, ultimately of a more rational form of political administration. The American contributors were not all of one mind; but the Editor clearly spoke for the majority.

The style of thought that we sketch has, of course, a wider habitat than political science alone—indeed we will see that it inclines to a sociological rather than a strictly political viewpoint. Merriam remarked in his UNESCO article on 'Political Science in the United States' that 'it is extremely difficult to separate political science from social science in the U.S.' Indeed, both Merriam and Lasswell have been noted leaders in what is sometimes called the 'social science' view of politics, or the advocacy of a 'unified science of society', an all-embracing science of society, or—a key word—the *integration* of the social sciences.

Related to the concept of 'a unified social science', and often a synonym, is the notion of the 'Behavioural Sciences'.[2] This notion seeks to imply that the social sciences, *qua* sciences—as is often said—

[1] UNESCO, *Contemporary Political Science*, pp. 2–3.

[2] See the reports that have been financed by the Behavioural Sciences Division of the Ford Foundation on the state and the needs of the 'Behavioural Sciences' at five leading universities: *A Report on the Behavioural Sciences at the University of Chicago* (Mimeographed, Chicago University Press: 1954); *The Behavioural Sciences at Harvard* (Cambridge, Mass.: 1954); and mimeographed publications under similar titles from the University of Michigan, Ann Arbor; the University of North Carolina, and Stanford. There is a fascinating review of these by Professor Arthur MacMahon, of Columbia, in the *APSR*, XLIX (Sept. 1955), 857–63.

can only be concerned with observable and measurable behaviour. Professor David Truman writes on 'The Impact on Political Science on the Revolution in the Behavioural Sciences' and says: 'the phrase refers to those bodies of knowledge . . . that provide or aspire to provide "verified principles" of human behaviour through the use of methods similar to those of the natural sciences'—so the viewpoint is essentially the same.[1] Truman pictured traditional political science as narrowly concerned with mere 'institutional description', lacking a scientific approach to the whole 'political process'. 'What was known for a time', he says, 'during the 1920's and 1930's as the "*Chicago School*" of political science, gathered around the stimulating person of the late Charles E. Merriam, represented a fairly explicit revolt against the established tradition.' [2]

The Social Science Research Council in 1951 organized an 'Inter-University Summer Seminar on Political Behaviour' whose published report well illustrates most of the dominant tendencies of American political science. 'Political behaviour research', the seven members reported, requires 'a systematic statement of hypotheses and a rigorous ordering of evidence' so as to allow: (1) 'the effective identification of behavioural uniformities' and their conditions; (2) 'ease of replication and validation in successive researches'; and (3) 'an accretion of systematic knowledge of the institutions upon which attention is fixed'.[3] There was, however, some doubt about the significance of this work, for the committee then wrote: 'These aspirations do not *necessarily* imply that it is possible to reduce all political behaviour to known causal relations and thereby achieve complete predictability and control in the political process.' [4] But, once again, there is a tribute to Merriam: 'The path of political behaviour research was, indeed, staked out by Charles Merriam in his Presidential Address to the American Political Science Association in 1925.[5]

Merriam himself had offered, in 1923, a brief account of the stages in the development of American political science. It has been much quoted as an authority. He distinguished four general periods of development. The first, extending to about 1850, was one in which '*a priori* reasoning' and 'the deductive method' were emphasized. The second, from then until about 1900, was the period of 'the

---

[1] This is published as No. 8 of the Brookings Lectures for 1955, under the general title *Research Frontiers in Politics and Government* (The Brookings Institution, Washington, D.C.: 1955), p. 202.
[2] *Ibid.*, p. 215.
[3] 'Research in Political Behaviour', *APSR*, XLVI (Dec. 1952), 1006.
[4] *Loc. cit.*, my italics, for I am assured by one of the participants that the word 'necessarily' was not in the first draft but was inserted to gain unanimity.
[5] *Ibid.*, pp. 1004–5.

historical and comparative method'. The third period, which began with the Progressive Era in about 1900, was concerned with 'observation, survey and measurements'. And the fourth period, which was just dawning, was characterized, specifically, by the beginnings of the psychological treatment of politics; and, generally, by the attempt to make political science more scientific.[1]

But this account, we will see, is a misleading over-simplification, and its principle of classification hides more than it reveals: for the classification according to methodology is itself the expression of some substantive political beliefs, characteristic of American political thought.

In a sentence: the science of politics assumes a peculiar four-fold relationship between a common notion of *science* as it is found in ordinary American social thought; the idea of a common *citizenship* training; the generalization of the habits of American *democracy*, and, tending to embrace all these, the common belief in an inevitable *progress* or a manifest destiny for American society. It is necessary to begin at the beginning to understand the logic of this relationship and what the terms in it mean.

[1] Merriam, 'Recent Advances in Political Methods', *APSR*, XVII (May 1923), 286, as quoted by *Goals for Political Science, op. cit.*, p. 8; by Marshal Dimock in another UNESCO Report, *The Teaching of the Social Sciences in the United States* (Paris: 1954), p. 56, and Raymond Gettell, *History of American Political Thought* (New York: 1928), p. 616.

PART ONE
Origins

I

THE SCIENCE OF POLITICS IN THE EARLY REPUBLIC

The assembly to which I address myself is too enlightened not to be fully sensible how much a flourishing state of the arts and sciences contributes to national prosperity and reputation. . . . Among the motives to . . . [create a national University] the assimilation of the principles, opinions and manners of our countrymen, by the common education of a portion of our youth from every quarter, well deserves attention.

The more homogeneous our citizens can be made in these particulars, the greater will be our prospect of permanent union; and a primary object of such an institution should be, the education of our youth in the science of government.

WASHINGTON before Congress, December 7th, 1796

In the selection of our Law Professor we must be rigorously attentive to his political principles.

JEFFERSON to Madison, February 17th, 1826

1. Pedagogy or Practice?

RIGHT FROM the founding of the new Republic there were good reasons why the study of politics should grow into a distinct, large and powerful academic discipline, something very different in both content and size from almost anything, then or now, in European education.

In the Ninth Paper of *The Federalist*, Alexander Hamilton had written of a 'science of politics' which had sprung from the precepts of Harrington, Locke and Montesquieu and which could be maintained and extended:

The science of politics, however, like most other sciences, has received vast improvements. The efficacy of the various principles is now understood, which were either not known at all or imperfectly known to the ancients, the regular distribution of power into distinct departments, the introduction of legislative balances and checks; the institution of courts

3

composed of judges holding their offices during good behaviour; the representation of the people in the legislative by deputies of their own election; these are wholly new discoveries, or have made their principal progress towards perfection in modern times.[1]

As early as 1774 John Adams had spoken of 'the divine science of politics', a phrase that he uses several times in his many writings; and Thomas Jefferson in a letter to Thomas Mann Randolph had recommended Montesquieu's *L'Esprit des Lois* to give an understanding of 'the science of government' and had added, in the same context, that 'Locke's little book on Government, is perfect as far as it goes'.[2]

There was a clear case that the learning of these principles, of 'the science of politics', should not be left to chance or private initiative, but should form part of the institutions of the new Republic. George Washington had himself fruitlessly addressed Congress on this very theme, and had even renewed the argument from the grave. In his Will he lamented that young men had to be sent abroad for their education, 'contracting not only habits of dissipation and *extravagance*, but principles unfriendly to Republican government and the true and genuine liberties of mankind'. Therefore, he would leave land and money to found a 'National University', if Congress would agree to match his grant, a university 'to which youth of fortune and talent from all parts . . . might be sent for the completion of their education in all branches of polite literature in arts and science—in acquiring knowledge in the principles of politics and good government'.[3]

In a young Federation of States, where many were fully conscious of how much its tenuous national unity depended upon deliberate political arrangements, it would not have been unexpected to see such a study at once spring forth, like a new Pallas Athene from the brow of Zeus, adult and fully armed. But Congress, through parsimony and indifference, did not act. And the few existing universities remained firmly attached to their traditional curriculum, which, they no doubt felt, had been good enough to educate the men of 1776 and still more so the men of 1787. So the birth of the new goddess was, after all, not so swift, although the circumstances, right from the beginning, were propitious. The narrow curriculum and the low intellectual vitality of the existing universities (rather, 'colleges')

---

[1] *The Federalist* (Modern Library Edition, N.Y.: 1937), p. 48.
[2] Adams, *Works*, ed. C. F. Adams (Boston: 1854), IV, 193, and IX, 339 and 512; and Jefferson, *The Writings of Thomas Jefferson*, ed. A. E. Bergh (Washington, D.C.: 1907), VII, 31.
[3] See Washington Chauncey Ford, *Wills of George Washington and His Immediate Ancestors* (Historical Printing Club, Brooklyn, N.Y.: 1891), pp. 90–1, and Charles Kendall Adams, *Washington and the Higher Education* (Ithaca, N.Y.: 1888).

gave little encouragement to such a new study: America set no example to France in this. While the title of an academic disputation at Harvard in 1788 can show that Washington was not alone in his wish: '*Is it more necessary in a Republic than in any other form of government that young men should be instructed in political science?*', and though the motion was carried, yet, to judge by the curriculum of the next eighty years, the Harvard Board of Overseers were not impressed.[1]

But there is a more profound reason for this initial suspicion, restraint or indifference—a reason that underlies the whole difference between the traditions of the American and of the French Revolutions, as seen in the *immediate concern* of the French leaders to create a system of compulsory patriotic education. For, in America, *political science was felt to exist already in the conduct of her own statesmen*, not in the books of the professors. Indeed, when all excess of praise and disparagement is done, it is hard to deny that the men of the Constitutional Convention at Philadelphia together exhibited a political ability and a practical wisdom unrivalled by any group of statesmen in modern history. Lord Acton's testimony is significant: 'it is in political science only that America occupies the first rank. There are six Americans on a level with the foremost Europeans, with Smith and Turgot, Mill and Humboldt. Five of these were Secretaries of State, and one was Secretary of the Treasury.'[2] For Acton, in bestowing his liberal praise, almost inevitably fell into the early American usage of the shifty phrase 'political science': he clearly did not refer to a literature of treatises and monographs, nor to mere practice unexpressed in literature at all; but rather to a vindicatory literature of speeches and State Papers.

By 'political science' both Acton and Hamilton would be at one in meaning the expressed *maxims* of statecraft as derived from history and experience, not the 'laws of nature' applied to the construction of the 'artificial animal' of Hobbes, Bentham, Comte and then the American social scientists. The short-lived *American Review of History and Politics* of 1811 promised its readers in the 'Prospectus' to the first number: 'Whatever maxims of wisdom applicable to our institutions the best writers either ancient or modern can afford on the science of government, will be industriously sought and quoted.'[3] Indeed, this was also, in essence, political science to Jefferson, at

[1] Quoted by William Coolidge Lane in his *Early Harvard Broadsides*, American Antiquarian Society (Worcester, Mass.: 1914), p. 38. See also Samuel Eliot Morison, *Three Centuries of Harvard* (Cambridge, Mass.: 1936), p. 136.

[2] Lord Acton in a review of Bryce's *American Commonwealth*, see *English Historical Review*, XIV (April 1889), 390.

[3] *American Review of History and Politics* (Philadelphia: 1811). It only survived two volumes until 1812. It called itself a 'general repository of literature and State papers' The maxims of political science were in the State papers.

least in the reflective tranquillity of his retirement. This is clear by the great agreement reached about the nature of the American Revolution in the ever-astonishing correspondence of his last days with the octogenarian, John Adams. Jefferson might flirt in his study with the *Idéologie* of Destutt de Tracy, but in practice his 'science of politics' was, like that of Hamilton and Adams, composed of flexible maxims, not inflexible axioms. Jefferson was the typically American figure of the temperamental and intellectual rationalist tempered by a prudence born of political responsibilities and by a deep respect for the Common Law. A pure science of politics was to him an interesting speculation, but not a practical possibility, however much circumstances in America might seem, superficially, to be favourable. John Adams, in contrast, was the temperamental conservative, but was tempered by the need not merely to 'reform in order to preserve', but actually *to create* in order to preserve. Adams was himself ironically aware of this apparent oddity, as is seen in his account of the time immediately after the Revolution:

> I knew that every one of my friends . . . had at that time no idea of any other government but a contemptible legislature in one assembly, with committees for executive magistrates and judges. . . . I answered [their questions] by sporting off-hand a variety of short sketches of plans which might be adopted by the conventions; and as this subject was brought into view in some way or other almost every day, . . . I had in my head and at my tongue's end as many projects of government as Mr. Burke says the Abbé Sieyes had in his pigeon-holes, not, however, constructed at such length, nor laboured with his metaphysical refinements. I took care, however, always to bear my testimony against every plan of an unbalanced government.[1]

Burke, surely, would have been desperately unhappy to have had to picture himself in even remotely the same circumstances as Sieyes, or, indeed, as Adams. But Adams, the American Whig, kept his nerve and sailed with success closer to the shoals of 'ideology', 'rationalism' or 'mechanism' than the European conservative would think possible.

For in European terms, and in the way that many Americans have continued to think in European categories, there was an inherent tension in such a practical political science. The conservative in America appeared to be like the doctrinaire in Europe, the archcodifier; but equally, the doctrinaire in America sought to conserve a genuine tradition of liberty. Both clung to the hopes for a victory of 'Reason' over tyranny and superstition in France, but both told

---

[1] *Works*, III, 20.

les philosophes to mind their own business when these worthies were disappointed, as was Condorcet, that the American Constitution was not, after all, 'pure reason'.[1] The object of the *Declaration of Independence*, wrote Jefferson in 1825, was 'not to find out new principles, or new arguments, never before thought of . . . ; but to place before mankind the common sense of the subject . . . it was intended to be an expression of the American mind'.[2] But while the 'common sense of the subject' was a summary of the specific practices of the Englishman-in-America, the appeal to 'mankind' gave to American thought an aura of generality as well; inevitably a particular justification, out of 'a decent respect for the opinions of mankind', became seen as a generalization. This is the root of the confusion in American thought between sociology and philosophy. There was the paradox of a successful 'isolation' appearing to be an international advocacy of a particular body of beliefs. Nobody doubted that these beliefs existed and were precise, least of all the European conservative as anti-American. To the Americans these beliefs were 'self-evident', which, at first, was more to say 'taken for granted' than 'axiomatic'. Granted a relative isolation and the possibility of mass immigration, this dual aspect did not involve practical contradictions for either the American or the European liberal. Only much later, when American tradition became revered almost to the degree that a critical history was neglected, and when American nationalism prevented the free immigration of 'the naturally American everywhere', did this paradox involve something like ideological double-identity.

In the early days of the Republic, however, there was such a wide agreement in a common pattern of successful political practice that no challenge arose to create either a doctrinal crystallization of practice, such as Locke had attempted for early Whiggery, or a dialectic denial, such as Marx hurled at European liberalism. When De Tocqueville observed that America was 'the country in the world where philosophy is the least studied', he was a witness, less to *youth* as Jefferson had defensively maintained in his *Notes on Virginia*, than to the remarkable *unity* of belief in social and political ideas. As has often been said, though the consequences of it were rarely appreciated, the area of disagreement in the framing and acceptance of the Federal Constitution was trivial compared to the extent of the agreement. Amid agreement legalism flourishes; only from conflict, or the fear of conflict—of powers or of moralities—does political philosophy emerge. There was felt to be no need for a critical

---

[1] See Zoltan Haraszti's *John Adams and the Prophets of Progress* (Cambridge, Mass.: 1952).
[2] From a letter to Henry Lee of May 8th, 1825, *Writings*, ed. Bergh, XVI, 118.

and speculative activity of political philosophy in the United States: the *Declaration of Independence* had promulgated natural rights for all time and the Federal and State Constitutions had codified positive law, even leaving room for the equitable procedures of the old Common Law. Jurisprudence would be a necessary explicative study, indeed a directly practical study as well; but the direct study of politics, in either the Aristotelian or the modern American sense, was unnecessary. Most American statesmen felt with Edmund Burke that: 'One sure sign of an ill conducted State is the propensity of the people to resort to theories.'

Despite the passionate literary attempts to create a sense of a distinctive American nationalism, the novelty of American ideas was at first nothing more than the novelty of a circumstance in which it seemed possible to preserve all the most liberal elements of Europe while discarding the remnants of Feudalism. Only after the new circumstances of American independence had worked upon the character of European liberalism for several generations did there come a clear national need for an actual teaching of the 'principles of politics', such as Washington had advised. By the third generation of the life of the Republic the circumstances that had given clarity to the 'science of politics' of Hamilton and Adams had so changed, and the attraction of politics for men of ability had become so much less, that there was felt a need to re-create them in the classrooms, in consequence tending to formalize the original principles, rendering them into a written ideology. Sectional strife, western expansion and the beginnings of mass immigration all presented a challenge that made, by the middle of the century, the response of a formal, pedagogic political science seem an obvious thing. But when this response did come, there still remained underlying it such a massive agreement about the nature and aims of American life, that, almost from the beginning, it was conceived as a mere method—a technique for sustaining a pre-existent American liberalism, not as a critical or speculative discipline.

Such a change was bound to come about, so perhaps Washington was more far-sighted than the Congress that neglected to vote funds for the project of his Will. But, equally, it is not hard to see why Congress in the 1800's should have regarded this as an expensive and dispensable luxury.

2. Citizen Literature and the Lockean Unanimity

Thus at first American 'political science' lay enshrined not in the writings of scholars, but in what Bliss Perry once aptly termed, 'citizen literature'. By this he meant patriotic writings and explanations of the *Constitution*. These were, at the most, pragmatic argu-

ments based on differing interpretations of the agreed premises—
and, indeed, De Tocqueville was not wrong, much of the political
education was practical and participatory. There was no American
De Tocqueville, but there was the *Constitution* itself, the *Federalist*
papers, the Farewell Address of Washington, the Virginia and the
Kentucky Resolutions and the decisions of Chief Justice Marshall;
the speeches and public letters of Jefferson and of the Adamses, of
Calhoun, of Clay, of Webster and then of Abraham Lincoln; later
there were the editorials of Garrison, Greeley, and then Godkin,
all in the same tradition. It was a tradition that could not challenge
the measure of the eighteenth-century Enlightenment, nor yet the
music of the German Romantic political philosophers, but it had no
wish or purpose to: sober, commonsense, middleground, accepted
but expanding truths, these were their sound stock in a profitable
and enviable trade. This 'citizen literature' was like the house that
Jefferson spent a lifetime building himself at Monticello; its external
appearance was strict pseudo-classical; but the domestic and internal
arrangements showed an ingeniousness of invention and convenience
that bespoke the blending of the Gentleman with the Frontiersman
to make the new American Commonman.

American political literature seemed in little need of a philosophy.
There was no need even for Benthamite Utilitarianism: for, in
American terms, even Andrew Gallatin and John Quincy Adams
could appear Benthamites already—could appear, when in London,
as natural friends of Bentham, without, when in Washington, involving themselves in either the detail of his thought or the ostracism
of his social position. When Jeremy Bentham described himself to
Andrew Jackson as 'more of a United-States man than an English-
man', he was unwittingly giving a convincing reason why no one in
America should trouble to read him.[1] Before the Civil War, even the
theories and polemics of Ricardo and the English Liberal Economists
appeared as either platitudinous or as irrelevant to American experience. American political literature could be 'citizen literature'
because it was needed only *to mirror* the political thought of more
or less *all* Americans; the European liberal, struggling for ascendency
and not enjoying an exclusive and original dominance, had to provide both polemic and theory.

The models of such citizen literature are to be found in Commonwealth England more than in Revolutionary France, but in America
they grew *to seem* completely timeless and general, even rationalistic,

---

[1] Quoted by Merle Curti, to an opposite effect, in his *The Growth of American
Thought* (New York: 1943), p. 373. Professor Curti regrets that the reception of
Utilitarianism into the United States has never been systematically studied. He ignores
the obvious reason: because there was no marked reception; they were Utilitarians
already.

almost scientific. For the opposition on which the slogans of American liberalism had originally thrived had been left behind, so they had moved from being the dissidence of dissent to becoming the harmony of national purpose. There was little need to study the history of American thought as it was palpably so rational and *had been* transplanted to an unspoilt garden; and there was little need to study how to apply its principles to circumstances, because they were applied already. A 'genteel anarchist like Locke' had said most of what there was to say about the division of political powers and the grounds of human liberties; and the *Constitution* had turned these static assumptions into a living law that was a mirror of the natural law. Locke's *Second Treatise on Civil Government* in England always remained something of a Party pamphlet, or at least subject to partisan interpretation. But in America it was almost a descriptive work of sociology. It was as if Locke had failed to paint an accurate picture of England in 1688, but had instead foretold theoretically the shape of things to come in early America.

The question here is not of the direct or the literary influence of Locke, but rather an assertion that the premises and postulates of Locke were realized to a remarkable degree in the thought and circumstances of the Englishman-in-America—far more so than in the English Constitution of the eighteenth century. There is a deep incoherence or contradiction in Locke concerning whether Parliament or the 'People' was sovereign. This was to recur again and again to bedevil the English Whigs; but it was actually to be a source of strength to American Whiggery, even if, like the Constitution of 1787 itself, it was a strength of compromise between things that in England and Europe would be irreconcilable.[1] If 'all the world was like America' the meaning of Locke's assertion that 'the *community* comes to be Umpire' would be plain. For, in America, the *people* did seem to be both the community and, in so far as there was one, the State: they were Umpire over themselves, they bound *themselves* with the rigid rules of a written Constitution. The great Whig magnates of 1688 who in England may have been Locke's only effective 'Umpires', in America had no counterpart. The awkward confluence in Locke of the cross-currents of community-power, individual natural rights and the Legislative power—this was the very place in the stream where Americans were deliberately resolved to float. There was to be not merely 'division of powers', in several senses, but 'checks and balances' as well. The Constitution itself actually thrived on incoherence and compromise simply because individuals

---

[1] G. H. Guttridge has well shown in his *English Whiggism and the American Revolution* (Berkeley, Cal.: 1942), pp. 10–12 *et passim*, how Locke's doctrines were used by English and American publicists to almost opposite effect.

in fact thought so much alike and were so equal in status that there
was no great crisis of State power against either communal power or
individual rights. Because of this unanimity people were even willing
that some of the most important political questions should be treated
as legal and not legislative questions.

If the War of Independence can properly be called a Revolution at
all, then it is a Lockean sense of Revolution—the community *resum-
ing* its rights—and neither an Aristotelian nor a Marxian. Both
American and Lockean political thought are remarkably free of
thoughts of history, dilemma and crisis; revolution to them is not
an upturning of social strata in the name of an ideology, but is, as it
were, merely the release of a well-proportioned wheel, already built
and free from arbitrary friction, along a flat and straight road; variations of speed will be enjoyed and expected, but not of direction.
Form and principle are not suffered and recreated but are merely,
and happily, reaffirmed.

The American had been given certain final political and social
principles: 'The government of the United States', said Professor
Woodrow Wilson, 'was constructed upon the Whig theory of political
dynamics, which was a sort of unconscious copy of the Newtonian
theory of the Universe. . . . Politics is turned into mechanics under
his touch.' [1] But they were mechanics who thought of a pre-existent
'sweet harmony', more than of a future rebuilding of the machine.
The American might not attempt to give a rational structure to 'a
never ending *wonder* at the starry heavens above and the moral law
within', as did Kant betwixt Newton and Rousseau, but he did accept
them *both*, sometimes stolidly, sometimes eagerly. American 'political science' at this time, like much of American Protestantism and
Unitarianism, was an easy and harmonious blending of faith and
works; it was supremely self-confident, at times even aggressive in
tone, but it was the quality of harmony that was felt as the thing
unique and dominant, not a tension or even an imbalance between
'faith' and 'works' such as might lead, one day, to an affirmation of
one over the other, or even to a deep exploration of the content of both.

The famous second paragraph of the *Declaration of Independence*
had laid down the moral and political conditions for the obedience
of law. So, for a political education, the universities needed only to
study and to teach what the Constitution and the laws actually were,
and, as the actual political harmony threatened to grow less while
the belief in it remained strong, also something about *good citizenship* and the need thereof.

[1] Quoted approvingly by F. S. C. Northrop, *The Meeting of East and West* (New
York: 1947), p. 139, from Wilson, *Constitutional Government in the United States* (New
York: 1908), pp. 54–6.

3. The Teaching There Was

Until after the Civil War political science scarcely existed as a subject in the teaching of American colleges. 'Moral philosophy', usually a compulsory course, would consider something of the moral obligations of man as citizen. But the curriculum was in all cases prescribed and rigid, narrow and school-like. A textbook of Moral Philosophy would be read, the teacher himself drawing heavily upon the *Ethics* and the *Politics* of Aristotle and upon the great Whig publicists and divines, but his students would be kept close to their secondary text. The method of study was all too often a mere catechism from such a text. The whole College curriculum consisted of studies in Latin, Greek, Mathematics, Logic and Moral Philosophy, with only minor local variants from this common and compulsory fare, such as 'Political Economy' in a venturesome few. To judge by the lack of distinguished teachers, by the lack of important original writings and by the types of books in use, these studies kindled neither enthusiasm nor scholarship and had no discernible effect at all on American political thought.

The Elements of Moral Science by President Francis Wayland of Brown (New York: 1835) was one book widely used up until the 1850's. Its sections on Civil Polity contain well-worn homilies and precepts on the relation of liberty to order. It shows no critical technique at all, nor even a compulsion to advance rational evidence— except a quasi-theological proof that the accumulation of property was simply God's reward to especially deserving Christians. William Whewell's *Elements of Morality, including Polity* (London: 1845; New York: 1856), an English textbook, divided the 'general trunk of morality' into five parts: Jurisprudence, Morality of Reason, Morality of Religion, Polity and International Law. This was a more systematic and well grounded book, but was also conventionally didactic; it was a world away from the excitement and achievement of historical and political speculation in Germany of the time, and even from the best minds in England and, in other fields, New England, too. At Harvard, for instance, in 1846, Whewell's book succeeded William Paley's renowned *Principles of Moral and Political Philosophy* (London: 1785; Philadelphia: 1788) as a text for the senior class. It remained in use until 1856, in which year it lapsed into a Freshman text for religious instruction. Another text towards the end of the period, Joseph Haven's *Moral Philosophy: including Theoretical and Practical Ethics* (Boston: 1859) summed up in its prefatory remarks both the aims and the lack of achievement of political studies at this time:

Of the several classes of duties, that class which pertains to the State

12

—or Political Ethics—has received in these pages a fuller description than is usually given in works of this kind; yet not fuller, perhaps, than its relative importance demands. It has seemed to the author that the youth of a free country should be carefully instructed in the first principles of civil government, and in the rights and obligations of the citizen. It is the proper province of Moral Philosophy, which treats of the various duties of life, to do this. Yet, strange as it may seem, no branch of moral science has probably received less attention, in this country, than Political Ethics.[1]

Another negative factor was that Law Faculties were ceasing to be the sustaining ground for traditional political theory. Law Faculties, even then, were increasingly becoming technical professional schools, and they paid less and less attention to that 'Jurisprudence' which, in the great Roman and German manner, can embrace so much of politics. Political science in part arose as a separate discipline to fill this gap in learning left by the decay of Jurisprudence in American Law Schools.[2] By way of contrast, the vitality of Jurisprudence in German universities largely explains why 'political science' there has not found a separate identity, either conceptually or departmentally, until our own generation—and then largely under American influence. Even the Constitutional disputes which led up to the Civil War, and the fact that the United States was enduring as a *Federal* system, did little to stimulate a fundamental study of the relation of Law to political obligation. Once again, the pre-existent unity of American liberalism, what Professor Daniel Boorstin has called 'the givenness' of American experience, came into play. For the American, when faced with apparent grave contradictions of belief or interest in his way of life, has shown a peculiar genius for appealing not to the authority of Jurisprudence or Philosophy—or of trying to reconstruct either, but rather to trusting soberly in a Supreme Court to reach any decision and to declare (by five to four) that there is no real contradiction.

The most determined attempt to carry out the maxim that the study of politics should have a peculiar importance for American life was, as can readily be expected, in Thomas Jefferson's own University of Virginia—the founding of which was one of the three things for which he himself wished to be remembered. One of the eight chairs was to be a Chair of Law and Civil Polity. The filling of

[1] Quoted by Anna Haddow, *Political Science in American Colleges and Universities, 1636–1900* (New York: 1939); the monograph simply lists the names of courses taught and books prescribed.

[2] By 1892 Ernest Wilson Huffert in an article on 'Jurisprudence in American Universities' written for the *Annals of the American Academy of Political and Social Science*, II, laments that 'too much of the teaching in Law Schools is purely empirical and consists in the conning of rules and the framing of formulas'. In particular he notes that American Law Schools provided no courses in Political Theory such as there were at 'Oxford and Cambridge, and at Heidelberg, Leipzig . . .' (pp. 488 ff.).

this proved an unexpected difficulty to the great advocate of liberty, for he sought 'to guard against the dissemination of . . . [Federalist] principles among our youth, and the diffusion of that poison, by a previous prescription of the tests to be followed in their discourses'.[1] Jefferson was too conscientious a proprietor to risk so much expense and work being spoiled by—as another would have said—an 'unregulated liberty'. Joseph Cabell, one of the Board of Visitors, agreed with Jefferson that 'prescription' was necessary for the Professors of Law and Civil Polity and also of Moral Philosophy, because they were 'connected with a science calculated to give tone and direction to the public mind, on the most important subject that can occupy the human understanding'.[2] So we owe to his discussion with James Madison, Joseph Cabell and other Visitors of the University about what texts to prescribe, a remarkably illuminating statement of what were considered by the gentlemen of Virginia in 1825 to be 'the principles of government' and a proper way to teach and to insist upon them. This was the resolution that the Visitors finally approved:

Whereas it is the duty of this Board to the Government under which it lives and especially to that of which this University is the immediate creation, to pay especial attention to the principles of government which shall be inculcated therein, and to provide that none shall be inculcated which are incompatible with those on which the Constitutions of this State and of the United States are genuinely based, in the common opinion; and for this purpose it may be necessary to point out specially where these principles are to be found legitimately developed: Resolved, that it is the opinion of this Board that as to the general principles of liberty and the rights of man, in nature and in society, the doctrines of Locke in his *Essay concerning the true original extent and end of Civil Government*, and of Sidney in his *Discourse on Government* may be considered as those generally approved by our fellow citizens of this, and the United States, and that on the distinctive principles of the government of our State and of those of the United States, the best guides are to be found in (1) the *Declaration of Independence*, as the fundamental act of union of these states, (2) the book known by the title of *The Federalist*, being an authority to which appeal is habitually made by all, and rarely declined or denied by any as evidence of the general opinion of those who framed, and of those who accepted the Constitution of the United States, on questions as to its genuine meaning, (3) the *Resolutions of the General Assembly of Virginia* in 1799 on the subject of the alien and

---

[1] Quoted by N. F. Cabell in his *Early History of the University of Virginia* (Richmond, Va.: 1856), p. 482; see also Herbert B. Adams, *Thomas Jefferson and the University of Virginia*, U.S. Bureau of Education Circular of Information, 1888, No. 1 (Washington, D.C.: Government Printing Office, 1888); Roy J. Honeywell, *The Educational Work of Thomas Jefferson* (Cambridge, Mass.: 1931), p. 973; and Haddow, *Political Science*, pp. 127–9.

[2] Quoted by N. F. Cabell, *ibid.*, pp. 303–4.

sedition laws, which appear to accord with the predominant sense of the people of the United States, (4) the valedictory address of President Washington, as conveying lessons of peculiar value; and that in the branch of the School of Law, which is to treat on the subject of Civil Polity, these shall be used as the text and documents of the school.[1]

In other Faculties, however, the choice of books was left to the Professor. This attempt at Republican prescription was obviously an extremely fit choice of books for American higher citizenship and was a splendid evocation of what Jefferson had called 'the American mind'; but it was none the less flagrant prescription and indoctrination. These writings did indeed well sum up 'the predominant sense of the people'; but the careful references to popular opinion that qualify every assertion of this resolution only underline how little even Jefferson's concept of political studies was an educative or learned discipline in its own right. He wrote to Madison: 'It is in our seminary that that vestal flame [of 'true Whiggism'] is to be kept alive. . . . If we are true and vigilant in our trust, within a dozen or twenty years a majority of our own legislature will be from one school, and many disciples will have carried its doctrines home to their several States, and will have leavened thus the whole mass.' John Adams had good cause to protest that in the Visitors' Resolution Jefferson 'carried his patriotism rather too far . . . he was guilty of narrowing political science to a party platform'.[2]

It is as if the Visitors of the University of Virginia wanted to make sure that the American liberal must forever say 'ditto to Mr. Jefferson'. Those who do say so too unreflectively should ponder this incident well. All this was still, however, the citizenship literature of unanimity: there was as yet no distinctive and systematic American scholarship in politics.

4. The Founding of the Study

From this period one figure of specific importance does emerge, whom Charles Merriam was to call 'the founder of the systematic study of government'—Francis Lieber. He was one of the first among those periodic influxes of scholarly refugees from Germany who were to do much to add to American political studies a strength of critical method and a depth of history.[3] His *Manual of Political*

---

[1] Quoted by Haddow, p. 129, and Honeywell, pp. 121–2.

[2] Jefferson, *Writings*, ed. Bergh, XVI, 156; Adams, quoted by H. B. Adams, *Thomas Jefferson and the University of Virginia*, p. 139. Even Madison had remonstrated with Jefferson that the inclusion of the Virginia Resolutions might brand the University as purely partisan; only at his suggestion did Jefferson then include Washington's Farewell Address as a kind of venerable makeweight. [See *Letters and Other Writings of James Madison*, ed. Gaillard Hunt (New York: 1900–10), III, 481–3.]

[3] He came to America after being expelled from Prussia after a short period of imprisonment in 1827. He taught in the Chair of 'History and Political Economy' at the

Ethics (1839) achieved little repute, but his *Civil Liberty and Self Government* (1853) gained him national recognition and a Chair of 'History and Political Science' at Columbia, renamed from 'History and Political Economy' at his own request. Herbert B. Adams, a generation later, was to sum up Lieber's achievement well:

> These works represent the first real transmission of German political philosophy to the New World through the clarifying experience of English history and American life. This was the first great original production of political science in America. This creation came from the contact of a philosophic German with the historical realities of Anglo-American liberty.[1]

The two books and his many pamphlets and addresses showed Lieber to be a liberal nationalist of the generation of the Diet of Frankfurt, and, more philosophically, a Kantian republican—like Kant always torn between the authority of learned knowledge and a belief that the moral law lay clearest in the breast of the 'common man'. In a sense these qualities were well attuned to his enthusiasm for American life. But his books remain the attempt of an outsider at synthesis; in their formalization of experience they were only acceptable to Americans at a moment of peculiar crisis. For in applying them as principles he makes the traditionalism and 'givenness' of American life something falsely rationalistic. It was all too often the *European* liberal who tried to treat ' "the rights of Englishmen" living in America' as though they were the universalized Rights of Man, whether of Condorcet or of Kant.

Yet Lieber's *Civil Liberty and Self Government* was then easily the most systematic and well grounded study of politics to emerge from an American university. If it reached the same basic conclusions as Jefferson's Syllabus of politics was intended to inculcate, yet it did offer grounds—indeed novel grounds—for propositions whose native grounding was beginning to oscillate only between habit and incantation. He did challenge the accepted 'Social Contract and Natural Rights' theories, trying instead to show the historical reality of liberty and nationalism elevating each other in an evolving organic community. He sounded at times in his patriotic orations during the Civil War like a German-American Mazzini. But the educated public were not overly eager to discriminate between any reasons as long as

College of South Carolina from 1837 to 1857. For twenty years he strove to get North so as to be free to speak out in the 'Great Debate'. Only in 1858 was he given a new Chair of 'Political Science and History' at Columbia. See Frank Freidel, *Francis Lieber: Nineteenth Century Liberal* (Baton Rouge: 1947); Thomas Sergeant Perry, ed., *Life and Letters of Francis Lieber* (Boston: 1882).

[1] H. B. Adams, *The Study of History in American Colleges and Universities*, Bureau of Education, Circular of Information, No. 2 (Government Printing Office, Washington, D.C.: 1887).

the results of the reasonings coincided with a belief in a manifest destiny for a nation of individualists. Also, Lieber was not a man to despise a certain politic ambiguity.[1] His was not a great revivifying or creative effort of political thought, but it was sufficient to establish political studies at Columbia as an autonomous discipline.

As a pupil and protégé of Niebuhr, the German historian, and a correspondent of De Tocqueville, Bunsen and Mittermaier, he led his students 'between German culture and American wants through Anglo-Saxon training'.[2] He liberated both history and politics from being a mere equipage to language, literature, philosophy, theology or law, and justified the status of political science on sound, specifically Aristotelian grounds, arguing that politics is the rational application of historical experience to the moral problems of ordering the priority of differing interests in one ever-changing society.[3]

His Inaugural Address at Columbia revealed more than most such lectures. He bore out its title, *History and Political Science, Necessary Studies in Free Countries*, by arguing that Europe had reached the highest state of freedom and culture ever known in World History, and that the United States was bound for greater heights, predominantly due to a political ability, of which an enlightened liberal nationalism was the most complete form. He sternly warned his audience that the study of politics was no light thing, either physically or morally—it was no mere relaying of accepted common opinion. 'The large field of political science', he said, should aspire always to 'political philosophy':

Man's moral individualism and the sovereign necessity of his living in society . . . lead to the twin ideas of Right and Duty. Political Science dwells upon this most important elementary truth, that the idea of right cannot be philosophically stated without the idea of obligation, nor that of duty without that of right, and it must be shown how calamitous every attempt has proved to separate them.[4]

In keeping with the commitment of philosophy, he argued that the study of politics will kindle in its students a love of it for its own sake. But he ended with the firm qualification (to his audience, surely a reassurance): 'Need I add that the student [having studied political science] . . . will be better prepared for the grave purposes for which this country destines him, and a partner in the great commonwealth

[1] His *Civil Liberty and Self-Government* was perhaps overly high-minded when, in 1853, it could satisfy both Northern and Southern reviewers that he was 'sound' on their major concern.
[2] See H. B. Adams, *The Study of History, loc. cit.*
[3] See Lieber, *The Ancient and the Modern Teacher of Politics*, an Introductory Discourse to a course of lectures on the State (New York: 1860).
[4] Lieber, *History and Political Science, Necessary Studies in Free Countries*, an Inaugural Address delivered . . . [in] 1858 at Columbia College, New York, pp. 42–3.

of self-government. If not, then strike these sciences from your catalogue. . . . NON SCHOLAE SED VITAE, VITAE UTRIQUE' [Seneca].

Political science was not to be stricken from the catalogues: it was to multiply upon them in the coming two generations, even separated from the guiding hand of history, and this for reasons still more in keeping with the closing passage of Lieber's Inaugural Address than with the middle.

II

CITIZENSHIP AND NATIONAL EXPANSION

We ought to teach history in such a way that it can be applied to the immediate needs of our time. The period has hardly arrived for elegant and learned investigation on points of mere scholarly interest.
ANDREW D. WHITE, President of Cornell

The disregard of special fitness, combined with an unwillingness to acknowledge that there can be anything special about any man, which is born of equality, constitutes the great defect of modern democracy.
EDWIN L. GODKIN, *Unforeseen Tendencies of Democracy*

Shakspere was all right in his way, but he didn't know anything about Fifteenth District politics.
ALDERMAN GEORGE WASHINGTON PLUNKETT,
Sachem of the Society of Tammany

1. The Expansive Setting

THERE WAS a rapid and eager expansion of Higher Education in the United States from about the time of the ending of the Civil War. It was part of a national expansion and energy in all fields, not alone in business enterprise. The leading sections of the country came out of the carnage of the Civil War stronger than before, having found their strength and regained their confidence. The Morrill Land Grant Act of 1862 was the Homestead Act of education; its provisions were eagerly made use of in the new post-War atmosphere; from it sprung at least sixty-nine land-grant colleges. The American passion for education was given material capabilities. There was a great generation of German-trained educational leaders, notably Charles W. Eliot, Daniel Coit Gilman and Andrew D. White, to guide this expansion, which was not only of the new State universities but also of new and old private foundations. Colleges and universities were becoming as much the monumental posterity of the Hopkins, the

19

Cornells, the Stanfords, the Vanderbilts and the Rockefellers as the stranded churches and cathedrals of the English countryside were once of the merchants of the Calais Wool Staple. Before the Civil War there had been, by and large, only small colleges, mainly devoted to an education thought fit for Ministers of Religion; after the War, large, multi-purpose, mainly secular, genuine universities emerged. It is important in understanding the subsequent prestige of the social sciences to realize that the secularized American universities first arose in this expansive era, and, right from their birth, for the first time in America created *both* original scholarly research and a growing body of purely professional and vocational schools and studies. This tension between pure and applied knowledge, this ambiguity about their function, was with them right from their founding or expansion. Also, in the State universities, an ultra-democratic assumption about entrance qualifications was often a founding condition. They were to be democratic agencies of social mobility. Even on the founding of Cornell in 1868—a private university—Ezra Cornell himself remarked: 'I would found an institution in which any person can find instruction in any study.'

A dynamic element asserted itself in American political and social thought that kept inflating the possibilities of the original American creed—though the relative proportion of the elements remained the same: there was a sense of expanding frontiers. By this is meant not merely the narrow thesis of Frederick Jackson Turner, expounded when it could no longer apply and largely mistaking cause for effect, but a wider national feeling of almost limitless possibilities, of living all the time in tomorrow in almost every sphere of life. That the 'frontiers of knowledge' about man-in-society would be expanded just as science and technology had expanded man's knowledge and control of the physical universe was a belief soon to be widely heard in pulpit and press as well as from academic chairs. The ground in popular educated sentiment was being laid for a future science of politics and of society, although the educational leaders of roughly the years 1860 to 1910 rightly did not all believe that to have their ears too close to the ground was always a becoming gesture.

The atmosphere of the time was to strengthen those series of marriages in American political thought that were always to seem somewhat incestuous to the European liberal: between an intense individualism and an intense conformism; between a commercial materialism and a religious sense of destiny; between natural law and progress; and between a real egalitarianism and an equally real trust in Capitalism. Whatever the tragedy of the Civil War, the most elementary contrast to Europe led to a great confidence in a shared destiny: 'Have the elder races halted, | Do they droop and end their lesson | Wearied over there beyond the sea? | We take up the task eternal . . .', as the sturdiest of democrats, Walt Whitman, was to sing, himself a symbolic figure in this New World expansiveness. This atmosphere, when given material possibilities, could stimulate the almost prodigal founding and expansion of colleges and universities with a speed and scale unique to the world, almost in pace with industrial expansion. And it could create a sentiment, even in conservative-minded scholars like the brothers Henry and Brooks Adams, that made modern history, social studies and political science achieve a great importance in the new educational order, even though their novelty in methods, for a while, lagged behind their change in importance and scale.

2. Inaugural Purposes

The coming of a higher academic learning to America is usually fittingly dated by the election of Charles W. Eliot, a Unitarian, to be President of Harvard in 1869, and the founding of Johns Hopkins in 1876.

For the third Anniversary Address of the founding of Johns Hopkins—a university intended solely for graduate and higher studies—Andrew D. White, the historian and first President of Cornell, chose a theme in which he himself was exerting great influence, *Education in Political Science*. White was a leading figure in the expansion and secularization of American Higher Education. His own *magnum opus* was, significantly, a *History of the Warfare of Science with Theology*, a stout rationalist and 'Darwinian' tract which, however, was careful to make clear that 'religion' was not necessarily involved in the area of folly and deceit termed 'theology'.

White thought that the systematic teaching of political science should be one of the leading tasks of the new universities. Within twenty years from the end of the Civil War, departments of Political Science, in one form or another, were, indeed, established at Columbia, Michigan, Cornell, Pennsylvania and Yale; and the growth of political science in History departments was marked at Johns Hopkins, Harvard and Princeton. Indeed, at Columbia the 'School of Political Science' under John W. Burgess led the way for all other departments in being the first to offer graduate instruction at all.

White, in his Johns Hopkins Address, broached, then, a typical theme of his day. He spoke of the difficulties of popular democracy as a form of government: while in America there was no lack of 'popular appreciation of close argument', he said, yet there was 'the frequent want among political leaders of adequate training for discussion'. He argued that the United States as a whole would profit by a close study in the colleges and universities of political science and political history: 'Thus alone can the experience of the past be brought to bear upon the needs of the present.' A political education also required, he continued, a comparative and historical study of the various schools of Political Economy, 'not the mere dogmas of this or that school'; it would also broaden out into directly practical consequences: ' . . . of what is generally classed a Social Science, including what pertains to the causes, prevention, alleviation and cure of pauperism, insanity and crime'.[1] And he also advocated a study of International Law:

> While the injunctions of the Father of this country to avoid entangling alliances has sunk deep into the American mind, there can be no doubt that before this nation shall have attained a hundred millions of inhabitants our diplomatic relations with many other countries will require much more serious thought than now. It is not too soon to have this in view.[2]

White meant by 'political science' something still quite close to the usage of Hamilton and, later, Lord Acton; but the applied art, or the statesman's knowledge of maxims, was becoming more formalized. It was becoming, in White's usage, an intellectual discipline, a 'science' not as directly practical as 'social science', but still far more practical, possibly vocational, than natural science or even conventional history. White does not treat of the demands of the discipline and the demands of good citizenship as if they could ever possibly diverge or even require a different type of education or training. His notion of a 'science' calls for a much more methodical exercise of rational intelligence than in the past, but the notion is not limited to a concept of the methodology of the natural sciences. He is closer to the *Sozialwissenschaft* of the German schools, and the 'objective' history of Ranke, than to natural science. To illustrate both the range of the concept's use and yet its general narrowing (or tightening), a famous series that began soon after his Address were the 'Johns Hopkins University Studies in Historical and Political Science'; but also there was White's own *History of the Warfare of Science with Theology*, in which the laws and inventions of science were only instances of a wider scientific spirit that he hoped to see extended more and more to the concerns of man.

At first glance, reading many such Addresses, there is a suspicion that 'good citizenship' is good bait for university benefactors, but that the meal actually devoured was of more solid stuff. When White accepted the Presidency of Cornell in 1868 one of the six departments

---

[1] *Education in Political Science*, an address delivered at the third anniversary of Johns Hopkins, Feb. 22nd, 1879 (Baltimore: 1879), pp. 9 and 16.
[2] *Ibid.*, p. 17.

then became that of 'History, Political and Social Science'. He had written to the trustees:

> In any Republic, and especially in this, the most frequent ambition among young men will be to rise to positions of trust in public service and the committee thinks it well at least *to attempt* to provide a department in view of the wants of these; a department where there should be something more than a mere glance over one or two superseded textbooks —where there should be a large and hearty study and comparison of the views and methods of Guizot, and Mill, and Lieber, and Woolsey, and Bastiat, and Carey, and Mayne, and others.[1]

But there was within White himself a latent tension between learning and direct practicality. While students were few in number and of such high calibre that this 'large and hearty' study could serve both ends, a conflict was not immediately evident. He did not need to make a choice between academic quality and civic quantity. The aim was simply seen as the need for 'the best men' to enter politics. So both the direct application of the studies of political science and history and the notion of a general civic enlightenment by almost any type of education well pursued, were pressed, side by side, without any feeling of incongruity. And, after all, men like White, Eliot and Gilman had a broad and elevated view of politics—the following generation was to call it 'unrealistic'—and a large measure of personal independence. The motives for political science as citizenship education can sometimes inspire trust, but sometimes not.[2]

But the ultra-practical cast of thought raised its head in the closing passage of White's Johns Hopkins Address. He discusses the prospects for this new education:

> First, the tendencies of large numbers of active minded young men favour it. No observing Professor in any College has failed to note the love of young Americans for the study and discussion of political questions. It constantly happens that the students who will shirk ordinary scholastic duties will labour hard to prepare themselves for such a discussion. So strong is this tendency that College authorities have often taken measures to check it. These measures have, to a certain extent, succeeded, yet I cannot but think that it is far better to direct such discussions than to check them. They seem to be a healthy outgrowth of our political life. I would rather send forth one well trained young man, sturdy in the town meeting, patriotic in the caucus—than a hundred of the gorgeous and gifted

---

[1] Quoted by Anna Haddow, *Political Science in American Colleges and Universities* (New York: 1939), p. 190.

[2] See a typical example amidst a vast and repetitive form of literature, J. F. Duncomb, *The Importance of Teaching the Science of Government in a University Supported by the State*, a Commencement Address (University of Iowa: 1885). 'Our University owes its existence to the government. Let her pay the debt by teaching its principles, its history, its purposes, its duties, its privileges and its powers' (p. 10).

young cynics who lounge about clubs, talk about 'Art' and 'Culture' and wonder why the country persists in going to the bad.[1]

Such bread-and-butter Puritanism was never far from the surface in a man like White. But a further paradox arises from the fact that these leaders of the educational expansion took their own graduate study in Germany at the very height of the great era of pure scholarship. They brought back methods, however, of educational reform quite as much as intellectual ideas, expanding them and adapting them to the requirements of American life.

White himself had led this new learned *Wanderung*. As early as 1853, on graduating from Yale, he heard lectures at the Sorbonne and the Collège de France, being especially influenced by the example of Laboulaye as a combination of publicist, historian and politician. He then spent a year at the feet of Ranke in Berlin. Typically, he first accepted a post in the Old Northwest, the Chair of History at Michigan, in 1857. 'He not only instructed,' wrote H. B. Adams of him then, 'but, what was even more important, he inspired. While he remained in the Chair perhaps no study was pursued with so much enthusiasm by the mass of students.'[2] However well trained, how could men become 'patriotic in the caucus' unless they were 'inspired'? His militant secular ethic, reminiscent of T. H. Huxley, must have been vastly impressive, particularly as his doctrine was relatively simple. He could urge both self- and civic-improvement, not by neglecting conventional education, but by following a youth of study with a life of *action*. How should one act? He seemed to argue that participation in politics was the important thing; once the educated man was in the town meeting and the caucus, he would know well enough how to act and would act for the best. A politics of responsibility and a politics of efficiency mingle together.

In 1881 a department of Political Science was opened at the University of Michigan with an Address by Charles Kendall Adams on 'The Relations of Political Science to National Prosperity'.[3] He repeats the arguments of White in favour of teaching political science at all; he ties this to a theme of an expanding national prosperity encouraged by a skilled and expert Civil Service; and he touches on the old Jeffersonian notion of an 'aristocracy of talent':

In nearly every one of the countries of Europe there is found a class, accustomed by tradition to positions of honour and responsibility, and,

[1] White, *Education in Political Science*, p. 19. (The reasoning of this passage is a fascinating example of the half-way house between the old education and the soon-to-come progressive education of Dewey.)

[2] H. B. Adams, *The Study of History, op. cit.*, p. 94.

[3] C. K. Adams, 'The Relations of Political Science to National Prosperity' (Ann Arbor: 1881). C. K. Adams had succeeded White in the Chair of History when White became President of Cornell in 1868.

for this very reason, living under especial inducements to fit themselves for positions of political trust. . . . With us there is no governing class. The son of the lowest has the same political pathway open before him as the son of the highest. The danger is, therefore, that the substantial benefits of a thorough education will be neglected, and that reliance will be based upon the baser arts of political manipulation.[1]

Political stability to Adams was a case of 'let us now educate our masters'. Education was to offer a conscious opposition to corruption in politics, to the general 'degradation of the democratic dogmas': it was an attempt to create a well-educated class of public servants in place of the responsible aristocracy America neither had nor wanted. It was a far from unworthy or uncalled-for idea; but it carried with it the danger of exaggerating its possible results and benefits, and, by this exaggeration, of neglecting the upkeep of the educational base from which this respectable expedition was to sally forth out into the Badlands of the City Halls and the Nominating Conventions. Perhaps the professed practicality of men like White and Adams did not involve the new education in pure vocationalism because of their very political impracticality; or, whatever White said about 'immediate needs', because the curricula they designed covered a high-minded notion of practicality and was concerned more obviously with indirect effects than with immediate needs—certainly when compared to 'citizenship training' today.

But the balance between education and training was not easy to strike. For instance, when the Wharton School of Finance and Economics was founded at the University of Pennsylvania in 1881, courses 'such as every American citizen should pursue in outline at least as preparation for the duties of citizenship' were listed in the catalogue as a mish-mash of Politics, Finance, Accounting and Constitutional History. But there was also a higher level of practicality at the Wharton School. The Juniors were to read Bagehot's *Physics and Politics* as well as Johnson's *History of American Politics*.[2] Bagehot's empiricism, which looked beyond Constitutional fiction into actual function, was a method congenial to American experience —despite his somewhat brash and somewhat ignorant strictures on the divisive effects of Congressional Government. His placing of government in an evolutionary context gave him an added suitability. He deeply influenced one of the first American scholars of great stature who regarded himself as wholly a political scientist, Woodrow Wilson.[3]

[1] *Ibid.*, pp. 11–12.
[2] Haddow, *Political Science in American Colleges, op. cit.*, pp. 186–9.
[3] See Wilson's two published essays on Bagehot: 'A Literary Politician', in *Mere Literature and Other Essays* (New York: 1896), pp. 69–103; and 'A Wit and a Seer', *Atlantic Monthly*, LXXXII (Oct. 1898), pp. 527–40.

Among many writings that seek to establish political science as an independent academic discipline, an article by the young Woodrow Wilson called 'Of the Study of Politics', in the *New Princeton Review* of 1887, stresses the theme of citizenship more subtly than most. Politics, Wilson wrote, was only to be understood by the scholar who was also 'a man of the world', a man of affairs, as were Burke, Mill, De Tocqueville and Bagehot. And he urged that 'students must go beyond the law' and must 'paint government to the life—to make it live again upon the page'. When Wilson sadly quotes Lord Elgin as saying, when he was Governor-General of Canada, that in Washington 'there was no Government to deal with', Wilson is not merely criticizing the diffusion of political authority in Washington, but also the irrelevant horizons and categories of the study of politics, the German theories of the State brought back by scholars and administrators like John W. Burgess. Both factors combined, in Wilson's view, to prevent an answer to Lord Elgin's practical problem of whom to do business with in Washington, of where the heart of political sovereignty lay.

John W. Burgess was the most able scholar among the returning *Herrn Doktoren*. He grew up in a Whig enclave of Tennessee from which he dangerously fled to serve with the Union Army in the Civil War. Like his French contemporaries after 1870, he saw the need for an education that would fortify national unity. After graduating and teaching at Amherst College in Massachusetts, imbibing the strange democratic and Puritan Hegelianism of Julius Seelye, he succeeded Lieber as Professor of 'History, Political Science and International Law' at Columbia. He had left Amherst because his eagerness to establish a seminar in political science had offended the old-time theologians and pedagogues who dominated the College. His description of the old order at Amherst shows well what the new generation felt it was up against:

They regarded the College as a place for discipline, not as a place for research. To them the truth had already been found. It was contained in the Bible and it was the business of the College to give the preliminary training for acquiring and disseminating it. Research implied doubt. It implied that there was, at least, a great deal of truth still to be found, and it was implied that the truth already found was approximative and in continual need of revision and readjustment. . . .

I did not see then, as I do now, that the struggle in this sphere between conservatism and *progress* had already set in. So long as it was confined to a competition between natural science and theology *and before natural science became biological*, an accommodation could be maintained, but when research undertook to account for life and morality, then its hostility to revelation was recognized, and its advance combatted.[1]

[1] *The Reminiscences of an American Scholar* (New York: 1934), p. 152, my italics.

26

As we will see later, Burgess was to appear as anything but an anti-conservative apostle of progress to the political scientists of the so-called 'Progressive Era', during which, after the turn of the century, the second wave of academic expansion took place. He was then seen as methodologically 'conservative', by his narrowly institutional view of political science; and as politically 'reactionary', by his quasi-biological notion of progress as the peculiar destiny of the Anglo-Saxon race. But this is another case of the Progressive historians' reading back subsequent prejudices into a previous era; in his day Burgess was among the leading ranks of the publicists of 'progress', a conservative-liberal perhaps, but in no sense himself a conservative.

Most of the trustees at Columbia became as eager as he, as he wrote to them, 'to prepare young men for the duties of public life'. To prepare himself for this, he first supplemented his German experience by studying for a year in Paris the organization of the new École Libre des Sciences Politiques. The École Libre had a syllabus mainly aimed at the training of a Higher Civil Service as a direct contribution to French reconstruction.[1] It can broadly be said that American Higher Education took from Germany the *method* of instruction by seminar and by an elective system of original lectures, but from France was taken, in Political Science and History, the *object* of a professional training for the Civil Service which was added to the *already existing*, more general, native idea of political studies as citizenship training. Burgess, on his return to Columbia, organized the 'School of Political Science', at first merely a collective name for Graduate and College courses in History, Political Philosophy, Economy, Public Law, Jurisprudence, Sociology and Diplomacy. But it soon became: 'firmly established as the leading Graduate Faculty and School in the University union and as a model for such Faculties and Schools throughout the country'.[2] The intense professionalism of the Law School at Columbia, originally intended to be a centre of legal theory, also acted as a spur in the founding and

[1] The Fifth Volume of the Johns Hopkins University *Studies in Historical and Political Science* published a long study, edited by Andrew D. White, 'European Schools of History and Politics' (Dec. 1887). It reprinted his Johns Hopkins address on 'Education in Political Science' together with reports on 'what we can learn from' each major European country. The longest of these was 'Recent Impressions of the École Libre' by T. K. Worthington. He is most interested in the School's preparation for the Government examinations, but he does note that: 'It should be clearly understood, however, that it is not the purpose of the directors to make the École Libre solely a preparatory school for the civil service. On the contrary, it is their ideal to make the institution a great University of Political Science. . . . There are many courses at the École Libre, which have a purely educational or non-utilitarian value' (p. 66).

[2] Burgess, *Reminiscences*, p. 244; see also Haddow, *op. cit.*, pp. 181–9, and Burgess, 'The Study of Political Science in Columbia University', *International Review*, XII (1882), pp. 346–51.

expansion of the School of Political Science. In 1886 the *Political Science Quarterly* was founded; it carried original research and also news, for the first time, of the 'political science profession'. It announced that the topics discussed would be 'primarily such as are of public interest in the United States', but made clear that the journal 'excludes neither European history, which is the history of our own civilization, nor contemporaneous events in any part of the world which throw light upon the problems and tendencies of our own country'.[1]

The new School was described thus by the 'College Handbook' of 1880: 'Its prime aim is . . . the development of all branches of political science. Its secondary aim is the preparation of young men for all the branches of public service.' The distinction is interesting. A. D. White would have put the 'secondary aim' first, but Burgess' own stress was reflected in this 'prime aim'. Yet the difference was treated as one only of stress or degree. A conflict of interest was not yet apparent, just as the notion of 'science' in both White and Burgess could still embrace many different points of view: it was sometimes a method, but in addition a temper of mind; it was sometimes no more than 'good scholarship', but in addition a belief that all sciences could share in the progress of natural science and biological science. But immanent in what were taken as differences of stress, there were profound differences of quality. However, at the time, political science as a social science was a prominent partner in a general growth of higher academic standards in the new universities. And it shared in what was at first as much a novelty of academic organization as of any new intellectual content to the things taught.

3. German Means to American Ends

An important condition of the change in American higher education was, as Burgess said, 'that our Colleges furnish annually several hundreds of students of the Universities of Germany'. The peculiar product of the old American colleges was passing away—'a hybrid somewhat between the drill-master of the Gymnasium and the University Professor', towards a new type of teacher who thought largely in terms of German methods of instruction and (Burgess should have added, but did not) the new French idea of a vocational training for public administration.[2] This was taken to mean the combination of studies at the election of the student; the giving of instruction by original lectures; and the use of the seminar as an

---

[1] A prefatory note to Vol. I, No. 1 (March 1886).
[2] Burgess, *The American University: when shall it be? where shall it be? what shall it be?* (Boston: 1884), pp. 3 ff.

activity of co-operative research. But this movement did not create in either history or political science an immediate concentration on specifically American problems and sources. It was here that serious scholarship differed most markedly from the aspirations of citizenship training. Many European topics were themselves new and exciting discoveries to the wandering American graduate students, and their intellectual prestige was far greater. (Had not a student of George Bancroft been appalled to be told by the omniscient Ranke that the *History of the United States* was the best such history that had yet appeared, 'from the democratic point of view'?) But the two questions were intermingled, as Burgess himself showed in drafting a Minority Report at one stage of the quarrel at Columbia about the status of the new Faculty of Political Science:

It is not creditable to this country that so many Americans should be forced abroad by lack of University instruction at home, and it is of doubtful benefit to this country that so many of its young men should be trained to regard our affairs at a foreign angle. . . . It is notorious that nearly all Americans who have studied political economy in Germany during the last decade, have returned to this country with a more or less pronounced leaning towards State Socialism. This evil is in process of remedy by the development of American schools of political science. . . . We are not disposed to deny the advantage of a foreign point of view in widening the student's mental horizon; but the question is not whether we are to have the foreign point of view in addition to the American, but whether the American point of view, now practically non-existent, shall be supplied.[1]

The desire to study American topics could only come to the fore when the yet freshly won victory of nationalism, consequent to the Republican victory in the Civil War, had had time to percolate into the Colleges. The victory of 'this indissoluble Union' over 'these United States' meant, for the first time, that the American scholar and writer could begin to feel himself securely a part of an American culture, could feel a synthesis at work of American political and geographical convenience with European scholarship and letters, no longer a bifurcation. The complaints of famously articulate Bostonians about the crudities of the new age should not detract from the general consolidation of nationalism, the vastly heightened political and economic confidence. If Henry Adams was to write his

---

[1] Quoted by R. Gordon Hoxie *et al.*, *A History of the Faculty of Political Science, Columbia University* (New York: 1955), p. 51, from a Faculty Report of 1889. Burgess must have had in mind the declaration of the American Economic Association at their inaugural meeting at Saratoga in Sept. 1885 that: 'We regard the state as an agency whose positive assistance is one of the indispensable conditions of human progress.' This was a deliberate challenge to the Spencerian orthodoxy of the time, as we will soon see. These economists had mostly been influenced by witnessing Bismarck's policies of 'State Socialism'.

bitter satire on Washington politics, *Democracy*, and his flight to the past of *Mont-Saint-Michel and Chartres*, yet there was also his monumental account of the *Administration of Jefferson and Madison* to show that even if he found American politics dirty and distasteful, yet they were unavoidably fascinating. If the Americanism of Fenimore Cooper could be pricked by the knowing wit of Mark Twain, yet there was Mark Twain himself far from *An Innocent Abroad* and aggressively the *Connecticut Yankee at the Court of King Arthur*. Twain's biting attack on political corruption, *The Gilded Age*, was genuine satire, it sprang from an alternative hope for America; whereas Adams' *Democracy* moved from the irony of genteel indifference to the cynicism of despair. Again, if Adams' friend Motley was to devote his great talents to a history of the Dutch Republic, yet there was Francis Parkman to put the whole North American continent upon his canvas with grace of style as well as with the spirit of Manifest Destiny. The American writer and scholar was beginning to strain at the leash of alien categories and topics of scholarship.

For American history was not the European concentration on the strengthening and then the unification of the State (in which even Machiavelli could be rehabilitated by Lord Acton), but was the story of a growing psychological identity of *society* (in which even the elementary achievement of Hamiltonian statesmanship could be safely attacked by those who benefited from it the most). The 'Union' was not the 'State'. Turner could see this identity of society as due to the Mississippi valley and the Frontier, ignoring the fact that the individualism of American society far preceded the frontier; but he was right, at this time, to look away from the political history of State sovereignty, the focus of the European and European-trained historians. The very rise of Social History was to be a sign of how much more the strength of American society lay and had lain at the sociological rather than at the central political level. The United States recovered from 'The War Between the States', flourished and expanded under national political régimes of an incompetence and corruption that would have endangered the entire life of most European nations.

The mild Hegelianism that Burgess had gained from Droysen and Treitschke, and from Julius Seelye in his Amherst days, was perpetually frustrated of an object. Despite the awakening of a national self-confidence in American learning and letters, it was hard for the historians and the new political scientists to avoid looking to European history for a State that had not been swallowed up in society. Burgess could view the outcome of the Civil War as an Hegelian would view the unification of Germany. He fully shared the Anglo-Saxon racialism of John Fiske's famous essay on 'Manifest Destiny'.

But to most Americans these things appeared to arise out of a demo-cratic, popular nationalism, not out of any sense of the purposes of the State. The American *Sittlichkeit* needed no State to express it. William Lloyd Garrison, the abolitionist, could with equal plausi-bility, even if with equal sterility, try to introduce Mazzini to the American public as the philosopher of democratic nationalism[1] (Garrison splendidly reproducing, in American terms, Mazzini's own ambivalence and confusion between nationalism and cosmopolitan-ism). When Burgess defined sovereignty as 'original, absolute, un-limited, universal power over the individual subject and all associa-tions of subjects', he was adopting a concept that, whatever its general import, was almost meaningless for *American* politics.[2] Burgess, for all his great influence as a university administrator and a founder of political science, left no intellectual disciples at all.

There was still a feeling that American history was of a simple greatness that left little room for diverse interpretations: an astonish-ing agreement reigned even about the nature of the framing of the Constitution. Only after a generation of study in the conflicts of established European history and historiography did historians begin to realize that there were great problems to elucidate in the national history that had not been settled on the bayonets of Grant's armies, and that a psychological unity of belief did not necessarily mean a clarity of knowledge. The young political scientists might have sought for this historical understanding—particularly of the nature of the Revolution; but they were less conscious of history than many historians were of politics. Instead of looking back into the nature of American historical experience as the needed founda-tion for their discipline, they began straight away in a time of great change to concern themselves with what seemed to be immediate practice; and, at the same time, they aspired to become more 'scientific', at the very time when the popular meaning of that term was shifting and hardening. Of the great achievement and the elaborate organization of German scholarship which was received at the same time as the whole social and industrial expansion of the nation after the Civil War, it was the organization more than the content that had a lasting effect, and then not so much the specific organization as the organizational frame of mind.

4. To Make the Best Men Take to Politics

Political science as citizenship training and as Civil Service pre-paration was given an added impetus by the growing concern of 'the

[1] Garrison, *Joseph Mazzini: His Life, Writings and Political Principles* (New York: 1872).
[2] See his *Political Science and Constitutional Law*, I (New York: 1891), p. 52.

better elements' with the problem of corruption in politics. A large number of the dissident Republican 'half-breeds' of the 'seventies and 'eighties, and of the 'Mugwumps' who assembled in proud convention in 1872, were college men, even though in '72 they turned down the impeccable Charles Francis Adams and ran the erratic Horace Greeley for President. Charles W. Eliot, the young President of Harvard, attended there at Cincinnati, as well as Charles Francis and Henry Adams; both Daniel Coit Gilman and Andrew D. White watched as if expecting Cincinnati to become a second Philadelphia. These men regarded themselves as the old Americans—they were in fact mostly of Yankee Protestant stock—who were now having to defend the public morals of the country against the new twin dangers of 'wild radicalism' and of 'irresponsible plutocracy'. Henry James (the nephew) placed an apt quotation from a speech of Francis Parkman's at the head of his biography, *Charles W. Eliot:* 'The presence of highly cultivated and vigorous minds is the most powerful aid to popular education. A class of strong thinkers is the palladium of democracy. They are the natural enemies of ostentation and aggressive wealth. The vast aggregate of average intelligence cannot supply their place.'

Even in the early 1830's, De Tocqueville had lamented the absence from politics of men like that 'remarkable generation' who had sat in Convention at Philadelphia. By the 1870's the harsh growing pains of industrialism and mass immigration had so changed, or, as many thought, corrupted, the style and tempo of early Republican politics, that the old 'political science' of precept and example in the practice of statesmanship was now felt to be insufficient. Political science must now be directly taught, not merely as 'civics' to the city offspring of the 'melting-pot', but also, though in a broader manner, to the native Americans in the colleges, men who, it was feared, had lost their early spontaneous political skill, responsibility and wisdom. Reform of the universities and reform of the Civil Service were to go hand in glove. The 'best men'—as College Presidents can at least be safely called—acted as if Jefferson's worst fears about the effect of a growth of the cities were about to be realized, although, at the same time, they were to a man sound on a national Capitalism and hostile to States' rights, eager to show 'The Relations of Political Science to National Prosperity', and eager to enlist, while civilizing them, the support of 'the men of unknown birth and notorious fortune'—the 'Robber Barons', soon to become the 'great educational benefactors'.

The publication of Dorman B. Eaton's *The Civil Service in Great Britain* (New York: 1880) was quite as important a preparation for the Pendleton Act of 1883 as the assassination of President Garfield 'by a disappointed office seeker'. Eaton's book broadcast the success of the British reforms of 1855 and 1870 and added to the knowledge of the Prussian system which the *Herrn Doktoren* brought back from Germany.[1] Politically, Civil Service reform was to prove disappointing as a sovereign balm, salve and remedy for all the diseases that the body politic is heir to; but it did directly stimulate the study of government. The 'silkstockings' would enter politics if made indignant enough; but, as Alderman Richard Croker once remarked in a bizarre conversation with W. T. Stead, they would never stay in: '. . . when mugwump principles won't even make mugwumps work, do you expect the same lofty motives to be sufficient to interest the masses in politics?'[2] Yet the failure of many local municipal reform movements to outlive the momentum of one campaign against the regular organization only increased the faith of 'the better elements' in the *long-run* remedial effects of Higher Education. Edwin L. Godkin, the editor of *The Nation*, spoke for the new College Presidents like Gilman, White and Eliot, as well as for his fellow-editors of the high-toned journals, when he wrote:

In the popular mind there is what may be called a disposition to believe not only that one man is as good as another, but that he knows as much on any matter of general interest. In any particular business the superiority of the man who has long followed it is freely acknowledged, but in public affairs this is not so much denied as disregarded.[3]

The oddness of the situation is reflected in that Godkin's 'superiority of the man who has long followed it' is clearly, in the context of his book, meant to be an argument for the greater participation of the *student* of politics, not for a greater trust of the political regular.

So, after the Civil War in the great period of national expansion, men like Godkin cast the universities into the role of De Tocqueville's 'aristocracy of intellect' or Jefferson's 'aristocracy of talent', a force to civilize both the politician and the capitalist. But Godkin in his *Unforeseen Tendencies of Democracy*, like C. K. and H. B. Adams, and Burgess in their College Addresses, never faced squarely the problem of size, the dangers of a dilution or even a regard for 'special fitness'. Did democracy mean, 'every man an aristocrat'—as many texts from Jefferson would say; or was there only a relatively small,

---

[1] Eaton later endowed a Chair of Municipal Science and Administration at Columbia, and one of Political Science at Harvard. He hoped that the Chair at Columbia would contribute 'to greatly reduce the number and frequency of elections in municipalities; to prevent the control of their affairs by parties and factions; and to make good municipal government the ambition and endeavour of the worthiest citizens. . . .' (Quoted from the terms of the Columbia bequest by Hoxie, *Political Science, Columbia University*, p. 69).

[2] Quoted by M. R. Werner, *Tammany Hall* (New York: 1928), p. 449.

[3] *The Unforeseen Tendencies of Democracy* (Boston: 1898), p. 44.

though socially mobile, 'natural aristocracy'—as many other Jeffersonian texts could support? Daniel Coit Gilman was almost alone in giving constant warnings about the dangers of an over-expansion of the colleges and universities.[1] White, on the other hand, and most of the State University Presidents, seemed inclined to demand as much expansion as physically possible. These differences became, however, like the differences between Federalist and Jeffersonian political thought, differences of stress and not of kind. Both were 'democratic' and both 'expansionist' in their attitude to education.

H. B. Adams' report of 1887 for the Bureau of Education, *The Study of History in American Colleges and Universities*, was in large part a mirror of the common ground in such sentiment. (He included Political Science as a part of History.) The final chapter of this report was entitled 'Carroll D. Wright on Political Education'. (Wright was the energetic Commissioner of the new United States Bureau of Labour.) Adams, with his eye for the significant detail, commendingly quotes from an Address of Wright's, 'The Study of Statistics in American Colleges': 'That College which comprehends that it is essential to fit men for the best administrative duties, not only in government but in great business enterprises which demand leaders of as high a quality as those essential for a chief magistrate, will receive the patronage, the commendation and the gratitude of the people.' It would have been academic for him to discuss whether patronage and gratitude are always given for worthy services, and to have distinguished some of 'the people' from others; but he does suggest something of the precise nature of these services:

> I would urge upon the Government of the United States, and upon the Governments of the States, the necessity of providing by law for the admission of students that have taken scientific courses in statistics as honorary attachés of or clerks to be employed in the practical work of the statistical offices. This is easily done without expenditure by the Government, but with the very best economic results.[2]

Wright saw the expansion of 'the statistical offices' as the key to good government, and the provision of such education as the primary role of political science in the universities. He exhibits the belief, soon to become widespread, that, quite simply, anything that is wrong with American government could be set right spontaneously if the facts were known. Of course, if we look back at the lack of written knowledge of 'how government really works', and at the lack of elementary statistics known to the government itself, there is at least a grain of truth, certainly of need, in Wright's position.

[1] See Abraham Flexner, *Daniel Coit Gilman: Creator of the American Type of University* (New York: 1946).
[2] Adams, *The Study of History*, pp. 265–6.

Yet here already is that self-defeatingly practical streak that made so many professional political scientists in the United States concerned merely with public administration, a concern whose narrowness was not apparent while it took place in the context of a wider reformism. But if that reformist temper were ever to wane, an event that they could not understand or control within their own terms, all that would be left would be a merely descriptive and classificatory study. The stress on a positive citizenship education can be a two-edged sword for the political reformer: the unexpected source of an involuntary conservatism. While not wishing to anticipate later discussion, yet a possible misunderstanding can be anticipated. In times when liberty seems in danger, a great deal is said about a study for its own sake alone. But it would be a mistake to view the 'operative ideals' of the early fathers of American political science as necessarily grossly indoctrinatory or thoughtlessly technical. Benjamin Jowett and T. H. Green at Oxford were known by American scholars to be also explicitly concerned with education as a vehicle for statesmanship and public service. The University had a duty to create, at least to encourage, minds likely to make good citizens and guardians. Allowing for differences in tradition, it was the same type of motive that lay behind the Inaugural Addresses of the American historians and political scientists. The vital distinction, most probably, lay not in the motive but in the manner. Jowett and Green, under the Platonic spell of the flowing dialectic between Law and Justice, discussed the moral bases of citizenship education as something wider than the mechanics of an agreed solution, whether this solution passed as conservatism or rationalism. Education, to them, involved a discussion of the nature of the good society, some sort of a discussion at least, even if perhaps not as bold or as precise as was once thought; it raised questions that turned upon the nature and conditions of individual virtue. Political philosophy and general education, rightly conceived, were to them inseparable. But to the English liberal idealists, the one could not be directly *a vehicle* of the other; they conditioned each other like the privacy and the mutuality of affection. Some types of citizenship could all too easily gain at the expense of philosophy, and some types of philosophy at the expense of civic cohesion. When there was a need to seek to apply either, the essence of its application was, paradoxically, indirection. In this lies much of the difference between a political education and a political training.

Pure education is, indeed, pure nothing; its claimants have only neglected to study the political and social conditions of its existence and its presuppositions. But the demand for the American universities to teach political science as citizenship took place in the context of a virtual unanimity of belief, though not of clarity as to what that belief was. The reformed educational structure of the leading universities was to be copied, with amazingly few important variations, by the new colleges and universities, one by one. The structure imposed its limitations without at the same time stimulating a critical study of the inherited political controls. Fortified, as will be seen, by a philosophy of *progress*, but with little philosophizing about *history*, the 'best men' tended to believe that corruption and all other 'mere frictions' would vanish once Civil Service examinations were substituted for the spoils system. To put the point perhaps over-simply, the deliberate advocacy of citizenship training and the critical study of the fundamental conditions, forms and aims of political society in the United States—these never took place at the same time in the same minds. Each lacking the other was only a partial mode of experience that would lead to a distorted expression in American political education.

However, if we accept in practice the inevitable tension between citizenship training and political education in any society that depends for its stability upon mass consent, the general passion for education thus revealed in American life in these years was and remains something fine and admirable. So, too, the growth of a formal political science as an attempt to codify a past practice was, in some form, not merely a necessity for cohesion in American expansion and integration, but was also, despite its dangers, out of its very size and thus variety, full of rich possibilities and alternatives.

The study of politics is everywhere a response to a belief that there is a crisis. The difficulty besetting American political thought is perhaps that while there has never been a crisis deep enough for a re-thinking of the original beliefs to take place, yet there has always been, underlying the massive surface confidence, enough frictions of adjustment and growth to make a formal political science seem needed, and needed on a uniquely large scale. But because these crises have been regarded as marginal or as problems to be clearly solved so as to maintain the validity of the old beliefs in new circumstances, this political science did not take the form of political theory or philosophy, but of citizenship education or training; and it mostly grew up not as a learned 'science', as Burgess mainly wished, but as a technological 'science', as Wright entirely wished.

III

AMERICAN LIBERALISM REFURBISHED BY PROGRESS: SPENCER AND DARWIN

It was reserved for Herbert Spencer to discover this all-comprehensive law which is found to explain alike all the phenomena of man's history and all those of external nature. This sublime discovery, that the Universe is in a continuous process of evolution from the homogeneous to the heterogeneous, with which only Newton's law of gravitation is at all worthy to be compared, underlies not only physics, but also history.

> From a review of the American edition of Spencer's
> *First Principles* in the *National Quarterly Review*

H. Spencer you English never quite do justice to, or at least those I have talked to do not. He is dull. He writes an ugly uncharming style, his ideals are those of a lower middle class British Philistine. And yet after all abatements I doubt if any writer of English except Darwin has done so much to affect our whole way of thinking about the Universe.

> OLIVER WENDELL HOLMES, JR., in a letter
> to Sir Frederick Pollock

1. The Role and Need of Progress

WHILE the colleges and universities expanded and reorganized and the systematic study of politics began, there were also, as conditions of this same age of enterprise, new intellectual doctrines that were widely and warmly received. These became so influential that, although at first rarely mirrored in the actual lectures offered in the new Political Science departments, yet they formed the foreground of an educated man's thought at that time and the background of ideas without which the distinctive development of the method of political science in the early twentieth century could not be understood.

The theories of a necessary progress and of a therapeutic science of society both appeared upon the scene. They were to result in a new split between political theory and political practice; a predilection to psychological explanation, and an antagonism to historical and philosophical explanation. They strengthened rather than created many existing attitudes that we will find systematized to a unique degree in subsequent American social thought. They were to furnish added conditions, in turn, for the emergence of a unique type of philosophy, pragmatism, and of a largely unsystematized but increasingly influential positivism. From the debates that attended the reception of Herbert Spencer's thought and from a social gloss on Darwinian biology, progress and social science jointly emerged as a rational structure fulfilling an immanence of already existing American sentiments. From this time on, 'Progress' and 'Science' become the master-concepts of a distinctively American social thought. It is impossible to understand the grounds for a 'science of politics' without studying the reception of the doctrine of Progress, even though its first appearance, strictly speaking, was in sociological theory. Later we will show that the American political scientists never reflected upon the meaning of the doctrine of Progress: they merely accepted it as an established part of American thought, showing by their own actions how deeply it was established, but how little understood. It is another case of the importance of popular thought in American intellectual development.

'Where there is no vision,' the Proverbs have said, 'the people perish.' The great industrial, geographical and emotional stirring that seized America after the trauma of the Civil War gave an apparent need for a secular religion—'secular', because there was no longer a common religion and because orthodox religious belief in general was on the verge of decline; but 'religious', because American national sentiment grew more, not less, in need of the assurance of a Manifest Destiny, a 'providential dispensation' that would both fulfil and transcend existing American experience, especially as, for the first time, this experience seemed almost at odds with itself. The tragedy of the Civil War, the bitterness of Reconstruction, the growth of the cities, brought obvious poverty and unrest as well as benefits. There was no desire to repudiate the past, the already established American creed, but a desire for an ideological restatement to fit the new conditions, to add a dynamic impulse to a formerly static pattern. The popular sentiments of optimism became hardened into a doctrine of Progress. The doctrine, of course, was not specifically American. J. B. Bury wrote in his *The Idea of Progress: an inquiry into its origins and growth:*

Thus in the 'seventies and 'eighties of the last century the idea of progress was becoming a general article of faith. Some might hold it in the fatalistic form . . .; others might believe that the future will depend largely on our own conscious efforts, but that there is nothing in the nature of things to disappoint the prospect of steady and indefinite advance. The majority did not enquire too curiously into such points of doctrine, but received it in a vague sense as a comfortable addition to their convictions. But it became a part of the general mental outlook of educated people.[1]

But, while this is true, Bury completely ignored any account of the unique vitality and importance of the doctrine in the United States— the reasons for which, surely, throw light upon the nature of the doctrine itself as well as upon American social thought.[2]

It must not be forgotten that the Industrial Revolution struck America later than it did England; the psychological crisis of industrialism coincided with the Civil War and created a fear that a break in the continuity of the American vision might have taken place. Against the spirit of Carnegie's *Triumphant Democracy*—the book that became a symbol of the optimism and expansion of the new era —there must be offset the famous passage in *The Education of Henry Adams* where he describes the utter strangeness of the America to which he returned after his war-time sojourn in the London Embassy as secretary to the last of the great Federalists, his father. But while the fears held by Henry Adams were more widely shared among the 'best men' than he himself supposed, yet it was the very practical friendship of Andrew Carnegie to Herbert Spencer that was to symbolize their popular solution, not that of Henry Adams for twelfth-century France.

2. The Plausibility of Spencer in America

By the incredibly eager reception of a far from easy system and book, Herbert Spencer's *Social Statics*,[3] 'evolution became a new

[1] J. B. Bury, *The Idea of Progress: an inquiry into its origins and growth* (London: 1920), p. 346.

[2] The First American Edition of Bury (New York: 1930), however, has a valuable supplementary introduction by Charles Beard. Also, Arthur A. Ekirch has shown in his monograph, *The Idea of Progress in America, 1815–1860* (New York: 1944), how very deeply the *sentiment* of progress has already been accepted on the level of popular thought, though not at the time as the general theory of social research that it later became.

An interesting exemplification of the idea, far from a critical study, is to be found in Harry Elmer Barnes, *Sociology and Political Theory* (New York: 1924), especially Chap. X, 'The State and Social Progress'.

[3] Herbert Spencer, *Social Statics, or, The Conditions Essential to Human Happiness* (London: 1851; first American edition, New York: 1866). Richard Hofstadter in his *Social Darwinism and American Thought* (Philadelphia: 1944) says that from its earliest publication in 1866 until 1903 the *authorized editions alone* of *Social Statics* sold 368,755 copies, 'a figure probably unparalleled for works in such difficult spheres as philosophy and sociology' (p. 21). Hofstadter's *Social Darwinism* is a brilliant and sensitive account of the actual doctrine in America, but it is less helpful in explaining why the ground was so fertile for such a strange growth.

religion, something for which the American people have always evinced a marked tenderness', as Professor Corwin has dryly commented.[1] It was truly the urban equivalent of the Prairie religions; not, however, a Social-Gospel, but initially an economic individualism, an explanation in terms of the best available scientific laws that gave some meaning to the half-lost small individual in the bewildering pace of the new expansion. Even a generation later, Spencer appeared to Jack London's autobiographical hero, Martin Eden, as 'organizing all knowledge for him, reducing everything to unity, elaborating ultimate realities, and presenting to his startled gaze a Universe so concrete of realization that it was like a model of a ship such as sailors make and put in bottles'.[2] He was to Andrew Carnegie, 'the man to whom I owe most'—a rare and telling self-effacement. John R. Commons was to reminisce in his old age:

> My father and his cronies talked politics and science. Everyone of them in that Eastern section of Indiana was a Republican, living on the battle cries of the Civil War, and everyone was a follower of Herbert Spencer, who was then the shining light of evolution and individualism. Several years later, in 1888, I was shocked, at a meeting of the American Economic Association, to hear Professor Ely denounce Herbert Spencer who had misled economists. I was brought up on Hoosierism, Republicanism, Presbyterianism and Spencerism.[3]

What was the peculiar attraction of Spencer that made his refurbishing and extension of *laissez-faire* more widely welcomed than the earlier English Utilitarian writings? In part, just a happy accident of a temporary vacuum of explicit social thought in America, giving rise to one of those periodic urges for self-justification that the would-be rationalist needs to justify his political and economic practices. But moreover, there was the added faith in those practices given by the demonstration that a great God, called Evolution, had the Universe in its grip, and so, if we observed the attendant laws, we would progress smoothly forward, following a logical expansion of existing practices, not a restriction. Bentham had applied *laissez-faire* to

[1] Edward S. Corwin, 'Evolution and Politics', in *Evolutionary Thought in America*, ed. Stow Persons (New Haven: 1950). This is, in some ways, a more helpful essay than Hofstadter's, despite its less comprehensive character; for it puts the significance of the reception of Spencer and Darwin squarely in the whole context of American political tradition. His identification of Darwin himself with social reformism seems, however, unwarranted.

[2] Quoted by F. O. Matthiesen in his *Theodore Dreiser* (New York: 1951), p. 39.

[3] Commons, *Myself* (New York: 1934), p. 8. (Perhaps this is why, as it was once said, Indiana always had first-class second-rate men.) The authority of the wisest of 'Progressive' scholars can also join in this chorus of mixed tributes: 'Spencer laid out the broad highway over which American thought travelled in the later years of the century.' [Vernon L. Parrington, *Main Currents in American Thought* (New York: 1930), III, p. 198.]

economics, but had claimed law and politics as the sphere of scientific *regulation*. But Spencer demonstrated laws of nature, first from biology and then from mechanics, which made progressive evolution dependent on non-interference by the State in all of those spheres. (Spencerianism was a kind of inverted Hobbism; an ironic occurrence for the Lockean world of America.) The real function of government was negative: it was only to furnish a transitional stage which, by securing free-play for the operation of natural laws, would increasingly render its own existence less necessary. 'It is a mistake to consider that Government must last for ever,' declared Spencer. 'It is not essential but incidental. As amongst bushmen we find a state incidental to Government, so may there be one in which it shall become extinct.' [1]

The logic of his explanation, clearest in his *Synthetic Philosophy* (1858), is expressed by mechanical terms of *force* and *equilibrium*, rather than by his earlier biological routes to a teleological standard of value. From the principle of the 'Persistence of Force', it is implied that all things tend ultimately to equilibrium, and, consequently, all things as they are in fact by this tendency alone will transform themselves, by a process called 'evolution', to a higher and a final equilibrium. Both the Solar system and the biological life of man inevitably act for the best in the best of all possible worlds, when left alone from politicians and reformers so as to evolve in peace. Fortunately, at the date of writing the most advanced societies had passed out of the *Kriegsstaat*, of war and strict State control, into the *Handelsstaat*, where industry flourishes in peace as the observance of contract in a civil society of men who, each as an end (or an atom) in himself, observe strictly voluntary association in a strictly limited number of common interests.

Spencer's most widely read essays were those that eventually appeared together as *The Man Versus the State*,[2] a commentary on the regrettable growth of 'Statism' in England. He argued that society was a system naturally so well ordered that attempts at 'reform' nearly always only substituted one 'evil' for another, or actually exacerbated them. A system was a system, and 'reform' was an external and arbitrary event. However, the social system carried its own remedies for apparent particular 'evils'; it was not static: it evolved. Evolution was a slow and painful process, but a certain, natural and efficient one because it ensured, in *his* pre-Darwinian phrase, 'the survival of the fittest'. Man and society as a whole must adapt to environment and to a recognition of nature's laws, and those unable to do so will be eliminated. Spencer even warned strongly

---

[1] Spencer, *Social Statics, op. cit.*, p. 69.
[2] *The Man Versus the State* (New York: 1884).

41

against apparently mild and beneficial forms of State regulation: State-supported education, the regulation of housing conditions, tariffs, municipal building projects, Government postal systems, and even large-scale private charity: these, all these, were interferences with the evolutionary laws of nature.

Spencer is thus the liberal sublime. For those who profited from the new expansiveness he gave self-justification, and, for the others, a theory that would somehow explain their relative ill fortune. Spencerism met both these needs by sustaining the deep common faith in the destiny of American democratic individualism. 'All would be all right in the end', are the simple tidings taken from the laboured gospel of Spencer; and this without need for a radical change in institutions or beliefs. Mr. Justice Holmes did not exaggerate: the Supreme Court did 'read Mr. Herbert Spencer's *Social Statics* into the Constitution'—the road from *Munn vs. Illinois* to *Lochner vs. New York*. But there was no inherent falseness in the latter interpretation of the 'due process' clause: there was much to be said for the case that America had had no great *laissez-faire* theorists because some form of *laissez-faire* was not a theory but, as Stephen Field argued in the 'Slaughter House cases', was a condition of American life.

Spencerism and the doctrine of Progress, then, grew to intellectual prominence in the United States at a time when some men had had a vision of an abyss beyond or in the midst of the fair and rolling fields of the ever more swiftly expanding West. J. W. Burgess recalled in his *Reminiscences* the violent and terrible times of his youth as a Whig on the border of seceding Tennessee: neighbour had killed neighbour and families had fought amongst themselves. It was as if the Lockean state of nature had plunged into the morbid powers of that of Hobbes—indeed the young Oliver Wendell Holmes had returned to the front, after his first wounds had healed, carrying the *Leviathan* in his knapsack. Burgess wrote:

Such experiences threw a sadness over my young life, and produced in me such an early realization of the innate hypocrisy of the human soul, that I wonder I have not dwelt always under a deeper pessimism than has actually possessed me. As it was, I early lost faith in the wisdom and goodness of the mass of men. I have always found many men ignorant, greedy, prejudiced, malicious, brutal and vindictive. The supermen, who make the ideas and ideals of civilization, I have found very few and far between.[1]

It was from the closeness of this vision that Spencer helped to save, or insure, America. Both the bloodshed of the Civil War and

[1] John W. Burgess, *The Reminiscences of an American Scholar* (New York: 1934), p. 12.

the unfamiliarity of the new industrialism served to undermine habit and to inflate it into ideology. Human society might be at times, like nature, 'red in tooth and claw'—in the phrase that T. H. Huxley made his own—but it was working for the best. Even the Civil War had worked out for the best. Even the leaders of the defeated South had embraced the Northern doctrine of Progress and the practice of business expansion: the nostalgia was to come only with the creation of a new and commercial basis for prosperity among the leading elements of the South.[1] When Daniel Coit Gilman cast around for someone to give a suitable address at the formal opening of Johns Hopkins in 1876, it was indeed a very apt choice, despite some religious grumblings, to invite T. H. Huxley.[2]

And for the somewhat reflective man it was the greatest comfort of all that both the new industrial technology and the theories of Mr. Spencer could be accepted as 'scientific' and not merely political.[3] Indeed the word 'political' throughout this age is largely held in contempt. Not merely in this period but throughout American history, the strength and cohesion of the community seem to lie less in the political institutions and laws than in the popular opinions of mass society. The sociological cast of American political science and the impetus given to the study of sociology by Spencer are no accidents. Both the achievements of the industrialists and those of Spencer's syntheses gave an even greater authority to the word 'science', an authority that from this date was to become a lasting and a leading part of the culture. The 'Manifest Destiny' of which Jefferson had spoken in his First Inaugural Address, which meant to him the geographical uniqueness and opportunity with which America had already been blessed, now became subsumed in the doctrine of Progress-through-Science. This doctrine went beyond, but did not necessarily contradict, the earlier Deistic Jeffersonian sense of the peculiar dispensations of 'overriding Providence'.

3. Spencer and the Providential Dispensation

At the heart of American social thought there was, and has remained, a belief in themselves as a chosen people. This aspect of the Puritan foundation, indeed of the early Calvinist orthodoxy, has remained—perhaps this aspect alone: a certain sense, in the phrases of Cotton Mather, that every detail of life in 'this Israel in the Wilderness'

---

[1] This is decisively shown in C. Vann Woodward's masterly volume, *The Origins of the New South, 1877–1913* (Baton Rouge: 1951). See especially pp. 143–4.

[2] Abraham Flexner, *Daniel Coit Gilman: creator of the American type of University* (New York: 1946), p. 84.

[3] Ekirch expresses an obvious but important truth when he says: 'To the generality of the American people it was the *practical application* of science that furnished the most obvious evidence of progress' (*The Idea of Progress in America*, p. 106).

exhibited 'wonderworking Providences' and 'Illustrious Dispensations'. It meant that if ever there had been an open and public warfare of Science and *Religion* (as thought distinct from *Theology*), such as many of the English Darwinists had tried to stage, Science might well have lost. Secularism in the United States has rarely meant agnosticism; it has usually meant a kind of non-denominational Protestantism, or a vague but powerful Deism. And Unitarianism has been of far greater significance than the actual numbers of Unitarians would suggest—even including the unbroken succession of Unitarians as Presidents of Harvard from 1869 to 1954.

Spencer, as not the least of his achievements, avoided that *odium theologicum* that so often struck Darwin, who loftily took no pains at all to smooth the ruffled feathers of mistaken religiosity. Spencer avoided this. His doctrines of the 'Unknowable' or 'the First Mover' (in which he happily felt originality) plastered over, as it were, Hume's simple doubt about *the uniformity of nature* with a first principle that could be taken as a sufficient condition for any religious metaphysic by those who cared to, or as something like a 'rule of thought' by those who quietly cared not. The compatibility of Spencerian social science with the Providential dispensation of American Protestantism is well shown in some 'critical notices' of his *First Principles* that were inserted by the publisher as end-pages to the first American edition of his *Illustrations of Universal Progress* (New York: 1864). The *Christian Examiner*, the leading Methodist organ, spoke of Spencer 'bringing a flag of truce and presenting terms of agreement meant to be honourable to both parties'. And the *New Englander* gives some hint of what these terms were: 'While showing the *unsearchable nature* of the ultimate facts on which religion depends, he demonstrates their *real existence* and their great importance. . . . We certainly would not charge him with theoretical atheism, holding as he does this religious idea.' While the *Christian Spectator* threw discretion to the wind:

. . . Like Moses, when he came down from the mount, this positive philosophy comes with a veil over its face, that its too divine radiance may be hidden for a time. This is Science that has been conversing with God, and brings in her hand His law written on tablets of stone.

It was even in such terms as this that America's most influential pulpit was at once to thunder and to reassure when Henry Ward Beecher decided to accept the Spencerian Universe.[1] Perhaps there was something more deep-rooted in the acceptance of Spencer by respectable Protestant pulpits than a mere yielding to the spirit of the times. For the 'respectable Protestant divines' had always been care-

[1] See Beecher's *Religion and Science* (New York: 1873).

ful to maintain an alliance with learning, a welcoming of 'natural reason as a supplement to faith' (in Cotton Mather's words), against the inroads of the 'unlearned Ministry', the fundamentalist revivalists. If the learned pulpits had ever been forced into an open warfare with 'Science', they would only have strengthened the self-confidence and self-righteousness of their main opponents *within* Protestantism. To the Fundamentalists the struggle against 'Science and Evolution' was only one incident in a more general good fight against the carnal presumption of reason in questioning the spirit and the word.

Spencerism could thus be used as a synthesis of low Protestantism and of a high rationalist Scientism. Spencer justified the assumptions and met the speculative needs of an age. Even after his fall from educated grace, he left permanent streams of tendency upon the *tabula rasa* of the Lockean mind. When a doctrinal replacement came, it came in his own terms of Science and Progress. The Spencerians established the authoritative idea of a 'science of society'.

It should again be stressed that while the doctrine of Progress arose from the same factors as conditioned the rise of political science as citizenship education, yet it did not at once directly affect political science. For political science was restrained, at least in part, by the newly imported German historiography. The doctrine of Progress, at the time of its reception, was not widely subject to the checks and balances of academic debate. But it captured popular thought and became part of the new climate of Americanism into which the universities fell when later they turned against what they had come to feel was the irrelevance of European learned experience. If, in the 1870's, the new social scientists had immediately created a uniquely strong and nationalistic discipline, then their primary Americanism might have remained the political writings of the Federalist and Jeffersonian era; but by the time they returned to study, and then to teach, matters American, they were already looking at a world in which 'Progress' and 'Science' had already become dominant operative ideals of American culture.

4. Darwin as the American Hegel

'The government of the United States was . . . a sort of unconscious copy of the Newtonian theory of the Universe'—as we have already quoted Woodrow Wilson. But he continued: 'In our day, whenever we discuss the structure or development of anything . . . we . . . follow Mr. Darwin. . . .' [1] The publication of Charles Darwin's

---

[1] *Constitutional Government in the United States* (New York: 1908), p. 55; see also an Address of 1912 in *The Public Papers of Woodrow Wilson: College and State*, II, eds. R. S. Baker and W. E. Dodd (New York: 1925), p. 434: '. . . what we have been witnessing for the past hundred years is the transformation of a Newtonian constitution into a Darwinian constitution. [Applause.]'

The Origin of Species in 1859 appeared to Spencer not as a rival theory, but as a complementary theory. Darwin was a specialist with a biological theory of evolution; Spencer was a philosopher with a universal theory of evolution—the one was an instance of the other.

But Darwin, unlike Spencer, was in fact a scientist, in the tradition of the geologists and botanists. His theory was based on a hypothetical process of the natural selection of fit biological strains; it sought to explain a limited range of biological phenomena. It was largely people's ignorance of the implications of previous evolutionary theories—the same 'accident' of time as made Spencer's theories welcome—that made Darwin appear as the guarantor of the *eventual* social good. Progress (by which is meant the belief that goodness is historically cumulative) was not necessarily implied by Darwin's early formulation of his theory of evolution, his attempt to explain how variations occur within species. But the Spencerians soon obliterated any distinction between evolution and progress, in time affecting even Darwin's own thought. 'Darwinism', as distinct from the work of Darwin, became a philosophy and a methodology of human history.[1] Darwin shares the fate of Freud in that although he was mainly a painstaking worker in a specific field of truth, his name has become more often a synonym for the distortions of his ideas. Mr. Justice Holmes was once asked whether it was Voltaire who had influenced him towards scepticism. ' "Oh, no, it was not Voltaire—it was the influence of the scientific way of looking at the world—that made the change. . . . *The Origin of Species* came out, I think, while I was in College—H. Spencer had announced his intention to put the universe in our pockets—I hadn't read either of them to be sure, but, as I say, it was in the air." ' [2]

Edward Youmans, the zoologist, virtually abandoned his own researches in order to popularize, and thus extend, the message of Spencer and Darwin. This 'message' became one that told of the inevitability of Progress so long as sentimentality did not artificially prolong the existence of competitively unfit strains. And John Fiske levied reasons from Darwinism to support the argument for the dominance of the Anglo-Saxon race in his famous essay on their 'Manifest Destiny'.[3] The Rev. Josiah Strong, the Secretary of the Evangelical Society, sold 175,000 copies of a book which added to

[1] A similar collection of extravagant reviews in religious journals to those of Spencer (cited above) were bound into Nathan Sheppard's widely read anthology, *Darwinism Stated by Darwin Himself* (New York: 1886), pp. vii–viii.

[2] 'The Holmes–Cohen Correspondence', *Journal of the History of Ideas*, IX (Jan. 1948), 14–15.

[3] John Fiske, 'Manifest Destiny', reprinted in his *American Political Ideas from the Standpoint of Universal History* (Boston: 1885); see also his *Darwinism and Other Essays* (New York: 1879).

all this the deep-rooted belief of American Protestantism that they were a Chosen People destined to unique greatness.[1] Thus many American scholars, publicists and preachers made of Darwinism an irrational but compelling synthesis of Spencerism, Nationalism, Protestantism, Scientism and Capitalism.

Few people took the precise structure of Spencer's arguments from the Second Law of Thermodynamics very much to heart or mind, but his political conclusions were clear and *popularly* trusted. Darwin seemed to provide a simple foundation for these conclusions. Man survives as the fittest by adapting himself to his environment; the environment weeds out the worst and nourishes only the best. It was a crude interpretation, and there was little specific to be gained from the strict Darwinian scheme which was of relevance to social values or to happiness. The survival of the fittest merely means the fittest to survive in a particular environment; moral worth and the purposeful alternation of environment are not considered in the strict biological hypothesis.

Darwin himself in time became affected by the climate of opinion that his collision with Herbert Spencer and the American publicists helped to produce. In the Sixth Edition of *The Origin of Species* he wrote: 'We may look with some confidence to a secure future of great length. And as natural selection works solely by and for the good of each being, all corporeal and mental endowments will tend to progress towards perfection' (p. 428). But the remark, in the context of his book, is cryptic more than elucidatory; it bears no relation to his type of evidence for natural selection among certain species of animals. He began to see the fertility of his ideas, without himself submitting them to a philosophical criticism. Clearly he was personally more flattered than alarmed by appeals to his authority in the new social sciences—which authority, in some small way, he tried to live up to.[2] The attempt to draw social and political consequences from his work was aided by the admitted common roots of both his own and Spencer's theories in Malthus's theory of population. The idea of natural selection through the struggle for existence had come to Darwin while reading the *Essay on Population* which contains the celebrated thesis that a population unchecked by war, vice and disease would increase in geometrical proportion, whilst its means of subsistence can increase only in arithmetic proportion. This thesis at least focuses attention on the biological quality of the survivors. Darwin's idea of natural selection was broader than this. Climatic

---

[1] *Our Country: Its possible future and its present crisis* (New York: 1885), cited by Hofstadter, *Social Darwinism*, pp. 153–4.
[2] See, for example, his reference to Spencer on p. 252 in the 6th edition of *The Origin of Species* (New York: 1875).

conditions could 'select' without reference to competition with other individuals or species.

But the two distinct factors of 'natural selection' and 'the competitive struggle for existence' were often all but indistinguishable in his thought, as the full title of the *Origins* illustrates: *On the Origins of Species by Means of Natural Selection, or the Preservation of Favoured Races in the Struggle for Life*. The title alone expressed the meaning of Darwin to most of the publicists of Darwinism. They found the very notion of 'the biological' a sought-for bridge between the physical and the social, a frame of thought congenial to a technically minded nation who had experienced the struggle against environment and the conquest of the frontier far more than class, religious or national struggle.

Much that is typical of political theory in the United States as it appears in the restrictive disguise of a science of politics may be seen already. If every political theory relates a particular view of human nature to a particular style of ordering the institutions of government, then the view of human nature found here is the simple sensationalism of Locke. Also, every political theory that strives to rationalize new things tends to create an at least partly novel conceptual language. For American political theory this language is increasingly drawn from the vocabulary of natural science, at first largely from biology. And if to the purpose and the language of political philosophy the concept of its own directly political role is added, then in the United States this is found to be originally didactic: an apparatus for teaching the style and content of a particular politics to American youth. The amalgam of the movement for a direct citizenship instruction with the reception of Social-Darwinism was to have great consequences, both for American political studies and education in general. Perhaps as codifiers and reinterpreters of the American tradition Spencer and Darwin were the most influential theorists since John Locke. *Progress*, from this time on became the self-evident, taken-for-granted article of faith, the great 'inarticular major premise' underlying both common social thought and the systems of the new social sciences, political science eventually not least.

IV

AMBITION AND AMBIGUITY IN THE FOUNDING OF SOCIAL SCIENCE: SUMNER AND WARD

Education must assume . . . as basic premises the validity of the concept of progress and the . . . achieving it artificially by social effort. It must inculcate those facts and principles which sociologists have agreed are indispensable to progress . . . This notion of socialized education . . . for progress was developed by Comte, but it was reserved for Ward to make the subject almost his own. . . . It is . . . essential to bear in mind that education in the past and at the present time is far less devoted to inculcating the information necessary for social progress than to handing down tradition, inspiring a love for the past, eulogizing the *status quo* in social institutions, and uttering warnings against the very idea of progress. . . .

From HARRY ELMER BARNES, *Sociology and Political Theory* (1924)

The ideas of progress and of the indefinite perfectability of the human race belong to democratic ages. Democratic nations care but little for what has been, but they are haunted by visions of what will be; in this direction their unbounded imagination grows and dilates beyond all measure.   ALEXIS DE TOCQUEVILLE

1. Sumner opposes Sociology to the State

WRITING IN 1919, Professor Harry Elmer Barnes, the most tireless anthologist and impresario of the new social sciences, drew attention to the great importance for 'contemporary political theory' of the 'school of writers calling themselves, since the time of Comte, *sociologists*'. To them 'the State appears not as some metaphysical "ethical being" or as a purely legalistic entity emitting the commands of a determinate superior,' said Barnes, 'but as a purely natural product of *social evolution*. . . . The only sound criteria for estimating the value and relative excellence of the State is', he agreed with them, 'its adaptability to the function of promoting the progress and basic interests of the group at any given time.' [1] Barnes was writing about the doctrines of William Graham Sumner and Lester Frank Ward, 'two of the most distinguished of American sociologists'. Barnes' volume of 1925, *The History and Prospects of the Social Sciences*, which was something between the Manifesto and the Encyclopaedia of social science, bore as its reverent frontispiece a photograph of Lester Frank Ward.

Barnes had recognized his intellectual parents aright, indeed, the American parents of the whole social science movement. But he added a revealing (and an unnecessary) excuse for considering them together: 'In order to avoid the charge of advocating any specific interpretation of political theory these writers have consciously been chosen as representing widely different points of view.' However, it is not really the case that the liberal Barnes, having heard one orthodox Geographer, now wishes to give a Flat-Earth man a chance to make his obvious points. Even though Sumner and Ward are at polar antipodes on the issue of weak-State or strong-State, and even though, despite his 'purely descriptive approach', Barnes has stacked the cards in Ward's favour, yet, of more lasting importance, they shared a faith in inevitable progress and a scepticism about the utility of the practice and the very concept of politics.

Sumner was the first to recast Spencer in American terms so as to create a specifically American sociology; Ward was the first to advance an equally systematic criticism of the *laissez-faire* content of this analysis, and, beyond this, to put the case that 'progress' meant government by skilled social scientists—'Sociocracy'.

It was not until Sumner accepted the Chair of Political and Social Sciences in Yale College, in 1872, that he read Spencer's *Study of Sociology* as it was serialized in the *Contemporary Review*.[2] The naturalistic evolutionary view now appealed to him strongly, in contrast to his earlier disappointment with Spencer's more dogmatic *Social Statics*. Sumner, while never a slavish Spencerian in every detail, yet drew all his most general notions from the Spencerian sociology. He was a disciple more precise and lucid than the master, with a greater grasp of the function of actual institutions. He had little inclination to be *a priori* about the Post Office. His major contributions to systematic sociology were not published until after his death, but his teaching, together with his numerous essays and

[1] Harry Elmer Barnes, 'Two Representative Contributions of Sociology to Political Theory: the doctrines of William Graham Sumner and Lester Frank Ward', *American Journal of Sociology*, XXI (1919), 2; see 1–23 on Sumner, 150–70 on Ward.

[2] He had graduated in theology at Yale in 1859. He studied theology at Geneva, Göttingen and Oxford while a substitute served for him in the Army of the Republic. He was Rector to an Episcopalian Church for a short time, then, in 1868, became a tutor at Yale, in 1872, a full Professor. See Harris E. Starr, *William Graham Sumner* (New York: 1925).

addresses, commanded a wide audience, especially in the 'eighties. His one viewpoint that did stir up antagonism, and even attempts by Wall Street Yale Alumni to force his resignation—his opposition to tariff protection in any form—only shows his independence and integrity. He was in no manner the mere apologist for 'Big Business' that some have tried to paint him.[1]

Sumner's morality and his methodology rode together in constant war against the State, to preserve, as he said, 'true liberalism'. To Sumner any form of State intervention must have the presumption against it of being a danger to liberty. He levels great polemical skill and biting irony against the automatic reformers and 'do-gooders'— he may have been the first to use the phrase.[2] He argues three general propositions. Firstly, it is morally wrong to extend State activities when the effect will be, as is usually the case, to distribute benefits with no relation to burdens. Secondly, the State is proved by history to be usually incompetent; if a Statesman had perfect knowledge, he might plan rationally to maximize the social good, but this is never conceivable: the unintended effects of intervention always outweigh the intended. Thirdly, the obvious inequalities in society are a demonstration of the selectivity of social evolution: attempts to remedy inequalities by legislation or by large-scale charity only perpetuate the unfit. Although he clearly confuses 'ethical principles' with a hypothetical rational economic structure, yet he does advance what some economists would still feel is the deepest objection to any purportedly entirely rational theory of planning. 'It is characteristic of speculative legislation that it very generally produces the exact opposite of the result it was hoped to get from it,' he says. 'The reason is that the elements of any social problem which we do not know so far surpass those which we do know that our solutions have a greater chance to be wrong than to be right.' [3]

What Social Classes Owe to Each Other (the title of his most widely read book) is nothing but respect for the full liberty of one another. And the State owes nothing to anybody, except 'peace, order, and the guarantee of rights'.[4] Here is a complete *laissez-faire*, rounded out with an evolutionary dynamic of change, and remarkable

---

[1] For instance, Robert MacCloskey, *American Conservatism in the Age of Enterprise: a study of William Graham Sumner, Stephen J. Field and Andrew Carnegie* (Cambridge, Mass.: 1951).

[2] See especially his *The Challenge of Facts, and Other Essays* (New Haven: 1914).

[3] *Ibid.*, p. 215. I think of the critique of planning that the writings of Professor Hayek advance. But Sumner, like Hayek, to a certain extent misses the point by imputing to all planners his own notion of rationality, indeed his own rationalism. The Populist States, for instance, of the 'eighties and 'nineties were concerned to gain *political control* over Rail-road rates—an understandable motive; they were not claiming to create a more rational economic order in transportation.

[4] Sumner, *What Social Classes Owe to Each Other* (New York: 1883), p. 12.

for its frank recognition of class structure and of class hostility—though the classes are classes of success and failure, not of birth. Sumner denied the competence of the majority class—of failures—to make decisions that would go against the natural interests of the successful minority. This majority will probably be ignorant of the laws of evolution and may be stampeded into unnatural attempts to remedy in the mass what is their individual failure of application and diligence. He bluntly discards the democratic dogmas of equality. In no one is the split in the dominant liberal-Whig doctrines between the apparently equally valid inferences of *liberty* or of *equality* accepted with less misgivings—misgivings that have always perplexed and tortured American liberals of either wing. He substitutes for the Jeffersonian agrarian equality of situation a kind of methodological equality of industrial enterprise. All things that are done freely and do not prevent the equal freedom of others are equal in status. 'The Challenge of Facts' demands that we do not discriminate between one set of free-moving facts and another. Quantitative differences of facts are of interest only to the competitors *within* the system; qualitative differences are extraneous; the sociologist views the total system as moral because, by the automatic elimination of the unfit, it ensures Progress.

On the face of it, the sociologists' arguments would either justify the dominance of the millionaire—as the selected bloom of the evolutionary process; or else their own dominance—as those who understand the formula for universal betterment. But the scientific method that they espoused could also *itself* appear democratic, for it was based on an atomic individuality, was open to all, fully public and purged of mystery, authority, tradition and subjective hierarchy. The 'Age of Science' and the 'Age of Democracy' became commonly seen as all but identical concepts, the complementary progenitors of Progress—without any realization that to do so was to turn Science as knowledge into technology, and was to elevate a form of government called 'Democracy' from a technique into an end in itself.[1]

To Sumner, then, social classes were the 'facts' of Democracy and so must be viewed with the same cold objectivity as the constants in any scientific theory. 'Democracy,' he says, 'in order to be true to

[1] An interesting example is an address by Denison Olmsted, the Professor of Natural Philosophy and Astronomy at Yale, entitled 'On the Democratic Tendencies of Science' (no date, *circa* 1870), bound in a collection, *Pamphlets on Education*, V, University of California at Berkeley, Library. It begins: 'It has been but too common in our country to raise an outcry against the colleges and universities, as being aristocratic institutions, designed for the benefit of the rich. The same charges have sometimes been brought against science itself, as tending to produce and perpetuate invidious distinctions between men. . . . My object . . . is to prove that science, in its very nature, tends to promote political equality; to elevate the masses; to break down the spirit of aristocracy. . . .'

itself, and to develop into a sound working system, must show the same cold resistance to any claims for favour on grounds of poverty as on grounds of birth or rank.' [1] Or, as he sarcastically adds: 'There is an old ecclesiastical prejudice in favour of the poor and against the rich.' Liberty must be maintained against such prejudices—liberty, as it were, might rely on Faith and Hope, but must beware of Charity. 'The notion of civil liberty which we have inherited', he says, 'is that of a status *created for the individual by laws and institutions*, the effect of which is that each man is guaranteed the use of all his own powers exclusively for his own welfare.' [2] But he does not stop to notice how, in this definition, his notion of how liberty came about considerably modifies his notion of what liberty is.

This definition shows how Sumner became involved in a not un- expected ambiguity about what he meant by a 'law of nature'. For probably his major contribution to sociology was his attempt to purge the Spencerian system of its elements of natural law—even in a Lockean sense; he argued that there was no need to go beyond the observable pattern of 'mores' and 'folkways' in understanding social structure and its order. The sociologist would discover the true nature of these patterns, but, he thought, discovery of folkways can no more abrogate a law than can discovery in Physics: all that can follow is that frictions will be reduced by ending foolish attempts to regulate the inevitable selecting process of the law of evolution. So his laws are at the same time both laws of the *physis* and of the *nomos*. Social laws appear as conventional, as liberty is 'a status created for the individual by laws and institutions'. But if they are to be 'good laws', then they must also, presumably, be in conformity with the law of evolution, which is not conventional, but natural. In other words, Sumner can approach the study of society 'naturalistically' because, whatever happens, he thinks that there is a natural tendency towards betterment—the choices of ethical theory are irrelevant. 'Liberty' is stripped of all the ethical content that comes from historical understanding and becomes, at least potentially, every- where the same, despite its creation by various laws in various societies. It is the liberty of freely moving forces to continue moving freely. Liberty becomes another way of saying that sociology is the science of a closed system free from any 'extraneous' moral or physical interventions of force such as would prevent a natural equilibrium. 'Progress', no longer religion, comes near to becoming the opiate of the people.

Although Sumner rejects all religious and metaphysical sanctions upon social behaviour, and though to him history is merely a chronicle of near disasters due to rash State intervention, yet

[1] Sumner, *What Social Classes Owe*, p. 37.   [2] *Ibid.*, p. 12, my italics.

53

throughout his work there is a dominant hortatory tone, an enthusiasm and persuasive zeal that became almost the hallmark of the advocates of a science of society. It was clearly not so much the case that Sumner's 'forgotten man'—the individual—was '*guaranteed* the use of all his own powers exclusively for his own welfare', but that, come what may, he *should* use them so. Sumner was preaching the arrival of the Millennium-in-equilibrium through the evolutionary efforts of those who knew themselves to be the fittest-who-had-survived. The more strongly he urged *the need* to be purely objective and scientific in studying or practising the skills of society, the more the need became *a duty* to exhibit a kind of inverted moral integrity.

But, sooner or later, out of the very unpredictability of a society bent upon Progress, conflicts and changes occurred that made even the unreflective man wish to escape from such rationalistic codifications and to rationalize a changed experience. A popular opposition to all forms of State intervention in commerce, industry and social status could become considerably diluted in times of economic depression. There was no turning to 'Statism' and 'Socialism', as Spencer and Sumner feared, but in the thought of the 'nineties there was a growing sense that the case for individualism had been overstated, or had posed a false or over-sharp antithesis. Once voluntary agreement in it was shattered, the whole claim of Spencer and Sumner to be scientific had to be modified or had, as it did, to descend from the Hall of Science lectern and appear as a partisan idol of the market place. In political terms, the lack of clear agreement appeared at a most sensitive spot in the national mythology: Populism showed that the individualistic capitalist-farmer was beginning to realize that in times of tight credit he needed considerable help to remain a doctrinaire individualist.

Sumner, indeed, had seen clearly the poignancy of the dilemma of the American liberal individualist: 'The freeman in a free democracy, when cut off from all the ties which might pull him down, severed also the ties by which he might have made others pull him up. He must take all the consequences of his new status. He is, in a certain sense, an isolated man.'[1] Sumner, with an Hobbesean perversity and strength of will, was prepared to face this isolation rather than to live with the enervating 'fallacy of human fraternity'. But, occasionally, some of the giant-like creatures of the mythology of individualism lost such nerve, or, like Marlowe's Mephistopheles, stirred restlessly for companionship in their loneliness.

2. Some Seeds of Hesitancy

At the very time that Sumner was writing, one of those almost

[1] Sumner, *What Social Classes Owe*, p. 39.

periodic swings of group consciousness that complicate the nature of American individualism began to stir. Observers as different as De Tocqueville and Ostrogorski could note how an extreme individualism could also lead to an almost indiscriminate gregariousness, membership in a group for the sake of membership. This tendency of opposites to meet at their extremes has provided, from this time on, the greatest perplexity for American political and social thought. As we will see, Pragmatism itself only recreated this dilemma; the passionate individualism of William James was not at all the same thing as the group-consciousness of John Dewey.

The attempt was far afoot, from a variety of motives both political and theoretical, to strike some middle way between a strident individualism and an alien strengthening of the central State. Socialisms there were, and the Social Gospel revived to bring some ministers out of their 'Acres of Diamonds' into Christian-Socialism; but these were symptomatic extremes, greatly overemphasized and probably overstudied too. For, as Washington Gladden rightly protested: 'We may go far beyond Mr. Spencer's limits and yet stop a great way this side of socialism.' [1] But it was very hard for the type of social theory that Spencer and Sumner had popularized to strike any empirical middle ground between the annihilation of community responsibility, which is the ultimate end of an extreme individualism of method, and the dissolution of man into his social functions alone, which was to take place in much of subsequent social science.

The success of Spencer and Sumner had been a product of their ability to comfort traditional Americanism in a time of considerable social strain, and of how well the notes of their individualism fitted into the Jeffersonian scale. But this comfort was not to last, for Jeffersonianism itself was in process of reinterpretation, turning from the realm of localism and *laissez-faire* into the realm of Federalism and regulation. The Spencerians' very need for such vehemence and polemical violence after the Civil War was, perhaps all along, a sign that a challenge to their assumptions was implicit in the very conditions that they sought to justify. In a sense, they explained too much: for the formal domination of their words was so great that some men came, without wishing to deny their basic individualism and dedication to Progress and to Science, to wonder whether the actual system of American institutions was yet prepared enough for this fine natural system to work. The damning day was to come when Gifford Pinchot, a millionaire but a supporter of Theodore Roosevelt,

---

[1] Quoted by Richard Hofstadter, *Social Darwinism* (Philadelphia: 1944), p. 86. See generally, John D. Hicks, *The Populist Revolt* (Minneapolis: 1931) and Grant McConnel, *The Decline of Agrarian Democracy* (Berkeley, Cal.: 1953), Chapter I.

was to call Spencer 'a visionary'. All too clearly there was still need-less unhappiness and constraint in a system whose ideology had for twenty years been promising a natural equation of social happiness together with an all but complete liberty for each individual—per-haps positive acts of government were needed to create this harmony. As it arose, American Progressivism recreated for itself Bentham's idea of the 'sinister interests' that can spoil, temporarily, the liberal equation. There was no revolt 'against the system', as in Europe; but there was at the least a growing realization that Big Business—hitherto the fittest of the selected giants—could spoil the equilibrium that could and should be regulated in the interests of Small Business.

The growing importance of the Granger, the Agrarian, the Popu-list, and the Labour Movements could not be ignored, although they were movements of protest more than of drastic reform or of real power. There was a telling refutation of Spencerism in the industrial disputes of the 'eighties and 'nineties; and after the depression of 1887, Sumner and the Spencerians were forced more and more into the unreal position of appearing reactionaries, not liberals, trying to theorize both reformers and abuses out of existence. The exhaustion of free land, the social stratification of the rapidly growing urban populations, and the splitting up of the business 'community' into separate and conflicting groups were creating the need for a sociology that would at least touch upon regulation and positive acts of reform *as well as* still testifying to an underlying spontaneous betterment. Both the Sherman Anti-Trust Acts and the Protective Tariff were possible aspects of liberalism that threatened to outbid the Spencerian ethos.

When a full and strong criticism of Spencerian sociology did come, at least from an academic quarter, significantly it abandoned neither the idea of a science of society nor yet the idea of Progress. The growth of the American social sciences in their modern form was fully immanent the day that Sumner was brought to task for his elementary lack of observation by the palaeobotanist, Lester Frank Ward.

3. Ward turns Sumner Upside Down

The publication in 1883 of Ward's *Dynamic Sociology* marked the first significant attack on Spencer and Sumner as themselves un-scientific.[1] He is able to see them, quite correctly, as sons of their

---

[1] Ward was the son of an itinerant mechanic and a clergyman's daughter. His child-hood and early manhood were of intense poverty, but he educated himself at night school, taking diplomas in Arts, Law, and then Medicine. He continued scientific study and gained a distinguished reputation as a palaeobotanist, becoming in 1883 the chief Palaeontologist in the United States Geological Survey. Thus he was, unlike so many of the interpreters of biological law, himself a trained and practising scientist. See Emily Palmer Cape, *Lester F. Ward, a personal sketch* (New York: 1922). The

father Malthus, and to reject their inherited fatalism and unction by stressing purpose and control. He substitutes the *Positive Philosophy* of Comte for the *Essay on Population* of Malthus as a handbook for scientific Statesmen. Ward was not immediately to gain the ear of the ordinary educated public in the way that Spencer and Sumner had done. But he was to gain the allegiance of a new generation of teachers in these new subjects in the newly expanding universities, so that, when the time came when almost more than could be called 'the ordinary educated public' were attending the universities as a matter of social habit, his influence was to be, though indirect, massive.

Ward's attack began with a simple and basic observation. Just as Kropotkin, journeying on the Steppes, was to notice with the splendour of simplicity the fact of *mutual aid* amongst wild animals, so Ward, as a palaeobotanist, was to notice the prodigality and wastefulness of nature.[1] He noted that some lower organisms give off as many as a million ova of which only very few develop into maturity; the rest succumb in the vaunted struggle for survival. The waste of matter and reproductive powers appeared to him as fantastic compared to the conservation apparent in the intelligent purposes of man. Haphazard human strife, whether in warfare or in industrial competition, was similarly wasteful. Ward, instead of seeing man as an isolated individual struggling with a fixed environment, saw him as an active agent who fought back with 'creative intelligence' to shape environment to his purposes.

He distinguished between 'telic' and 'genetic' factors. The former were those governable by human will and purpose, the latter the result of material forces. He turns Sumner upside down as surely as Marx did Hegel. Environment need not wholly determine social reactions; society may react positively against natural limitations and deprivations by way of deliberate control: 'A close analysis shows', he said, 'that the fundamental distinction between the animal and the human method is that the *environment transforms the animal, while man transforms the environment.* ... *The paradox, therefore, is that free competition can only be secured through regulation.*'[2] For the coercion of natural laws, which in Spencer's eyes doom State action to impotence or disaster, human purpose is substituted: 'mind' capable of controlling matter within the limits of its

importance of Ward in relation to the origins of scientism in American political studies is noted by Hans J. Morgenthau in his *Scientific Man vs. Power Politics* (Chicago: 1946). Henry Steele Commager also treats of Ward in his *The American Mind* (New Haven: 1950) as an intellectual synthesis of a common type of American thought.

[1] Ward, *Glimpses of the Cosmos* (New York: 1913–18), III, 47–51; VI, 58–63.

[2] Ward, 'The Psychologic Basis of Social Economics', a paper submitted to the American Academy of Political and Social Science, *Proceedings*, No. 77 (1893), p. 81.

own intelligence. 'Co-operation is an artificial principle, the result of superior intelligence. Competition is a natural law, and involves no thought.' [1]

It was at this level of a politically progressive social-psychology that most American social scientists have accepted Ward. His *Psychic Factors in Civilization* tried to find a 'fundamental level of explanation' in which common biological drives create the reality of group and social action from out of the appearance of individual actions. But, in these terms, any statement about a psychological disposition can equally well be stated overtly and descriptively. 'Fundamental instincts' can be seen as behaviour in certain patterns. To call anything in Ward's system 'psychologic' may not add to our knowledge of it at all; it may just constitute a tautology, although an emotive one. (It is only with the reception of the Freudian doctrine of the subconscious, it may be argued, that a genuine new level of 'psychologic' explanation is added.) The important point for the moment, however, is to show that Ward's appeal to the level of the 'psychologic' does not in any way point to an irrationalism in human behaviour, but rather strengthens belief in man's control of the Universe, limited only by his intelligence. It is a 'psychologic' law that man shall act increasingly to achieve such control. And from this it followed, for Ward and his successors, that understanding 'the law of mind' led more directly to 'social amelioration' than any mere participation in conventional politics.

It is interesting to see the use that a contemporary American Hegelian, W. W. Willoughby, can find for Ward—one young man typical of many of the old-style teachers of politics at the time. Willoughby, in his *The Nature of the State* (1896), developed a gently Hegelian interpretation of 'General Will'. He treated of the foundation of the State as a unity created out of a mere collection of individuals by means of 'a sentiment of community of feeling and mutuality of interest, and this sentiment finds expression in the creation of a political power, and the subjection of the community to its authority'.[2] He then quotes approvingly from Jellinek's *Die Lehre von den Staaten Verbindungen* that the State 'gives expression to this unity by organizing itself as a collective personality, and constituting itself as a volitional and active person'. But when he comes to criticize the 'extreme *laissez-faire* of Spencer', it is to Ward that he turns:

The most thoroughgoing criticism of Spencerian doctrine is that of Professor Lester F. Ward . . . So satisfactorily has this writer laid bare

[1] Ward, *Dynamic Sociology, or Applied Social Science as Based upon Statistical Sociology and the Less Complex Sciences* (New York: 1883), II, 594.
[2] W. W. Willoughby ,*The Nature of the State* (New York: 1896), p. 257.

the inaccuracies and insufficiencies of this doctrine that in the following paragraphs it is necessary to do little more than reproduce his arguments.[1]

. . . which Willoughby proceeds to do. He sums up the argument of Ward, as far as he takes it: 'The fact is, that when we reach man, the competitive biological law holds good and is beneficial rather in its psychic than in its physiological aspects, while with Spencer and his followers the physiological features are emphasized and the psychic factors almost ignored.' [2]

But there was both more and less in Ward than Willoughby used him for. Certainly, in many places Ward does identify the 'psychic factors' with a group mind or with the concept of a general or a generalized will, as Willoughby's Hegelianism appeared to do. Ward spoke of the need for the individual member of society to know the true principles of social science, and for there to be 'a fearless application of these principles by the collective mind of society as embodied in its form of government, in the interest of the whole social organism'.[3] This 'collective mind' is not merely 'public opinion', as Barnes illicitly and democratically translates him. But, equally, to give it an Hegelian exegesis would be to confuse either the obscure with the Hegelian or else, more certainly, the biological with the ethical. Ward's phrase, 'social organism', is certainly an improvement in descriptive imagery upon the mechanics of Spencer's *Social Statics* and physiological biology, but it is the peculiarity of the cohesion of human society that neither biological nor mechanical imagery exactly expresses its nature. They are images to be used with caution, never literally, at the danger of becoming illicit inferences. The 'social organism' and the 'collective mind' of Ward are verbal attempts to bridge the gulf that he has dug for himself, of which one side is the determinism of causal laws upon society, and the other side the 'fearless application' (or not) of, as he soon makes clear, the sociologist as Statesman.

Ward becomes involved in the same kind of difficulty as Mannheim's 'sociology of knowledge' was to be later, and he can only offer the same kind of solution: the 'unattached intellectual' and the 'free-floating' social scientist. Ward exchanges Spencer's necessary determinism by nature for a necessary determination of natural environment by the most intelligent men: for Huxley's 'administrative nihilism' is substituted the rule of the sociologists. If existing

---

[1] *Ibid.*, p. 329.

[2] *Ibid.*, p. 335. I am aware that there is an unexplored relationship between neo-Darwinism and Hegelianism. D. G. Ritchie's *Darwin and Hegel, with other philosophical studies* (London: 1893), is clearly relevant.

[3] Ward, 'The Great Social Problem', an unpublished paper given at Brown and quoted by Samuel Chugerman in his *Lester Ward: an* [sic] *American Aristotle* (Durham, N.C.: 1939), p. 327.

social conflicts and limitations are only a function of as yet inadequate human intelligence, then conditions for expanding intelligence must be studied (by those of an already expanded intelligence):

The social will is, therefore, a mass of conflicting desires which largely neutralize one another. . . . The social intellect proves a poor guide, not because it is not sufficiently vigorous, but because knowledge of those matters which principally concern society are so limited, *while that which exists is chiefly lodged in the minds of those individuals who are allowed no voices in the affairs of state.*[1]

He has already pointed out in his *Dynamic Sociology* that the condition for a socially conscious State is 'the universal diffusion of the maximum amount of the most important knowledge'. Who are 'those individuals' who have the knowledge, and what is 'the most important knowledge'? These are questions of peculiar importance, especially when the State is resurrected as the repository of intelligence to counter the extreme individualism of Spencer and Sumner, indeed to counter, in the name of its fulfilment, the whole tradition of Constitutional-Democracy in America. Ward's answer is at first sensibly cautious: that we will not know the precise form of such a State until we reach it. But reach it we will: evolution may depend on increasing knowledge, but it is a psychic fact of man that he seeks for knowledge:

It is only after the mind of society, as embodied in its consciousness, will and intellect, shall, through the application of this formula for a sufficiently long time to reach the desired result, come to stand to the social organism in somewhat the relation the individual mind stands to the individual organism, that any fully developed art of government can be expected to appear.[2]

This seems to open the door for an Hegelian 'suspension and synthesis' of Ward and, at least, raises more questions than it solves. These ambiguities he attempts to resolve a little by supplying certain specific conditions. It is important, for understanding this next step, to realize that he felt himself neither an idealist nor yet an empiricist in the art of government. He had little faith in any 'mere tinkering' with the political or economic machinery of society.[3] He looked forward to the 'manufacture of intelligence, and its application, through scientific planning, to the whole life of society'. At one point Ward specifically attacks the empirical orientation of contemporary

[1] Ward, *The Psychic Factors of Civilization* (Boston: 1897), pp. 315–16, my italics. By 'those who are allowed no voices' he clearly means the sociologists and not the Negroes.

[2] *Ibid.*, p. 316.

[3] See Commager, *The American Mind, op. cit.*, p. 213, for a discussion of Ward's impatience with conventional politics.

Progressivism by stating that: '... *if government would be in the hands of social scientists*, instead of social empiricists, it might be elevated to the rank of an applied science'.[1] It is for this end that society, to Ward, 'deals with the artificial means of accelerating the spontaneous processes of nature',[2] to the end that society may emerge through the stages of 'physiocracy and plutocracy into sociocracy'.[3]

Once the logic of guided evolution is accepted, and the self-interested individual of Spencer is replaced by the group-intelligence of Ward as the methodological basis of social science, there is no flinching the consequences:

> Desires there will be, for so is man constituted, but these seek only their own satisfaction. .... It is true that the desires of men can be changed in their nature. The same individual will have entirely different desires if reared under one environment from what he would have if reared under an entirely different one. And this constitutes the over-whelming argument for the creation of a proper social environment.[4]

This will depend, he says, upon the education of man in a sound manner: '... it should consist in furnishing the largest possible amount of the most important knowledge, letting the beliefs take care of themselves'. But, again, the criterion of 'importance' is left undefined, or, rather, in the hands of the teacher-administrators, 'the sociocrats': 'It must be recognized that the legislator is essentially an inventor, a scientific discoverer. His duty is to be thoroughly versed in the whole theory and practice of social physics.' He is called upon to devise 'ways and means' for securing the true interests and improvement of the people for whom he is to legislate. This cannot be done within the existing framework of institutions:

> A public assembly governed by Parliamentary rules is as inadequate as could be conceived of for anything like scientific legislation. Imagine all the inventors in the country assembled in a hall acting under the gavel of a presiding officer to devise the machines of the future and to adopt the best by a majority vote. Or think of trying to advance scientific discovery by general convention![5]

He points out that actual research is done in laboratories or in small committees, and thus should it be also in government. The legislative committee 'really deliberate', they investigate questions, collect and hear testimony, and 'weigh evidence'. 'This is truly scientific and leads to the discovery of principles involved.

---

[1] Ward, *Dynamic Sociology*, II, 249.
[2] Ward, *Pure Sociology* (New York: 1903), III, 431.
[3] Ward, *Psychic Factors*, pp. 316–19.   [4] *Ibid.*, p. 308.
[5] *Ibid.*, p. 309. One is reminded of how Marx contrasted the institutions of the Commune of 1870 to Bourgeois Parliaments: 'They are representative without being Parliamentary ... they are working assemblies, not talking shops.'

less biased by Party leanings [cf. 'desires there will be'] they are very likely to reach the truth and report practical and useful measures.' Committee work is, therefore, 'the nearest approach we have to the scientific investigation of social questions. It is on the increase and is destined to play an ever-increasing role in national legislation.' [1] If the caucuses might demur, yet the campuses of today should give more honour to such a remarkable prophecy.

It is worth recounting Ward's ideas in such detail precisely because they offer a rational and systematic justification of an approach to the study of politics and sociology that a subsequent generation exemplified but scarcely paused to justify. Some of the details with which he works out his theory make it clear why Harry Elmer Barnes was so eager to revive a knowledge of Ward to the generation of Arthur Fisher Bentley, Charles Merriam, Stuart Rice and Harold Lasswell:

> Again there is statistical method. No one will deny that this is rapidly becoming a leading factor in legislation. Statistics are simply the facts which underlie the science of government. They are to the legislator what the results of observation and experiment are to the man of science. They are in fact the inductions of political science, and the inductive in that science is of the same value that it is to science in general, its only true foundation.[2]

This is, indeed, an interesting half-truth. But it contains two purely logical confusions. Firstly, a statistic is not *used*, primarily, as a *fact*, although it can be *mentioned*, secondarily, as a fact. It is a symbol of quantity attributed to a class of objects that we consider as a class for certain purposes; for other purposes the facts may fall in different classes. More helpfully, it could be said that principles of classification, not classes of statistics, partly underlie the science of government. Secondly, the Baconian notion of science as pure induction is false. There is never a mind so empty of prior theories that it can passively watch, as it were, a mess of facts arrange themselves into a well-baked theory. There is always some existing theory that is being tested, and some interest that has led to the particular investigation. These confusions become endemic—speaking historically as well as logically—in attempts to apply biological or physical metaphor or method to politics. They militate against consideration of both presuppositions and evaluative judgements. 'The beliefs take care of themselves', as Ward said, but only at the believer's peril—*caveat emptor*.

4. The Charms of Sociocracy

Ward proclaims: 'The individual has reigned long enough. The

---

[1] Ward, *Psychic Factors*, p. 310.　　　　　[2] *Ibid.*, p. 311.

day has come for society to take its own affairs into its own hands and shape its own destiny.' He regards democracy as a stage which society must pass through *en route* to 'the ultimate social stage which all governments must attain if they persist'. He asks:

How then, it may be asked, do democracy and sociocracy differ? How does society differ from the people? . . . But that shibboleth of democratic states, where it means anything at all that can be described or defined, stands simply for the majority of qualified electors, no matter how small that majority may be. . . . At least there is no denying the right of the majority to act for society, for to do this would involve either the denial of the right of the majority to act for all, or the admission of the right of a minority to act for society. But a majority acting for society is a different thing from society acting for itself, even though, as must always be the case, it acts through an agency chosen by its members.

Again, this is an interesting half-truth. There is, indeed, no necessary legitimacy in rule by a majority; but neither is there in rule by the expert. Ward shows the growing anti-historical temper of social thought in that he does not even stop to consider that the debates at the Philadelphia Convention and the Federalist Papers were also very much concerned with the problem of the relationship of the majority to society as a whole, and, indeed, made a lasting contribution to the Constitutional aspect of the problem.

Ward attacks 'Party politics', as much as any of the Progressive reformers, as the supreme example of the part acting for the whole. 'Sociocracy', he concludes, 'will alter all this. Irrelevant issues will be laid aside. The important objects upon which all but a few are agreed will receive their proper degree of attention, and measures will be considered in a non-partisan spirit with the sole purpose of securing those objects.' [1]

The uncritical faith of Ward in the Sociologist-Legislator is astonishing; in many ways it is a caricature more than a crystallization of a widespread longing among Americans to replace the realm of politics by the reign of technocracy. But precisely because the sentiment, if not the theory, was already so widespread, it was easy for the 'scientist' Ward to flourish in a highly individualistic society and yet to speak of 'the social will' as the ultimate and evolving reality. And the sources of this social will seems, from Ward's writings, to be the knowledge of how society works more than any generalized emanation of particular wills. 'Society acting for itself' is a product, then, of knowledge, not of will. His 'social will', in a sense is misnamed; he means 'social reason' or 'social knowledge'. This is not a polemical subterfuge on his part, but a sign of how completely he failed to see any possible tension, or even distinction,

[1] *Ibid.*, pp. 323–6.

between *will* and *reason*. He has no sense whatever, after the Christian or Kantian manner, that *any* individual will has within itself an *essence* of value. To Ward value is attached only to the *potentiality* of social reason or 'social will', 'society acting for itself'.

This is not to say that the sociologist, of any persuasion, may not be able to gain a greater knowledge of many conditions and relationships in society than the ordinary citizen. He can establish by his knowledge a legitimate claim to be consulted. But, even leaving aside the question whether this gives him any special operative political wisdom, there remains the practical question of whether particular sociologists are any more likely to agree amongst themselves than any other group. A Parliament of sociologists and technologists, even divided entirely into specialist committees, is surely no more likely to reach agreement and avoid party alignments or factions than is a Parliament of politicians. (As Madison had argued in the great Tenth Paper of *The Federalist*, factions are natural, and cannot be eliminated except at the cost of eliminating liberty; they can be constrained, but not destroyed.) The rival claims to scarce resources by different sciences will always stimulate the search for principles on which to establish priorities, and, in the long meanwhile, for a framework of law in which to arbitrate peacefully; to do this is no more than to paraphrase Aristotle's reasons for calling 'Politics' the 'Master Science'. Every theory of society and every social problem is inevitably a partial view: it will be based on a selection, not an exhaustion, of the evidence relevant to the solution of anything thought to be a problem. There is actually a danger to freedom when the ever-recurring search for legitimacy in politics is entirely subsumed in the quest for certainty.

Ward can only resolve the dichotomy between the majority will and the real will of all by trusting the particular wills, or, rather, knowledge, of the Sociocrats—the possessors of an *Arcanum Imperii* who will not have to be dragged reluctantly to office. The Sociocrats of Ward are no novelty, even if they are, in a wide sense, modern: these Platonic Guardians without the Platonic education are the type of Machiavelli's Prince and Rousseau's Legislator, only now become bureaucratized. They are chosen men who can transcend necessity. Ward has no sense of the importance of Constitutions, whether written or unwritten, and so cannot relate the largest achievement of Western politics to his Sociocracy at all. Here in Ward is the first sign of that tendency of political and social science, soon to become common, which under-estimates completely the importance of institutional factors, and, dissolving all content and structure away into biological-like 'process', looks only for a 'real level' of politics and social life where measurable behaviour is to be explained in terms of 'psychologic factors', socially conditioned, alone.

Clearly if Ward were removed utterly from the tradition in which he was born—about which there is no word in his writings—even totalitarian inferences could be drawn from his system. He shows the same epistemological certainty in a total system of social explanation and, also, the same rejection of the political for the meaningless ideal of the rule of society itself as a whole, via its mediators. Logically his route is the same as that of Comte towards his 'Priesthood of Science', although he felt no need, like Comte, *to create* a religion of Progress.

The above discussion of Ward was, of course, partial. No attempt has been made to give a full appreciation of the scope of his work and of its importance for descriptive sociology. In unfolding one great error he may well have discovered twenty or thirty lesser truths, certainly some. But the error that creates his 'Sociocracy' is a great one and one that was often to be repeated. This 'Sociocratic' element necessarily arises once a theorist clings to a belief in a necessary Progress after rejecting the equally false, but possibly less dangerous, Spencerian account of spontaneous Progress. Progress is *possible*, but to regard it as *necessary* and as *cumulative* is to destroy any possible meaning or place for individual morality: morality can only become what the Sociocrats regard as 'the artificial means of accelerating the spontaneous processes of nature'; and Progress, similarly, can only become what the Sociocrats say it is. In the scheme of Ward, evolution ultimately becomes the same as Progress. For if there is no standard independent of evolution that can say when evolution is beneficial or not—that is to say, when evolution becomes Progress, then *all* change must be seen as Progress. Of course, some 'natural' evolution, some unasked-for changes in fact appear palpably disastrous or cruel; so the doctrine of necessary Progress crystallizes, in Ward, into the form that all *deliberate* changes are progressive.

Many writers, as we have said, share Ward's premises, but wish to avoid his conclusions. Harry Elmer Barnes did just this when he drew Ward's work to the attention of political scientists in the 1920's as an ally of democracy and as a theoretical foundation for their own practice:

Sociocracy is the next logical step in political evolution. It is in reality the *ideal democracy* from which the present partisanship, ignorance, hypocrisy and stupidity have been eliminated. . . . The scientific statesmanship of the future must attempt to guide and utilize social force and energy in the same manner as the applied scientists of today control and utilize the physical energy of nature.[1]

[1] Barnes, 'Two Representative Contributions . . .', *op. cit.*, p. 162, my italics.

To add 'ideal' to 'democracy' is not to make the resulting concept sound any the less dubious. But even if, in his undeniably good democratic heart, Barnes really meant all that he said as mere analogy, yet he should have seen another side to his vision; if not the problem of the meaning of morality in such a brave new world, yet certainly the massive potentiality for control that modern technology has given the State. The temptation of certainty may reach its salvation in the predictable order not of a model, or of a speculative ideal type, but of a totalitarian régime. The Utopianism of Marxism, which breeds its cruelty, is strangely paralleled in the formal thought of those who followed or shared the premises of Ward.

Professor Samuel Chugerman in 1939 paid eloquent testimony to the importance of Ward, both as person and as type, in a book firmly called: *Lester Ward: an American Aristotle*:

> With such truths as those of dynamic sociology, the era of positive science and constructive ethics cannot be far away. *Public opinion (we have called it social will and the social mind often enough)* is waiting to be substituted for the individualistic hit-or-miss method of competition, a method which had been proved beyond any doubt to be cruel, restricted and blundering. Co-operation, education, and melioration essentially grounded in sociology are here to show us the way to the promised land of a humane moral order, ruled by society, for society. For formulating that system of social science and philosophy Ward should be forever enshrined in the hearts of humanity.[1]

The preface to this volume, however, out-Herods Herod. Professor Barnes dialectically synthesizes his understanding of Ward with his understanding of the New Deal:

> The vision of Ward came to naught for years. . . . But President Roosevelt's New Deal, as a gesture to remember the forgotten man, is a tiny fragment of Ward's sociology and a larger segment of the philosophy of the Founding Fathers. At last the United States seems to have given official recognition to the necessity of knowledge and insight for intelligent government. The vision which Ward, the still unknown Darwin of Sociology, wrote into his works . . . has developed into a vast mass of data, many specific surveys and plans under government sanction, and a complete overhauling of classical social reformism. If we drift again into something even worse than the period of 1914 to 1933, no one can say that we have not been adequately informed or powerfully warned.[2]

A man should not be judged by what use others make of his ideas,

---

[1] Samuel Chugerman, *Lester Ward: an American Aristotle*, p. 327, my italics. This is no work of phrenological eccentricity. By weight, format, footnotes and sponsors it is a scholarly volume. Professors Charles Ellwood, Howard Jensen and James Dealey introduced it to the world and it had, also, a special Foreword by Harry Elmer Barnes.

[2] *Ibid.*, pp. 11–12, a Foreword by Harry Elmer Barnes.

but ideas of such constant recurrence and gross vigour are never the possession of one man alone, though we study closely the man who makes of them the best or the most famous system. Barnes was directly influenced by Ward, but many others, not directly influenced, undergo, as we will see, the same experience of thought. Both Ward and Barnes present a caricature of the normal American political tradition, a tradition that in many ways Franklin Roosevelt, whom Barnes so enthusiastically misrepresents, himself best represents. He represents it by his 'try this, try that, but try something' pragmatism in the New Deal, something broadly successful, not disastrous, because it merely reasserted a timeworn faith in 'the common man', or rather, a faith that the common man would maintain his faith in Progress and American nationality, given a minimum of material help and a fair amount of governmental bustle that looked like progressive action. We have already seen enough to understand the plausibility of the caricature and something of why so many American political and social scientists should try, nevertheless, to recreate Roosevelt in their own image, rather than to reject him. The deeper problem is why, in rejecting the actual type of politics that Roosevelt himself practised, did they try to transcend this tradition by the path of positive science and not of speculative philosophy? It is the roots of this scientism in American academic thought in the years of roughly 1860–1900 that we have already been exploring, but the abundant flowering of it can only be understood in the context of the subsequent 'Progressive Era'.

5. Concluding Remarks

We have discussed Spencer, Sumner and Ward in these last two chapters because they drew the greatest theoretical coherency out of prevailing American thought. Ward, especially, influenced and expressed the coming pattern of ideas among American social and political scientists which began to differ from the common political tradition. In all three figures the insistence on a strictly scientific methodology is, in fact, a reflection of an idea of a particular political order. However logically invalid direct inferences for politics may be from such vast *a priori* systems of analogy from *Science*, yet historically the system of Spencer and Sumner did have great popular appeal, and that of Ward, great academic influence. But in drawing attention to a difference between the two systems, we still want to stress, yet again, their common conjuration with 'Science' and 'Progress'.

These first American sociologists clearly showed that any methodology of how to study society, however 'objective' and 'academic', must have political consequences—consequences which they drew firmly, too firmly. The idea of the 'neutrality of Science', which Chauncey Wright was then arguing vainly against James and Peirce in the Harvard Metaphysical Club, was scorned, almost without discussion.[1] Science was viewed as the technologist of Progress; and Progress was the cumulative achievement of both ethical and material goods. Of course, it should be granted that in Western culture since the Renaissance the vocabulary of political thought, of all schools, has tended to be highly coloured by concepts and analogies drawn from a contemporary understanding of the nature of natural science. And, equally, 'Progress' has its roots as deeply in the Protestant Millennial writings of the seventeenth century as in the writings of the Enlightenment of the eighteenth. But in political and social thought there is no need to mistake the analogies that we cull from either Science or Religion as necessarily meaning the realities that we are trying to express by them.

It could also be protested, and soon was, that such systems of thought, so vastly synthetic, were themselves unscientific; they neither experimented, measured nor accurately predicted. This is strictly true, but those who confined themselves to measurement, pure description and to what could pass as experiment did so because they had been convinced by such writings as Ward's that prediction would be possible. It was not a folly of Ward's to remain on the level of theory rather than of practical research; it was a recognition that the case for the new science or sciences had to be made good in principle and had to establish some criteria of meaning and verification before there was any use or any purpose for the strong young men to sally out with questionnaires upon the sociable doorsteps. We may doubt, philosophically, whether the case was made good; but, historically, we cannot doubt that it was made plausible.

'Progress', too, could synthesize as many things as Science. It was the shibboleth of both Democrat and Republican from California to Maine, of both those who wished to 'stand pat' with Mark Hanna or to reform (currency and electoral law) with William Jennings Bryan. But if it seemed to blur distinctions, it certainly set firm limits: under the spell of 'Progress' reformers would not become Socialists and corporate wealth would not become Conservative. The 'Progressives', like Charles Beard and Barnes, wished for more Federal regulation of monopolies, so as to ensure a truly *free economy*; the so-called Conservatives (i.e., the ultra-Liberals) believed that the monopoly question, if given time enough, would work itself out into the common desired *free economy*. There was a question of trusts and monopolies, but not a 'Social Question', as in Europe. In Europe, by

[1] See Philip Wiener, *Evolution and the Founders of Pragmatism* (Cambridge, Mass.: 1949), *passim*.

contrast, only sections of the middle classes spoke the language of Progress. Certainly, in late Victorian England up to 1914, they were large and influential sections, but they were constantly challenged: from below, by slogans of 'rights' and 'equality', and from above, by a lingering Conservative-Aristocratic scepticism about the spontaneity and inevitability of economic and moral betterment. European Socialists and Radicals were far more concerned with gaining an immediate equity, which compared to the American (middle-class) labourer they palpably lacked, than with learning the lulling incantation of 'Progress'—although admittedly with the growth of Communism, out of the frustration of many of these movements, something parallel to the function of Progress in American thought does arise. But it was then a divisive factor within the nation, not, as in America, an integrative one. 'Progress' in America was the response to the Industrial Revolution and its attendant expansion of a society *already liberal*; the original American did not need to be rescued or upturned by Revolution, but merely inflated and reassured by Progress.

In the United States in 1911, Truxton Beale, worried by a Progressivist monopoly of original scholarly writings, decided to gather together in print the most distinguished 'conservatives and individualists' of his day; Elihu Root, David Jayne Hill, Senator Henry Cabot Lodge, Judge E. H. Gary, Nicholas Murray Butler, Judge Harlan F. Stone, Charles W. Eliot and William Howard Taft—a roll call of Brahmin probity that could hold their heads high among the best men of Europe. But what did they write? Introductory essays to a new edition of Herbert Spencer's *The Man Versus the State* (1916)! (Barnes' invocation of Ward is the dialectic. counterpart of this.) When both 'left' and 'right' in America sung variants of a hymn to Progress and its consubstantial Science, no wonder a time could come when sceptics of Progress like Paul Elmer More and Irving Babbitt could be regarded by social scientists as between fools and knaves—and Henry Mencken, for that matter, as a *mere* comic.

Thus two great themes arise to dominate American social thought at the very time when it begins to become extended by and immersed in the growing colleges: Progress and the idea of a Science of Society. They did not immediately come to dominate political science; only after the turn of the century did the historical and philosophical German training begin to give way to something new. And this new style of political studies and would-be politics was not directly the positivism of Ward, though he helped to prepare the ground for what came. *Pragmatism*, indeed the whole special character of reformism in the Progressive Era, appeared as a synthesis between the idea of a Science of Society and the directly practical goal of political science, indeed of much of Higher Education in general, as citizenship training. As we will see, many of the new political scientists at the beginning of the Progressive Era seem merely to be moralists in practical action; but the spirit of Ward, and the whole body of common aspirations to which he gave theoretical expression, underlies them all, so that, by the end of the era and with little apparent change in formal doctrine, a full-blown vindication of a purely scientific approach to politics can appear in the pages of Arthur Fisher Bentley.

PART TWO
Conditions

V

THE CULT OF REALISM IN THE
PROGRESSIVE ERA

Philosophy in America will be lost between chewing a historic cud
long since reduced to a wooden fibre, or an apologetic for lost causes
(lost to natural science), or a scholastic, schematic formalism, unless
it can somehow bring to consciousness America's own needs and
its own implicit principle of successful action.

JOHN DEWEY, *Creative Intelligence* (1917)

I received a letter from an old friend who was in high glee over a
statement in some magazine that I had evolved a 'scientific theory'
as to why boys go to the bad in cities. It was plain that he was as much
surprised as he was pleased, and so was I when I heard what it was all
about. That which they had pitched upon as science was the baldest
recital of the facts as seen from Mulberry Street. Beyond putting two
and two together, there was very little reasoning about it.

JACOB RIIS, *The Making of an American*

1. The Progressives as Traditionalists

THE GENERATION after 1900 was to witness a spectacular increase in the teaching and literature of political science. It soon
became one of the largest departments on any typical campus.
Citizenship training was still the dominating purpose of this sheer
expansion, now stimulated by the debates about mass immigration
at the beginning of the period, and by the patriotism of both isolationists and interventionists at the end. But as it grew, it clearly
became addicted to techniques of study which were very different
from the original belief of the 'best men' of the 'seventies, 'eighties
and 'nineties that the problem of good government was, broadly
speaking, the problem of good men. In the midst of a national
enthusiasm for political reform, which political scientists themselves
shared in and led, they became possessed with the idea of a scientific
objectivity in which, as Dwight Waldo has well written, a 'new

73

amorality became almost a requisite for professional respect'. The demand arose on all sides to know 'how politics *really* works'; and this came close to being both the whole of the study of politics and the essence of reform. But what this demand itself really meant can only be understood in the whole context of the 'Progressive Era' and the American philosophy associated with it, pragmatism. Again our context may seem still to overwhelm our point, but this is something in the nature of American political science itself. Its concern with scientific method and its hope for a science of politics cannot be understood merely in terms of the intellectual trends dominant in the relatively few departments of Political Science already existing in 1900.

The Progressive Era saw a blending of the traditional Protestant moralism of American political thought with the modern technocratic frame of mind—a characteristic of modern social science. Scientism and moralism were to ride hand in hand, awkwardly but joyfully, upon pragmatism. 'As the philosophy of Spencer', Richard Hofstadter writes, 'had reigned supreme in the great age of enterprise, so pragmatism, which rapidly became the dominant American philosophy in the two decades after 1900, breathed the spirit of the Progressive Era.' [1] And to George Santayana, the pragmatism of Dewey was 'the devoted spokesman of the spirit of enterprise, of experiment, of modern industry . . . calculated to justify all the assumptions of American society'.[2]

William James and Charles Sanders Peirce, the real founder of American philosophic pragmatism, had only the remotest interest in systematic social and political theory. But the assertion that ideas were plans of action, not mirrors of reality; that all dualisms of *fact* and *value* are fatal; that the solving of *practical* problems, not the framing of definitions and the elucidation of metaphysics, was the purpose of man's highest activity—these were parts of the call for a 'new realism' that would give an era full of the spirit of reform the philosophic tools for practical political action. The instrumentalism of John Dewey was only a cultural extension of the 'pragmaticism' of Charles Sanders Peirce. James rescued Peirce's ideas from obscurity—though the man, alas, was impossible—and brought them into the decent and discriminating atmosphere of Harvard Yard, giving them affinity to the fierce individualism of the New England conscience. Dewey rescued them from even such obscurity, brought them on to the Court House Square and the School House Porch, and gave them affinity to the widespread stirrings for reform in

---

[1] *Social Darwinism* (New York: 1944), p. 103.
[2] See Santayana's contribution to *The Philosophy of John Dewey*, ed. Paul Schlipp (Evanston: 1939), p. 247.

national and municipal politics, in the practice of education, in the application of jurisprudence, and in the interpretation of the admittedly unique national history. The moralizing individual of the New England mind and the group-conscious reformism of the Prairie progressives, who dissolved the individual away into his social functions—these are the two sides of the pragmatist coin, a paradox flowing from a cultural ambivalence that was to have strange effects on the foundation and development of all the new social sciences.

Charles Beard, the supremely pragmatic figure of the scholar in action, wrote that: 'It was not the function of the student of politics to praise or condemn institutions or theories, but to understand and expound them; and thus for scientific purposes it [the study of politics] is separated from theology, ethics and patriotism.' [1] But the methodological separation became a practical separation: the business of pragmatism in the 1900's became to purge political thinking of 'theology, ethics and patriotism'—a triad that describes well enough the dominant interests of most American colleges in all subjects *before* the great educational reforms that began in the 1870's, yet one that had *already* lost its over-all dominance by the time that Beard was writing. Beard did not believe that he was condemning political studies to sterility by such a separation; on the contrary, only then could true reform follow. Pragmatism became a synthesis of many popular ideas about the authority of scientific procedure and an expression of national temperament by which reform became 'concrete', 'rational', 'demanded by the facts', even just 'scientific'. It eschewed the older moral reformism of the liberal Republicans like Greeley and Godkin, the 'Mugwumps' of the 'seventies and 'eighties, who began the movement for Civil Service reform; or the radicalism of Bryan and Champ Clark's Western democracy; or that Social Gospel movement of American Protestantism which reached its full flower in the writings of Walter Rauschenbush. Social ethics became secularized in the same manner that politics became regarded as potentially scientific. And yet pragmatism was far from untouched by the things that it formally rejected.

There was a renewed and deliberate attack on all previous notions of authority in favour of the name of both 'democracy' and 'science'. The word 'politics', in America so wrapped in derogatory connotations, began to be replaced by the word 'administration'. If, said one school of pragmatism, the *direct will of the people* was not interfered with by corrupt politicians manipulating complex and indirect electoral institutions, all would be well, the interests of the people

[1] Charles Beard, *Politics* (New York: 1908), p. 14.

and the actions of the legislatures would never part asunder. Initiative, Referendum and Recall became slogans of progressivism: South Dakota in 1898, Utah in 1900, Oregon in 1902, and, by 1917, over twenty States of the Union had adopted some form of initiative or referendum.[1] If, says another school of pragmatism, *experts* could replace elected politicians, and administration be separated from politics, then all would be well, the interests of the people would be calculated by their honest servants. The merit system of the Pendleton Civil Service Act of 1883 became expanded more and more by successive Presidents until by the time of Wilson's election it covered the majority of offices. And the 'commission plan' of city government began to spread after 1900, soon joined by the 'council-manager' form of government. Management by the people or management for the people might be debatable slogans, but they had a common belief that the people and their leaders, both in politics and in business, were grievously and needlessly at odds with one another. Politicians must be brought back to responsibility to the general will, as must even philosophy, religion and the idea of education itself. It was like the democratic protest of Jacksonian times, but now played out in the context of a country of vast industrial wealth, of a country growing rapidly every day more urban than rural, and of an already established national intellectual tradition.

But the Progressives were not sceptical about those goals of American individualism and mass prosperity that had become so vastly exaggerated and all-embracive in the 'Gilded Age' of post-Civil War democratic-capitalism. The success philosophy of Horatio Alger's *From Rags to Riches* was abhorrent both to the Wilsonian Democrat and to the Rooseveltian Republican *not* because the ends were unworthy of communal man, but because the 'survival of the fittest', which rationalized the complete opportunism of a Rockefeller, somehow had carried the inference that *all* were not fit to survive. It was not 'every man a brother' that the sound and fury of Progressivism preached, but, as Huey Long was later to give it its last and fullest expression, 'every man a King'.

Both Roosevelt and Wilson believed that there was a natural, smoothly working, indeed progressively expanding economy; though Wilson could think that some institutions had corrupted men, and Roosevelt that some men had corrupted institutions. Roosevelt could thunder in a letter to Taft that: 'The dull and purblind folly of the very rich men; their greed and arrogance . . . and the corruption

[1] See William Bennett Munro, *The Initiative, Referendum and Recall* (New York: 1912). He speaks of these devices growing in popularity as a 'logical by-product of a declining popular trust in the judgement and integrity of elective legislators' (p. 3). Also, a more critical but more comprehensive work, Ellis Paxson Oberholtzer, *The Referendum in America* (New York: 1912, 3rd ed.).

in business and politics, have tended to produce a very unhealthy condition of excitement and irritation in the popular mind, which shows itself in the great increase in socialist propaganda.' [1] But the legislative programme of Roosevelt was as anticlimatic and as firmly modified as that sentence itself. He was no enemy of business. The worst to fear from the present system was 'excitement and irritation'. His final boast was merely that he was 'as free from corruption as Washington or Lincoln'.

Wilson, on the other hand, could instruct the nation that: 'We must abolish everything that bears even the semblance of privilege, or of any kind of artificial advantage, and put our businessmen and producers under the stimulation of a constant necessity to be efficient, economic, and enterprising.' [2] Wilson, in other words, stood in that long and wishful line of liberal reformers who hoped to remove all imperfections from a naturally free market. He was no enemy of business. 'We deemed ourselves', he wrote, 'rank democrats, whereas we were in fact only progressive Englishmen.' Wilson's speeches and writings had stressed 'leadership', as much as Roosevelt's, as their scarlet letter of outraged principle; but there was no need to alter in any significant way what was led.

2. Herbert Croly and the Technical Tradition

Herbert Croly, a close friend of Roosevelt, the founder and editor of the *New Republic*, spoke well for the underlying moral temper of American progressivism. His *The Promise of American Life* is the semi-official theory of Rooseveltian reformism, the protest of the managers against the financiers and of 'old Americans' against the twin dangers of the new plutocrats and new radicals.

Croly distinguished between the *statics* and the *dynamics* of American life.[3] The first was the attained picture of Jeffersonian individualism; but the second was the promise of American life, whose spontaneous evolution could no longer be taken for granted: the manifest destiny set forth in Jefferson's First Inaugural Address now needed the direction of the Hamiltonian State to rescue these Jeffersonian principles from the antiquated Jeffersonian distrust of government. To Croly Progress appeared as a restrained immanence to be released only by sound and vigorous national leadership; it was not an involuntary and inevitable unfolding. Promise, not Manifest Destiny; Nationalism, not *laissez-faire*, are the concerns of Croly. With far more realism than the arch-realists Charles Beard, Thorstein Veblen or John Dewey, he recognized the progressivism of

[1] Quoted by Richard Hofstadter in his *The American Political Tradition and the Men Who Made It* (New York: 1949), p. 220.
[2] Woodrow Wilson, *The New Freedom* (New York: 1913), p. 22.
[3] Croly, *The Promise of American Life* (New York: 1909).

America as an underlying faith, 'religious, if not in its intensity, at least in its almost absolute and universal authority'.[1] He rendered explicit the blending of moralism and nationalism in the Progressive Era.

However, the great weight of historical and political analysis in *The Promise of American Life* in fact only argued for a degree of national, Federal leadership and regulation no more exceptional to American State tradition than the very moderate policy of trust regulation that the personal energy and force of Theodore Roosevelt's 'big stick' to industry boiled down to: 'the chauvinism and showmanism'. Croly, for all his elaborate historical analysis, was in fact just making two at first sight simple pleas: that the man of 'exceptional ability' should be more honoured, and that such men should themselves develop a craftsman's skill and delight in a particular vocation. This was not a counsel of perfection, for he tried to link his pleas to what he regarded as a tradition of technological competence, and he could even see the person of Marcus Alonzo Hanna as exhibiting some of the virtues he desires. Hanna was, to the radicals, the very symbol of the Wall Street money power, the gold bug that fed on the silver fields of the primitively virtuous West. But Croly pictures Hanna as really a force for a responsible conservatism in Republican Party councils:[2] he was the skilled technician in both business and politics who knew that there were proper technical limits to both. But significant ambiguities appear in this Industrial-Ruskinism, and ones related more to political science than to political practice, when Croly tries to make clear what he means by exceptional technical ability.

While Croly had recognized the faith of Americans in their unique destiny, he still went on to say that 'Americans have no popularly accepted ideals which are anything but an embarrassment to the aspiring individual'. Against the notion of 'accepted ideals', he posed that of 'an authentic standard of acquired knowledge'.[3] This he identified, seeing it as the true 'promise of American life', with 'technically competent work'—work, moreover, more concerned with competence than with mere production or, its corollary in politics, mere vote-getting:

The perfect type of authoritative technical methods are those which prevail among scientific men in respect to scientific work. No scientist as such has anything to gain by the use of inferior methods or by the production of inferior work. . . . In the Hall of Science exhibitors do not get their work hung upon the line because it tickles the public taste, or because

1 Croly, *The Promise of American Life* (New York: 1909), pp. 1–2.
2 Croly, *Marcus Alonzo Hanna* (New York: 1912).
3 Croly, *The Promise of American Life*, p. 435.

it is 'uplifting'. . . . The same standard is applied to everybody, and the jury is incorruptible.[1]

Technical standards in any one of the 'liberal or practical arts' cannot be applied 'as rigorously as can the standard of scientific truth', the fact that a man has to make choices in these arts is not 'an excuse for technical irresponsibility or mere electicism'. He urges, nevertheless, that 'a standard of uncompromising technical excellence' be applied in all arts, politics among the others.

Now, in so far as Croly himself went, this is unexceptionable. A craftsmanlike approach to politics could possibly furnish a splendid synthesis of the practical genius of Americans with the ideal image of America. Few conservatives, even, would wish to disagree with the definition of the Progressivist Croly: 'The authoritative technical tradition associated with any of the arts of civilization is merely the net result of the accumulated experience of mankind in a given region.' [2] But the danger is that, despite the broad and often clear vistas of Croly's view of American politics, it does not seem possible to state—certainly Croly himself does not—what in fact *are* the technical standards in politics. If it is technical, then it can, presumably, be taught. But can it be taught according to the same 'authentic standards' as, for instance, dentistry or accountancy? He praises the growing technical specialism of American industry; he notes that, thanks to a good engineering school at West Point, Army officers were once the best railroad engineers in the country; but he does not directly suggest that a similar specialist training could or should be applied to politics.[3] In fact, though he raises and makes great play with the idea of technology—typically and perhaps symptomatically of his time—he still proceeds to qualify it out of any special meaning. 'I have used the word not in the sense merely of Fine Art,' he goes on to say, 'but in the sense of all liberal and disinterested practical work . . . These qualifications . . . require that no one shall be admitted to the ranks of thoroughly competent performers unless he is morally and intellectually, as well as scientifically and manually, equipped for excellent work.' And, he adds, 'these appropriate moral and intellectual standards should be applied as incorruptibly as those born of specific technical practices'.[4] But he is back in the world of morality and tradition, and his 'technical standards' can now appear as no more and no less elusive than any maxims for statecraft offered by anyone whose learning, coherence, integrity and experience give him some authority to be heard. In

[1] *Ibid.*, p. 434.   [2] *Ibid.*, p. 433.
[3] See *ibid.*, pp. 428–30, for his praise of the industrial technologist and his mere comment that this 'transformation . . . *has not*' occurred to the same extent in 'business, politics and the arts'.
[4] *Ibid.*, p. 436.

other words, Croly should be criticized for mistaking a dilemma for a solution; his articulation is more interesting than his analysis. He is actually upholding a traditional American moralism, but he tries to reinterpret it to fit the sentiments of his own age, by talk of 'authoritative technical standards'. One moment he points to the shore, at another to the open sea; but he is really just riding with the tide.[1] Like his friend, Theodore Roosevelt, his inner consistency seems to be a profound admiration for activity, and still more activity, in any traditional American manner.

Even the great legislative activity and efficiency of Wilson's administration was no sudden intrusion of new categories of political thought upon traditional American liberalism. The emergence of strong and effective municipal reform movements, the new pragmatism, the new sociology, the new jurisprudence, took place in a still accepted tradition of political thought; indeed they are conceivable only as conditions of such an acceptance, as testimony to an unshaken underlying belief in the natural law of 1787 carried forward across all subsequent contradictions by a philosophy of progress. The absolute dominance of American liberalism 'was so sure of itself', Louis Hartz has well written, 'that it hardly needed to become articulate, so secure that it could actually support a pragmatism that seemed on the surface to belie it. American pragmatism has always been deceptive because, glacier-like, it has rested on miles of submerged conviction.'[2] Croly was not alone in demonstrating the difficulties, the almost inevitable self-contradiction in attempted 'articulation'. Woodrow Wilson said, in 1916: 'If I did not believe that to be a progressive was to preserve the essentials of our institutions, I for one could not be a progressive.'[3] And when Justice Holmes, himself the innovator of *New Paths in the Law*, read Charles Beard's *An Economic Interpretation of the Constitution*, the greater flower and symbol of progressive scholarship, he wrote sourly to his friend, Sir Frederick Pollock: 'He [Beard] mentions the amount of U.S. or State script held by them. Why? It doesn't need evidence that the man who drew the Constitution belonged to the well-to-do classes and had the views of their class. . . . Except for a covert sneer I can't see anything in it so far.'[4]

---

[1] He enters into his final pages by asserting: 'The conclusion is that for the present time an individual American's intentions and opinions are of less importance than his power of giving them excellent and efficient expression' (p. 438). But on the very last page he is echoing Montesquieu's saying that the principle of democracy is virtue, and assuring the 'common citizen' that he can become 'something of a saint and something of a hero' (p. 454).

[2] 'American Political Thought and the American Revolution', *APSR*, XLVI (June 1952), 337.　　　[3] Quoted by Hofstadter, *American Tradition*, p. 255.

[4] *Holmes–Pollock Letters*, ed. Mark de Wolfe Howe (Cambridge, Mass.: 1941), II, 237.

Wilson's legislative achievement is impressive: the Underwood Tariff Act of 1913; the Federal Reserve Act of 1913; the Federal Farm Loans Act of 1916; the Federal Trade Commission Act of 1914; and the Clayton (anti-Trust) Act of 1914. Even from the angry restlessness of Roosevelt's administration, the Federal Conservation movement of Clifford Pinchot emerged as of lasting administrative importance. But if a change in the style of political thought is looked for, then there is none more significant than the fact that Roosevelt and, more particularly, Wilson, could attain the Presidency at all. 'National leadership' to restore 'the rules of the game' are recurring phrases in both their speeches. 'Honesty in politics' and 'intelligent leadership in the national interest' are two typical slogans of the era. The roots of the Progressive Era are in the Civil Service Reform agitations of the previous three decades. From there came the movement that 'the best men should enter politics',[1] to which was later grafted the plea of Dewey that 'the *method* of intelligence should be applied to politics'. The tradition of the Jacksonian hope for rotation in office; of both the Tammany tiger and the Georgia red-neck distrust of 'the stuffed shirt' in politics; and of the continued suspicion of the 'egg-heads' in our own time—these were to some degree challenged and contained by the politics of the Progressive Era.

The lives of the leaders of political and social thought in the Progressive Era were an eloquent and often noble reply to the cynical realism of the political bosses. There was no doubt in the minds of men like A. Lawrence Lowell, Charles Beard and Arthur Fisher Bentley that if the 'first rule of politics is to get elected', yet a greater and more systematic knowledge of how men get elected—the study of political behaviour—would somehow lead to better men getting elected or to the national interest being mirrored more precisely than of old. But the social theorists carried the doctrine of the application of scientific intelligence to society to the lengths of a hoped-for release from party politics at all. There was a hope that intelligent methods of research and administration alone were needed. Croly's ambivalence between men and measures, between experience and technique, was magnified and torn apart. The new social sciences, building on the scientific canons of the evolutionary thought of the previous decades, historically were a force for political reform throughout the whole Progressive Era; but emotionally and philosophically they were more than that; they were in revolt against politics itself, full of a deep disgust at the dirt of politics that led to an aspiration to achieve the objectivity, dignity and authority of

[1] See James Bryce, *The American Commonwealth*, 2nd ed. (New York: 1890), Chapters LVIII, LXVIII, *et passim*, IV–XXXV; also E. D. Ross, *The Liberal Republican Movement* (New York: 1919); and C. R. Fish, *The Civil Service and the Patronage* (New York: 1905).

science. There was an almost Marxian fervour for replacing the reign of politics by the reign of society. It was a revolt made easy simply because there were no apparent deep issues of principle in American politics at the time, only questions of personal honesty and of pragmatic devices to make an agreed system work better. Perhaps the tragedy of the Progressive Era was that the doctrine of intelligent public administration based on technical 'standards' began more and more to supersede the doctrine of personal responsibility: the two halves of Croly fly asunder.

Now, to have asserted the fundamental likeness of policy between the competing parties of the Progressive Era (and to say that this is a vital condition for the plausibility of the idea of a science of politics) is no criticism of the sincerity and sometimes the effectiveness of the protagonists. Much of what is most admirable in American life is found in its deliberate rejection of the class dialectic of European politics. A large part of the spirit of the Progressive Era was a realization that American life and thought need no longer be expressed in European terms: a progressive liberal nationalism freed the political reformists from their taint of Anglophilism and gave even the radical a patriotism, even a jingoism, strange to his fellow of the European scene. Here lies the explanation of their involved paradox of claiming great novelty while all the time they exhibited traditional American traits or revived mid-century European views about the possibility of a science of society. Confidence had been gained that America need no longer half-apologize for her Statesmen, industry, colleges, literature and armies. The old American radical, like Bryan, Follette or William Allen White, was often angry, but he was always optimistic for America, and thus superbly American. The Progressive Era was not a rejection of the principles of the 'Gilded Age', as good New Dealing historians have hastily interpreted, but, as Woodrow Wilson clearly saw, an extension of the capitalist principle down to the many, in ideology if not always in strict economic fact.

Long before, De Tocqueville had written of his own comparative method of political interpretation: 'A new science of politics is needed for a new world.' A new science of politics, as will be seen, did arise, but it arose without either the need for taking sides that faced De Tocqueville or the benefits of the mingled comparative and philosophic method that he applied to the sociology of democratic institutions. It did not need to take sides in anything more fundamental than an advocacy of administrative reform and probity in politics. The method of intelligence of pragmatism was not formed in the desperate and creative circumstances in which Condorcet wrote his *Essay on Progress*; nor in the 'two Englands' of Chartist days; nor yet at the swan song of English Liberalism which saw the emergence of Fabianism. Intelligence and Science were no revolutionary slogans: they were dangerously near to platitudes.

3. Realism as Worthiness Through Facts

If the Progressive Era gave rise to no new political thought, it did spread the doctrine of innovation and activity as the signs of progress; law, government administration, journalism, and university and Protestant church life all showed increased and dedicated activity. And if they did not play with a new ball, yet the old one was so inflated that, while the proportions of the sphere remained constant, the displacement was significantly greater.

The importance of placing the founding and expansion of the new social sciences in the whole context of the Progressive Era can be underlined by examining a distinctive product of the period, the 'muckraking' journalism. The two things were by no means unconnected. Charles Beard in his *An Economic Interpretation of the Constitution* (1913) thought that he was *merely* uncovering the facts about the financial interests of the Founding Fathers, just as Lincoln Steffens thought that he was *merely* uncovering the facts about the financial interests of the city fathers of New York, Chicago, Philadelphia, Pittsburgh, Minneapolis and St. Louis. Lincoln Steffens wrote of his famed book, *The Shame of the Cities* (1903) that: 'It offered few conclusions. I could not interpret my own observations; so in the introduction I said that the book was printed as the articles were written, as journalism with a purpose: "to sound for the civic pride of an apparently shameless citizenship".' [1] Henry Demarest Lloyd's *Wealth Against Commonwealth* (1894) is not so much remarkable for the fervour of its condemnation as for the detail of its documentation. Ida Tarbell showed the detail and accuracy rather than the sensationalism of the new popular magazines—those that had risen largely on muckraking and on a political appeal to middle-class responsibility. Her famous *History of the Standard Oil Company* (1904) could stand in technique and 'factual authority' alongside the reports of the Interstate Commerce Commission or the monumental industrial histories of the school of John R. Commons in Wisconsin.[2]

[1] *Autobiography of Lincoln Steffens* (New York: 1931), p. 434. We find the doctrine of pure research first among the journalists. Steffens perpetually invites his readers to make up their own minds on the basis of the facts, but the conclusions of the book are glaringly obvious to anyone, not excluding the author.

[2] See J. R. Commons *et al.*, *A Documentary History of American Industrial Society*, 10 vols. (Cleveland: 1910–11); and his *History of Labour in the United States*, 4 vols. (New York: 1918–35). The example of Commons in helping to found and staff the first State Legislative Reference Library (in Wisconsin) and his career of public service on many commissions and as counsel to many investigations was formidable, stretching far beyond his own field of labour economics.

Gustavus Myers reached the climax of this whole muckraking movement with his three-volume *History of the Great American Fortunes* (1910). 'Like other critics of this school,' says a recent commentator, 'Myers had more faith in records than in rationalizations.' [1] When Walter Lippmann in his *Preface to Politics* (1911) called for more scientific studies of political realities, it was works like Tarbell's and Myers' that he saw as best portraying reality. The documentation of the muckraking journalism and its alleged objectivity makes it only in style and published location different from the empirical studies in city government that the sociologists and the new political scientists were beginning to interest themselves in. The deep and fearful picture of New York slum life in the journalist Jacob Riis's *How the Other Half Lives* (1897) was the pre-condition for the descriptive urban sociology of Robert E. Park, himself a former journalist turned social worker, then sociologist.[2]

Steffens himself grew to despair of the efficacy of mere muckraking. He found that it was not the politician who was corrupting the honest middle-class businessmen, but that it was as often the businessman who corrupted the politician. He began to see the attitude of his former 'chief', Lawrence Godkin, as futile:

Mr. Lawrence Godkin, the editor-in-chief, was a reformer Irish in breed, English in culture; his ideals both of journalism and of politics were those of an English liberal. He was against bad government and bad journalism which he attributed to bad men. His cure was to throw the rascals out and elect good men, regardless of party. Called a mugwump, he was really an aristocrat.[3]

To be an aristocrat was damning. Out of disgust with the recurring futility of liberal nostrums such as Godkin's, Steffens finally turned 'against the system', made his pilgrimage to Moscow, and suffered his double disillusionment according to the now familiar pattern. But Godkin's *Evening Post* and *Nation* were typical, not the eventual reaction of Steffens.

Some put their faith in the publication of 'facts' as alone sufficient to deal with, for instance, the problem of the trusts.[4] Most Progres-

[1] Irvin G. Wyllie, *The Self-Made Man in America, the Myth of Rags to Riches* (Rutgers University Press: 1954), p. 148.
[2] See Edward Shils, *The Present State of American Sociology* (Glencoe, Ill.: 1948), p. 10. Shils says of Park's and similar other works that though they made no 'direct contribution to the systematic theory of human behaviour' yet they have 'fulfilled a momentously important function in the development of social science by establishing an unbroken tradition of first-hand observation'. But this tradition of detailed first-hand observation when related to the moral purpose of a man like Park is one thing; when it can become divorced of any purpose, it is quite another.
[3] Steffens, *Autobiography*, p. 179.
[4] Hans B. Thorelli, in his monumental study, *The Federal Anti-Trust Policy, Origination of an American Tradition* (Stockholm: 1954), lists a number of prominent

sives, however, admitted that the people needed to be 'woken up' vigorously, though not changed—just as the 'facts' needed a lot of sweat, if little discrimination, to get at. True, business had failed to put its house in order, so, said right reason, the wide circulation of the new muckraking magazines would appeal to the people as a whole to assert their sovereign powers. Facts, once put before the people, would do their own work. The ground would be cut from under the feet of municipal graft, Congressional intrigue and—before long—secret diplomacy. Henry Demarest Lloyd pauses amidst his documentation to say of the great industrialists: 'Americans as they are, they ride over the people like Juggernauts to gain their ends. The moralists have preached to them since the world began, and have failed. The common people, the nation, must take them in hand.' [1] Mass journalism, originally radical more than reactionary, was the condition of a belief that if the facts were found the people would look after the conclusions. Similarly, the rapid growth of college education was a condition for a similar belief about *the study* of politics and society. And the conclusions that the muckrakers strengthened did not go beyond the demand for new political techniques and administrative agencies to carry forward existing democratic ideals.

The popular character of pragmatic realism as reformism can be seen most vividly in the literature of the era, in what Henry Steele Commager has well called 'the minority report of the novelists'. The methodology of the new novelists and of the new social scientists became almost identical, indeed many shared the same didactic aim. In the novel the cult of objectivity had arisen early and *realism* was a conscious slogan even in the 'eighties. Such novels as Henry Adams' *Democracy*, Mark Twain's *The Gilded Age*, or Winston Churchill's *Coniston* showed a substantial trend for the realities of Bossdom and no longer of Boston to become the central concern of the novelist. The 'slabs of raw and bleeding experience' thrown on the doorstep of the 1900's by Theodore Dreiser were different in content and approach from the restrained world of William Howells' New England Spas, but nevertheless both men called themselves 'realists', different though their respective worlds might be (for while to Howells manners still maketh man, to Dreiser, a generation later, the shaping force was social environment). The realism of Howells is

economists of the day who were cool towards the prohibition of trusts in the Sherman Act, or to any regulatory alternatives, but who believed that: 'Publicity would keep under control the abuses of over-capitalization.' 'It may be added', continued Thorelli, 'that publicity was a comfortable "neutral" policy for scientists to advocate and, incidentally, a policy promising to make the life of the economist more interesting' (p. 575). See also, Woodrow Wilson, *The New Freedom* (New York: 1913), pp. 115–16.
[1] *Wealth Against Commonwealth* (New York: 1894), p. 46.

that of 'the best men', genteel, optimistic, expansive and national. His writing was seeking, however, to become scientific, in the manner that his self-made man, Silas Lapham, could, when describing his new paint, pronounce '. . . the scientific phrases with a sort of reverent satisfaction, as if awed through his pride by a little lingering uncertainty as to what peroxide was'. The novel in general was becoming less interested in the philosophy and psyche of individuals, and more in the portrayal of social groups and forces, or of the individual as a type created by those forces. Even Henry James could say that the novelist is a 'patient historian, the living painter of his living time'; although James was always aware that all writing is selectivity: that the perceiver is prior to the perceived. But the 'tough minded' descriptive realism of Jack London's novels or of Frank Norris's novels of industrial oppression, *The Octopus* and *The Pit*, was a harbinger of the group-conscious pragmatism of the Progressive Era, a fusion of protest and description. The London *Times*, in reviewing Lloyd's *Wealth Against Commonwealth*, commented that 'it is as interesting and as disagreeable as a realistic novel'.[1] Both, indeed, believed that to show things 'just as they were' would in fact spontaneously create an urge to reform.

The novelists of Dreiser's generation, like the social scientists, fell heartily into the fallacy of naturalism that sees reality as an unambiguous picture of already arranged facts. They were slow to realize that every description implies a prior judgement. They accepted the naturalism of Zola and the French naturalists—*'L'art est une tranche de vie vue à travers d'un temperament'*—at a time when the theory was already discarded by European novelists precisely because it left out of account the extremely selective view of reality of the observer: neither the artist (nor the sociologist) was able to view total reality and depict it unsifted, but only a reality peculiar to his view, selectively and purposefully shaped according to some notion of importance, artistic or moral. But agreement was wider in American society as to what *'une tranche de vie'* was. Diversity of temperament was constantly being subsumed by 'the image of the common man', and the unity of reality was ensured, sociologically and not philosophically, by a belief in one 'American way of life', and was largely undisturbed by fundamental political and social disputes.

It is not really surprising that V. L. Parrington's three volumes on American literature should also be the best account of American political thought yet written[2]—for all his fond indulgences of agrarian romanticism; and that literary critics with a social theory of art, like

---

[1] Lloyd, *op. cit.*, Appendix of 'Notices by the Press' to the Second Printing, p. viii.
[2] V. L. Parrington, *Main Currents in American Thought*, 3 vols. (New York: 1927-30). See especially the third unfinished volume on 'Critical Realism'.

Lionel Trilling, Edmund Wilson and the late F. O. Matthiessen, should often be better guides for the student of 'the American political mind' than most of the statistically immaculate textbooks of the political scientists.

The pragmatic temper of both the new journalists and the new novelists somehow achieved for their age a happy marriage of fact and value, of descriptive and moral indignation—all this despite their over-simple belief in popular sovereignty and their too hasty scorn for the checks and balances of the classic Constitution. However much they professed an amoral attitude, to be in revolt against 'sentimentality' and 'moralism', their worthiness shone through appearances like the Anglican priest who doffs his collar for a Saturday afternoon game. But in the new social sciences the suppression of overt philosophizing was to be taken just as seriously and was to have even greater consequences than in imaginative literature.

If there was, then, in the politics of the Progressive Era, a 'Fair Deal' that anticipated many of the seemingly new rules and plays of Franklin Roosevelt's 'New Deal', yet the whole of politics was seen as having, at least potentially, the mechanical harmony of an agreed game, albeit a great game—*The Great Game of Politics*, as Frank Kent entitled his much-heard-of book. It was a game whose rules were already well established, even though it needed (in the words of Junius) 'an eternal vigilance' to see that the deal was fair—it needed further, as Locke has said, an 'Umpire', but no authority or officials more stern than that. The rules of play made neither for pure skill nor for pure chance, but were pragmatic, which is to say that a man by studying the game, both the constituted rules and the psychology of the play, would normally be more successful than if he played his cards by hunches or by 'outmoded superstitions'. Sometimes the runs of luck seemed to be so systematically discriminatory in favour of those who had won much already, that it took the ingrained optimism of the mass of Horatio Algers at the table to keep a demand for a change in the rules down to a futile minority grumble. The majority of players, fully accepting the game, merely felt that there was sometimes need for new deals to be made more swiftly so as to give the luck a chance to average out over large numbers.

To reduce politics to a technique of play was soon to stimulate a study of the factors unpredictable in those terms—the psychology of play, the 'psychic factors in civilization'. But psychology did not become a typical intellectual reduction of the Progressive Era, though such tendencies were afoot. This is to anticipate. The Progressive Era is marked by the moral fervour which is attached to particular techniques. And this fervour could be taken naturalistically, as is clear in the novelists even before the social scientists, by reason of the widespread popular agreement that some such techniques—of getting at the facts and of improving the articulation of popular opinion—were perfectly natural. Once again a substantial unity of sentiment, though now fastened on slightly different objects, passed for philosophy. And the philosophy that did come was a philosophy of method, something that was thought of far more as a way of realizing popular ideals than of explaining, evaluating and analysing them.

4. The Circularities of Pragmatism

By the early 'twenties there was scarcely a social scientist who did not consider himself to be, in some sense, a pragmatist. 'Practical, democratic, individualistic, opportunistic, spontaneous, hopeful,' writes Henry Steel Commager, 'pragmatism was wonderfully adapted to the temperament of the average American. . . . No wonder that, despite the broadsides of the official philosophers, pragmatism caught on until it became almost the official philosophy of America.' [1] To Charles and Mary Beard in their *American Spirit* and their *Rise of American Civilization* pragmatism was 'the American philosophy'. Both critics and advocates seem wholly agreed that pragmatism is not a 'basic', 'pure' or 'mere' philosophy, but is, in some sense, 'a mirror of America'. Even to discuss whether pragmatism should be treated as a social doctrine or as a philosophical critique is, indeed, to make the very kind of distinction that the pragmatist claims to have outmoded. And an obvious result of the pragmatists' insistence that the only meaningful 'experience' is social or cultural experience, is that the authority of the philosopher should be supplanted by that of the sociologist. In the same manner history could only justify itself against antiquarian irrelevance to 'America's own needs', in Dewey's phrase, in so far as it was contemporary history bearing on present and practical problems, better still, when it became political science.

It would be unjust and obtuse to offer any criticism of pragmatism without recognizing the apparent sterility of the contemporary discipline of 'philosophy' that it attacked, and without recognizing that for a brief period, the Progressive Era itself, pragmatism so coincided with a peculiar frame of mind and a particular politics that it was able to uphold an image of man that had almost the *arete* of the Greek world, a marriage of reason and action, as in Homer's Achilles: 'The doer of deeds *and* the speaker of words.' And it was an image less exclusive than the Greek, an almost Kantian image of

[1] Quoted by Arthur E. Murphy in 'Philosophical Scholarship', in Merle Curti, ed., *American Scholarship in the Twentieth Century* (Cambridge, Mass.: 1953), p. 184. Commager's account, he dryly comments, 'is hardly an exaggeration'.

the suppressed capabilities of 'the common man': adaptable, active, intelligent, co-operative.

But for pragmatism to do this in the form of an attack on the whole function of 'traditional philosophy', while itself offering no clearer criterion for practice than a common and popular notion of scientific method, was to create a view of 'thought-in-action' ultimately as all-embracive and as intangible as the image of 'idealism' which it attacked. To call philosophy back to account with practice is no bad cause to pursue. But 'practice' must then be defined. The original form of pragmatism, the most strictly 'logical', the claim of C. S. Peirce that the truth of an idea is its consequences—or the changes in other entities that result from its affirmation, came near to being a mere truism. F. H. Bradley, a surprisingly interested and careful critic of pragmatism, pointed out: 'Of course ideas involve physical change, in some sense, in me—but what are we to say about them? . . . The question is what are we to say about this physical event, and how otherwise it must be qualified, so that it is not merely a physical event but is a specially true or false belief or judgement.' [1] Dewey, of course, answered that we are not merely to say that a true idea is its physical consequences, but its social consequences also. And further, the *relevant* social consequences, out of an infinity of possible consequences, are somehow those that are beneficial to society. Pragmatism was not nihilism; it became a form of a particular optimism. 'Better it is', says Dewey in his *Quest for Certainty*—a statement paralleled again and again in his writings, 'for philosophy to err in active participation in the living struggles and issues of its own age and times than to maintain an immune and monastic impeccability.'

The reference of philosophy to social needs demanded a theory of what those social needs were. And Dewey's theory was almost exactly that of Lester Frank Ward. Social needs were not 'static' and thus potentially conservative, for the social system itself had the potentiality of progress if—and here science replaced mere ethical philosophy—intelligence, as a biological, not a philosophical force, was liberated from custom. Dewey's contribution to *Studies in Logical Theory*, his break with Hegelianism, was an apostrophe to evolutionary method:

The entire significance of the evolutionary method in biology and social history is that every distinct organ, structure or formation, every grouping of cells or elements, has to be treated as an instrument of adjustment or adaptation to a particular environing situation. Its meaning, its character, its value, is known when, and only when, it is considered as an arrangement for meeting conditions involved in some specific situation. This analysis of value is carried out in detail by tracing the successive stages of

---

[1] *Essays on Truth and Reality* (Oxford: 1914), p. 140.

development—by endeavouring to locate the particular situation in which each structure has its origins and by tracing the successive modifications, through which, in response to changing media, it has reached its present conformation.[1]

But the inherent difficulty with an appeal to evolution is as great for Dewey as it was for Ward. If the 'value' of the 'evolutionary method' is known 'when, and only when, it is considered as an arrangement for meeting conditions involved in some specific situation', how is one to know whether any specific situation is rationally preferable to another? This problem is made all the more acute because Dewey claims to relate philosophy not merely to practice in general—to looking after one's old fences—but to a reforming practice—to building new, more intelligent and scientific, fences for all. Of course, there was in Dewey an unpurged and admirable idealism; it was in the nature of things, or in the wishes of men, that true intelligence did not lead to degeneration but to progress. And there is no need to say that this idealism is a residue from his Hegelianism, as have some perhaps over-subtle critics: it was the same idealism as that of nearly all the new social scientists, the political reformers and the crusading or muckraking jouralists of the Progressive Era, the basic idealism or optimism of American political thought. Pragmatism assumed that very 'promise of American life' that it set out to vindicate and realize.[2]

Dewey, of course, believed that in looking for 'the objective needs of society' he had rescued pragmatism from the subjectivism, indeed the clear moralism, of William James's stress on 'the consequences of an idea for personal conduct'. But his own attempts to state a theory of *value* in fact only demonstrated the limits of pragmatism, or how the pragmatic judgement can only be one part of philosophy and not the whole, if it is to avoid defining these 'objective needs' simply in terms of what good men and true think these objective needs to be. He faced this problem explicitly in *The Quest for Certainty* of 1929. He held that not merely judgements of 'what *is* desired' are verifiable scientifically, but also judgements of 'what

---

[1] John Dewey *et al.*, *Studies in Logical Theory* (Chicago: 1903), p. 15.

[2] See, for instance, a typical passage in Professor Philip Wiener's able monograph, *Evolution and the Founders of Pragmatism* (Cambridge, Mass.: 1949)—he is defending pragmatism against the charge of 'scientific absolutism': 'the fallibility of the most exact scientific findings, so often stressed by the founders of pragmatism, was part of their *profound liberal aversion* to all forms of dogmatism, including that of overzealous lovers of scientific truth. They all objected to the hierarchical priesthood of social scientists advocated by Auguste Comte in his later years, for the same *democratic* reason that led them to reject theological and metaphysical dogmas. . . . The *common political faith* shared by all our early pragmatists was based on a utilitarian and democratic ethic of individualism to which all social institutions were subservient. It is a travesty on American pragmatism to condemn its philosophy as crass opportunism, as subordinating all truth to cash value.' (My sceptical italics.)

ought to be desired'. Science, he argued, does not attribute objective properties to things without being sure that certain test conditions are satisfied. Before calling an object 'red', we check that there are no extraordinary circumstances and that our eyesight is *normal*. In like manner, according to Dewey, we may argue that something is objectively desirable, when seen under normal conditions of moral life, 'thoroughly investigated'. In other words, he states that we ought not to equate the desired with the desirable except under certain ascertainable conditions—which then involves his whole theory of the community; but that when these conditions are realized, we both do and should desire something intelligently, scientifically—the sprightly rabbit at last from the dark hat. But the whole question of what are 'normal conditions'—which he sometimes calls 'laboratory conditions'—is surely what we want above all to pass judgements upon, and has been at all times, in one form or another, the constant and necessary concern of the great systems of speculative political philosophy. To say that conditions must be 'thoroughly investigated' is no more than a purely pragmatic axiom—'be diligent'—or even a trite moral one—'be honest'. But it became taken, amid an awareness that elementary thoroughness in the investigation of social problems had hitherto been all but non-existent, as somehow a vindication of 'social science' *against* 'philosophy'. But whether it is possible to define 'the normal' except circularly, as 'those conditions under which red will be red, the desired desirable', or sociologically in terms of an inevitably selective statement about the *mores* and *folkways* of a particular culture at a particular time, all this Dewey does not resolve.[1]

This pleasing circularity of argument, or rather, this implicit belief that normal society was itself immanently progressive, helps to explain something of the moralistic fervour with which the new social scientists could abandon the individual dilemmas of James for the apparent social certainties of Dewey. A school of political scientists arose who saw the individual, as in Dewey's theory of education, as solely the social product of functional groups. The group must have the purpose of enabling its members to widen 'their areas of shared concern'; to develop their social personality by means of improved communication of knowledge and increased participation in administration. Groups were all seen as interest groups, the relations between which could be seen best in almost Hobbesean terms—but an American Hobbes who believed in progress. The interest group became the

---

[1] My critique closely follows that of Morton White in his *Social Thought in America*, Chapter XIII, 'Is Ethics an Empirical Science?', *passim*. It is precisely the same logical difficulty about the assumption of a 'normal' that was to bedevil Harold Lasswell's attempt to apply psychoanalysis to the social sciences (see below, pp. 197–209).

mental level of social analysis. Professor Schneider has ob-
d:

ᴛ.ᴇ philosophy was given a more systematic and technical elaboration
as a theory of government by Arthur F. Bentley and by the Chicago
trinity, Charles E. Merriam, H. D. Lasswell and T. V. Smith. . . . Bentley,
Beard and Merriam have been leaders in formulating politics in terms of
the interaction of 'pressure-groups' and in thus providing a practical,
pluralistic substitute for the Marxian concepts of class-conflict in a society
where classes are vague, but conflicts continual.[1]

The Progressive Era that saw the ultra-individualistic attack by 'the
best men' upon almost any and all Party and pressure group
machinery, also saw the new university intellectuals begin to take
note of the resilience of some of this machinery, and of its variety
as well as of its abuses. Pragmatism could become far more realistic
about such groups and, indeed, see *all* experience and activity as
bound up in them, or in groups like them; it could be a telling
criticism of the 'organizations of the unorganizable' that were so
much of the ephemeral though vivid force of the Progressive movements.

But some pragmatists became so 'realistic' that they seemed to
close their eyes and refuse to judge anything except by touch, denying
any vision greater than particular concrete social experiences. So far
from emulating the formation of general theory in science, the new
political and social theorists, as good pluralists and pragmatists,
tended to eschew general theories and to concentrate on a piecemeal
empiricism—local, small-scale investigations: the study of public
administration and municipal government; the description of the
behaviour of small groups—these became the order of the day.
General theories, not merely metaphysical but also scientific, were
crowded from the field, or rather, pushed back into the subconscious
—in notable contrast, for example, to the course of scientistic thinking in German and French sociology. The broad sweep of the social
theories of the first two generations of Social-Darwinists became
suspect—though these theories settled down quietly and covertly to
form two vast 'inarticulate major premises': the *doctrine of progress*
and, as we shall later examine, the doctrine that the mere 'scientific'
discovery and description of facts about political behaviour is *therapeutic*, a restorative of 'the normal'. The fact of the matter is that
none of the pragmatists really thought systematically about scientific
procedures. They thought of science in a cant manner, as *the* method
of observation, experiment and *then* theory. The prior importance

---

[1] H. W. Schneider, *The History of American Philosophy* (New York: 1946), p. 568.
These four names are precisely those whom we will be studying in detail in Chapters
VII–X. Thus there is some agreement as to *who* is important.

of theory to observation scarcely occurred to them. To the pragmatist a prior commitment would seem like a prejudice: the task of the social philosopher was to let the facts bring themselves to order. Technology, more than scientific method, was the analogy that most obviously impressed them. Technology, as distinct from science; the pragmatic judgement, as distinct from the comprehensive philosophic judgement; administration, as distinct from politics—all these assume that social goals and limitations *are given* by some prior criteria or authority. Ultimately, pragmatism is less to be understood by what it claims, than by what it prohibits and attacks: it attacks the belief in criteria prior to practical social experience. It attacks the very activities that can give technology, the pragmatic judgement and administration a rational significance and purpose, philosophizing about history and philosophizing about ethics.

Dewey's attempted theoretical contribution to general philosophy was, then, his attempt to work out the implications of taking 'experience' as primarily the social experience of human communities: to treat of 'experience' as all that the anthropologist includes as belonging to human culture, not as 'sense data' or as 'introspective psychology'. But the great difficulty was, as the pragmatist should see more clearly than anyone, that experience—so treated—falls into many different patterns, conditioning different psychological and physical reactions. The consequences of such a view might seem to imply a pure relativism; but, as Bradley remarked, the American pragmatists were indeed not in earnest with their scepticism. To save themselves from complete relativism or irrelevance, they adopted one of many possible patterns. Some of the few continental pragmatists professed to adopt any such pattern arbitrarily, for the sake of action and activity as ends in themselves. But the American pragmatists, wisely, adopted the existing American pattern of belief and action; their experience was a nationalistic experience; indeed, they claimed to guide their nation, their admittedly unique nation, towards a yet more democratic and scientific future.

Ultimately, there is no more (and no less) to be said of pragmatism than that it was the prism through which the ordinary, common social thought of Americans was reflected upon the new social sciences; it was not in itself an understanding of that thought, although it provides a substantial clue by which a non-pragmatist can understand such thought. The very fact that the naturalism of pragmatism has a primarily popular and not so much an intellectual derivation is so important for the social sciences. This illustrates a seeming paradox of American political thought: the sameness of her individualism. Nowhere is individualism (of the Jamesean kind) more engrained in the hearts of both the people and the intellectuals;

but, equally, nowhere does it seem more easy to make sweeping and secure generalizations about the behaviour of the mass and of the groups of individuals. The conformity of American individualism has played a great role in the plausibility of both Dewey's pragmatism and 'the science of politics'.

VI

THE GROWTH OF POLITICAL SCIENCE

Colleges all too frequently confine attention . . . to a consideration
of abstract notions and principles which find scant place in the actual
operation of governmental affairs. . . . Political science, in some
quarters at least, has been too strictly confined to theories about civil
society and too little concerned with political affairs as they are.

American Political Science Association, *The Teaching of
Government* (New York: 1916)

We do not nowadays refute our predecessors, we pleasantly bid them
goodbye. Even if all our principles are unwittingly traditional we do
not like to bow openly to authority.

GEORGE SANTAYANA, *Character and Opinion in the United States*

1. The Inadequacy of the Old Order

IF WE HAVE taken so long and circuitous a journey towards
American political science itself, it is because none of those things
that predisposed it towards the 'scientific method' arose from within
itself. If political science has not been a necessary condition for
American life—as Washington had thought—yet its concern for
'science' is a consequence of American life, though not, as both the
extreme critic of America and the American social scientist often
maintain, a necessary consequence. The effect of 'the new realism'
and of pragmatism are dramatically evident when we now compare
the leading political scientists of the Progressive Era with the previous
generation. When the temper of mind of John W. Burgess, W. W.
Willoughby and Theodore Woolsey gives way to that of Charles
Beard, A. B. Hart, Frank Goodnow, A. L. Lowell and Arthur
Fisher Bentley, a profound change in academic political thought has
taken place. Bentley, indeed, was to synthesize the thought of the
social sciences of the Progressive Era in his *The Process of Government* (1908), and was to anticipate the transition from pragmatism
to positivism of the 'twenties and 'thirties.[1]

[1] *The Process of Government* is best examined separately in the last and following
chapter of this section.

The new political scientists looked no longer to the German historians; when they looked abroad at all, it was to a few British writers—though these were not original influences, but were revered as authorities for courses of action already under way, and then often more seemingly the same courses than actually the same. The work of both A. Lawrence Lowell, from New England, and of James Bryce, from Britain, was esteemed as the finest kind of 'realism', and even as a warrant for a future pure science of politics.

The older meaning of the concept 'political science' is seen in the title of Theodore Woolsey's book that grew out of his lectures on politics while he was President of Yale from 1846 to 1871, *Political Science, or The State*.[1] This double title seeks to find an English equivalent of *Staatswissenschaft*. The division of the first volume, he says, 'somewhat answers to the *Naturrecht, Staatslehre* and *Politik* of the Germans . . . it seemed more advisable to begin the theory of the state on the foundation of a concept of justice, than to work at this foundation while the theory was in process of construction'.[2] The book is vast and erudite, but its combination of a highly abstract discussion of rights with a narrowly legalistic discussion of institutions only shows how legitimate was the target for much of the pragmatic criticism. He shows well how juridical ideas of right give meaning and form to institutions as expressed in formal constitutions, but he fails entirely to show whether ideas of right give form to the patterns of activity by which institutions are actually worked and how they affect the character of the men who work them. He lacked that masterly sense of the relation between general political ideas and sociological institutions and behaviour that De Tocqueville had already shown—a strangely neglected example of method—or, indeed, lacked any corrective personal participation in public affairs, such as Wilson and Bryce were to insist upon as the sheet-anchor of the 'realistic' political scientist. Indeed his discussion of *Staatsrecht* is so alien to American experience and institutions, that it shows the failure of the German-trained scholars of his generation to establish any roots in American tradition, except those of method, a failure to show that the historical and political concepts that arose from totally different conditions in German history had any organic relationship to American politics. Albert Bushnell Hart (who during the 1900's taught a course at Harvard called 'Actual Government') could explicitly argue that the tradition and practice of limited and Federal government in the United States had precluded any 'State' in the German sense. And he can conclude a brisk philippic against the 'theory of the State' by saying: '*the most distinctive American theory*

---

[1] Woolsey, *Political Science, or The State* (New York: 1878), in two vols.
[2] *Ibid.*, p. vii; it went through many subsequent editions.

of Government is not to theorize.[1] In attempting to rescue political science from the sterility of work like Woolsey's, it is small wonder that Hart and his generation could mistake what in the long run was the predicament of American politics for its strength. The antagonism to theories of political right grew out of opposition to work that applied concepts of right to the formal legal institutions of society; but it is another matter to seek to avoid *any* discussion of theories of political right. Hart did not regard the *Federalist Papers* as theoretical, but many who accepted his general viewpoint did, or else they regarded them as unique, final and definitive, not as an example of a type of (theoretical) political activity.

John W. Burgess, as we have seen, did much to establish the academic respectability of political science, but contributed little to what became its dominant techniques and concerns. His major work, *Political Science and Comparative Law* (1890), shares Woolsey's defects, although his learning and expression are far greater. His teaching 'quietly slipped into neglect because of its irrelevance to newer research'.[2] For all his long tenure of the Chair of Political Science at Columbia he left no disciples and is spoken of by the present leaders of opinion in the political science profession with the respectful vagueness as to what were his actual views that well demonstrates his unshakeable position in pre-history. There was solid worth in his analysis of the post-Civil War constitutional settlement: he gave an unrivalled account of the devices by which the Supreme Court came to ensure national interest over sectional. But his own pronounced centralist views harked back to the old Federalists rather than heralded the new radicals.

If one aspect of his work was remembered, it was an aspect that when wrenched from its context only confirmed the worst fears of the pragmatists about what sort of abhorrent views such a man— a 'legalist' *and* an 'idealist'—was likely to hold. For he was one of those, like John Fiske, whose optimism, nationalism and belief in progress took the form not of a 'dynamic sociology', but rather of a theory of racial determinism. He can be found, as the first Theodore Roosevelt Professor at the University of Berlin, lecturing the Kaiser and assembled Court on the comradeship of Anglo-Saxon and Teuton and their innate superiority over the Latin and Slavic races[3] —the immigrant races whom the intellectual Progressives were beginning to defend against Anglo-Saxon Republicanism. In his

[1] A. B. Hart, 'The Growth of American Theories of Popular Government', *APSR*, I (Aug. 1907), my italics.
[2] David Easton, *The Political System* (New York: 1953), p. 71. See also Francis Wilson, *American Political Mind* (New York: 1949), p. 282, fn.
[3] Burgess, *Reminiscences of an American Scholar* (New York: 1934), Appendix II, pp. 368–79.

Political Science and Constitutional Law he explained political ability as an innate racial factor.

Such views were not allowed to slip quietly into the limbo of extraneous views, into becoming those pages that are passed over in an old author with no other harm but the tedium of irrelevance to the main corpus of his work. For the Progressives, involved in the changing nature of American nationality, had to challenge his racialism loudly, had to see it as central to his work. The leading wing of the Progressives was beginning to become self-consciously the champion of the minorities, and was beginning to realize, as one of the greatest glories of the American 'experiment', that the races despised by Burgess would soon become as good Americans as any. Nothing so clearly distinguishes the Wilsonian progressivism, and especially that of the colleges and universities, from both the older nativistic 'Mugwumpery' and agrarian Populism. They lost the struggle over the immigration laws in politics, but they gained their point overwhelmingly in the universities and colleges.

In this racial way, Burgess can show a type of Darwinism as plausible as that of any of the social scientists. Possibly his theory of progress had far more specific content to it than those of any of the political scientists of the Progressive Era (aside from the fact, of course, that much of this content was false). It would be unduly narrow not to say that his theories had as good a claim to scientific status as any.[1] In 1917 Burgess prepared for publication the more general chapters of his *Political Science*, reiterating that: 'In the study of general political science we must be able to find a standpoint from which the harmony of duty and policy may appear. History and ethnology offer us this elevated ground, and they teach us that the Teutonic nations are the political nations of the modern era. . . .'[2]

Hannah Arendt has well said that the nineteenth century threw up two main theories of ideological progress: a theory of the economic determination of history and a theory of the racial determination. The vast unity of American liberalism and the intensity of the theory of progress—these formed an ideology, and, in the manner of classical liberalism, an economic ideology. Perhaps the

---

[1] See Charles Merriam, *American Political Theories* (New York: 1903), p. 299, where he objectively relates: 'The nationalistic theory assumes its most complete and scientific form at the hands of J. W. Burgess.' This is a good remark, except that Merriam seems to confuse nationalism with racialism, so that in rejecting the latter he can deceive himself that he is rejecting the former also.

[2] P. 49. This was published as *The Foundations of Political Science*, strangely, almost grotesquely, not until 1933, when it was warmly introduced by Nicholas Murray Butler, President of Columbia, a long-lived anachronism who was probably the most well-hated man in American academic life. [See the six chapters hurled at him in Upton Sinclair's *The Goose Step* (New York: 1922).]

short phase of American adoration for the racial world of Rudyard Kipling and of Cecil Rhodes was an attempt by a frustrated conservatism to gain a perspective outside this powerful liberal ideology. But it failed. American economic liberalism, as we have argued, was all but universal: worker, farmer and proper-Bostonian were all democratic-capitalists. It was so universal that it could be taken for granted, so that where a purely economic interpretation of politics was everywhere acted upon, as something inherited from even the Lockean world of pre-industrial America, in that very place 'the economic interpretation of history' could be the most scorned, for it was unnecessary. Americans had had no experience of that crisis which made Marx seek to create the dialectic opposite of the liberal economy. Burgess' racialism could not be taken seriously for long in such an economic environment: it only made him look like an English snob or the German College Professor of the Yellow-Press cartoon. The 'free-play of ideas' which even Mr. Justice Holmes thought could not but lead to progress, was a play with counters of economic individualism, not of racial type. Even the too too solid South now offered no *theory* of racialism, only a massive indifference to the need for justification at all. Burgess thought himself a firm Northern nationalist, far from the habitual a-political racialism of the South; he believed in the 'American nation', not 'these United States'. But he was in the agonizing position of an Hegelian who was of a nation, but a nation which had no sense of the *State*.

It has been worth recalling these passages from Burgess because they illustrate clearly the break between the post-Civil War generation of political scientists and the pragmatists of the 1900's. Burgess was, after all, the acknowledged *doyen* of political scientists. Perhaps from his advocacy of the racial theory we can understand something of the thoroughness of the break; something of the politically radical hue that it first took; and something of the new distrust of all 'first principles' as somehow inevitably undemocratic.

Professor W. W. Willoughby's writings also throw light upon the change, particularly the reaction from political philosophy towards political science. Though his last work, *The Ethical Basis of Political Authority*, was published as late as 1930, yet, as he himself confesses, his ideas were still those of his volume of 1896, *The Nature of the State*. His was perhaps 'the last of the great efforts to interpret the state in terms of a juristic theory of a state personality endowed with a sovereign will'.[1] He came to represent to the young political science profession a strangely still living professor of ideas long ago refuted, by someone or other, and in opposition to which they gained

[1] Francis Wilson, *American Political Mind*, p. 415.

so much of their own *raison d'être*. *The Nature of the State* is much preoccupied with questions like 'The True Origins of the State', as one chapter is headed. '*Government* is mechanical . . . [but] the State, on the other hand, . . . has a will of its own, . . . there is life and volition both in itself and its members.' [1] His aim was 'the construction of a true system of political philosophy, the determination of the ultimate nature of the State and the grounds upon which its authority must be justified'.[2]

By 1927 his textbook, *An Introduction to the Problem of Government*, written in collaboration with Lindsay Rogers, is somewhat cut to the cloth of a pragmatic clientele; he divides political science into Descriptive Political Science, Historical Political Science, and Political Theory or Philosophy. The book strives to limit itself to the first category alone, but truth will out, and it has an historical and ethical tone that makes it highly untypical of textbooks at the time it was published.[3]

Looking at Woolsey, Burgess and Willoughby, we may better understand why Beard could demand that political science should be separated from 'theology, ethics and patriotism'. We may understand much of the fervour of the advocacy of the 'new realism' and of the new and more scientific political science.

But a revulsion from an extreme of abstraction and irrelevance explains only part of pragmatic realism; it does not explain why they ignored examples of political study that did in fact blend more judiciously ideas and institutions; why they passed so quickly over the massive example of De Tocqueville, much of the work of Wilson and Bryce—indeed, of Hamilton, Madison, Jefferson and Lieber, too, and went questing after a science more pure. The point of our tedious background chapters may now appear more sharply. The authority of a peculiar notion of scientific procedure became greater than that of a mere empirical or pragmatic realism and eventually, and ironically, greater than the test of political relevance. Ultimately, Bryce and Wilson were without a philosophical defence against being torn into their strictly verifiable and their strictly non-verifiable propositions. (Harold Lasswell became fond of using Bryce's *American Commonwealth* as a touchstone for the inadequacies of the 'old comparative method', regarding Bryce as rich in hypotheses but

---

[1] W. W. Willoughby, *The Nature of the State* (New York: 1896), p. 132.

[2] *Ibid.*, p. vii.

[3] He sees the interest in scientific political psychology stemming, he notes, from Bagehot, Tarde, Wallas, McDougall and Lippmann, and remarks with tact and caution: 'But the "science", if it be that, is as yet only in its beginnings, and beyond indicating that there are problems connected with man's actions in a group, the social psychologist has not produced any body of principles which may be used by the student of government.' [*An Introduction to the Problem of Government* (New York: 1927), pp. 8–9.]

lacking in statistical verification for his generalizations.)[1] When they were gone and the subject matter of their books was dated, nobody arose of like ability and authority who could paint a picture of the whole national political life—indeed, such an enterprise itself became suspect.

2. The First Political Scientists of 'Realism'

The American Political Science Association was founded in 1904. Its first President was Frank Goodnow, followed successively by Bryce, Lowell and Wilson. All these men had a strong belief in common that political studies must have direct relevance to practical politics.[2] It may be said that none of the previous generation would have disputed this. But the belief of most of those who founded the association was that a systematic understanding of politics (as a necessary prelude to reform) had been bedevilled by excessive discussion of how they *should* work. 'Political theorists and philosophical dreamers' had outlined 'various utopias' or else had arrogated the eighteenth-century Lockean concept of contract into an eternal and 'static' ideal.[3] 'One of the most salutary results of this vast accumulation of data on politics has been to discredit the older speculative theorists and utopia makers. . . .'[4] A firm separation was demanded between normative and factual propositions. 'Ends' were broadly a political question for popular electoral decision; 'means' towards those ends, and the knowledge that would contribute towards making these means efficient—these could be a much-more-than-less scientific question. But at first there was little dogmatism, merely a marked change in stress.

Bryce, Beard, Wilson, Goodnow and Lowell, and certainly historians of political thought like Dunning, and then MacIlwain and Sabine, were content to bring 'the facts of the case' before the bar—of what? Probably Bryce and Wilson would think of the bar of learned opinion, whereas the influence of Progressivism made Beard and Goodnow think first of public opinion, the 'real' political opinion. Beard is not merely one of the first scholars of the new

[1] See Lasswell's *Psychopathology and Politics* (New York: 1930), p. 251, and his 'analysis', 'The Comparative Method of James Bryce', ed. Stuart Rice, *Methods in Social Science* (Chicago: 1931), pp. 468–79.

[2] See Frank Goodnow's opening address to the first conference, *Proceedings of the American Political Science Association*, I (1904).

The first move in 1902 was to form an 'American Society for Comparative Legislation', but almost all those canvassed thought such a title far too narrow and suggested instead 'Political Science Association'. There were 214 founder members (*ibid.*, pp. 1–35).

[3] See Frank Goodnow, *Social Reform and the Constitution* (New York: 1911), p. 1; here all philosophers are dreamers, and a weight of sarcasm lies on the word 'theorists'.

[4] Charles A. Beard, 'Politics', in Columbia University, *Lectures on Science, Philosophy and Art* (New York: 1908), p. 8.

ism in history and politics,[1] but is also one of the first popularizers
of it. They all agree that it was enough to advance the facts. They
would all have disagreed firmly with Acton's dictum that the historian is both *judge* and witness.

But even if it is a fallacy to think that facts can be advanced without purpose, shape and tendency, this does not mean that much of
the work of those who believe it possible need necessarily suffer.
Beard, Bryce and Lowell were all men too learned and rooted in
their particular tradition to commit gross irrelevance. They wrote
with considered judgement about important matters. Whatever their
professed methodology, they were, in a manner, saved by their
prejudices. Yet there was a strain in American pragmatism such as
the 'realism' of Bryce in England did not exemplify, and which was
not satisfied with a commonsense realism; it began to stress more and
more statistical techniques of ensuring complete objectivity. There
was a feeling abroad, as the Benthamite radicals had felt of the
Whiggery of Macaulay, that the approach to politics by the study of
history was inherently and perniciously conservative. But Science,
which with steamboat, train, telegraph and harvester had made a
continent a nation, was the great radical, the great creator and
innovator: the progressive. 'It is . . . in the spirit of modern science
that the student of politics turns to the great divisions of his subject,'
wrote Beard, and he noted—as a modern commentator approvingly
quotes him—that the political science of his day differed from that
of twenty-five years earlier in 'the decreasing reference to the doctrine of natural rights as a basis for political practice'; 'increasing
hesitation to ascribe political events to Providential causes'; 'rejection of the divine and racial theories of institutions', and a persistent
attempt to get 'more precise notions about causation in politics'.[2]
But the consequences of such arguments were to be more extreme
than Beard himself came to welcome.

A. Lawrence Lowell's work well shows how this transition came
about, though he himself deliberately kept from crossing the bridge
that he helped to build. He was among the first systematically to
apply statistical techniques to politics. The mere obtaining and
ordering of reliable statistical evidence for administrative or social
problems by Government or philanthropic organizations had none

[1] See especially his 'Politics', *op. cit.*; his *An Economic Interpretation of the Constitution of the United States* (New York: 1913); and his *Contemporary American History*
(New York: 1914). Morton White writes of these last two books: 'The usual items in
history books were consciously omitted in order to treat more fully matters which
seemed important to a thinking man of 1913; . . . trusts, the money question, the
tariff, imperialism and the labour movement.' [*Social Thought in America* (New York:
1952), p. 33.]
[2] Quoted by Louis Wirth, 'The Social Sciences', *American Scholarship in the
Twentieth Century*, ed. Merle Curti (Cambridge, Mass.: 1953), p. 49.

too long a history. Lowell, almost for the first time, attempted to use statistical techniques as a method of positive inference.[1]

As early as his *Essays on Government* he clearly states his position: 'Anyone who attempts to study a carpet loom, or even an ordinary steam engine, when at rest, will find its mechanism hard to understand. . . . The same principle applies to the study of politics, for the real mechanism of government can be understood only by examining it in action.'[2] He then continues by quoting the remark of Walter Bagehot that, while the legal attributes of King, Lords and Commons had been often correctly described, yet their *functions* were entirely misconceived. ('Function' was beginning to be a much used word.) His best-known book, *Public Opinion and Popular Government* (1913), published when he was already President of Harvard, promises 'to look through the forms to observe the vital forces behind them'. It argues, without visible enthusiasm, that the 'essence of popular government may be said to consist in the control of political affairs by public opinion'.[3] But he makes clear that public opinion in a stable democracy must be not merely or necessarily the will of all, but, like Rousseau's general will, he says, a genuine consensus in regard to the legitimate character of the ruling authority, whether or not, on any particular issue, it coincides with the momentary wishes of a majority. This he summarizes by saying that an opinion must be public; and, also, 'it must be really an opinion'.

Lowell has been hailed by some as the father of Public Opinion analysis as the supreme guide to policy. But these distorting disciples must be shocked by his 'moralistic' insistence that opinion is not desire: that opinion is only a legitimate basis for authority in so far as 'it is only as a moral being that . . . [man] is fit for self-government. The great Statesman, like the great moral leader, is one who appeals to the higher emotions, to principle, to self-restraint, not to selfishness and appetite.'[4] It is in this light that Lowell says that 'devices for reform have rarely fulfilled the expectations they awoke' because of 'a failure to study politics scientifically, to investigate phenomena thoroughly. It is much easier to bring a railing accusation against men or institutions than to ascertain how far they are a natural product of the conditions under which they exist. To the scientific mind every phenomenon is a fact that has a cause, and it is wise to seek that cause when attempting to change the fact.'[5]

[1] See especially his 'Oscillations in Politics', *Annals of the American Academy of Political and Social Science*, XII (July 1898), 69–97.
[2] *Essays on Government* (Boston: 1889), p. 1. The most important of these took Wilson strongly to task over his advocacy of the Cabinet system for the United States.
[3] Lowell, *Public Opinion and Popular Government* (New York: 1913), p. 4.
[4] *Ibid.*, p. 27.
[5] *Ibid.*, p. 101; and see the whole of that section, 'Need of Scientific Study of Party Government', pp. 100–2.

His own position becomes more clear in his Presidential Address of 1910 to the American Political Science Association, called: 'The Physiology of Politics'. Lowell argues that academic sources are disregarded by men in public life because political scientists 'do not study enough the actual workings of government'. For example, he said, Direct Primaries were of burning interest at that time, yet, while political scientists 'are fertile with suggestions about the way it ought to work, [they] are almost dumb about its effect in practice'. The only helpful study he can think of on the direct primary movement is a book by a young man, Charles Merriam.[1]

He then makes some remarks that would seem trite if we were not aware of the type of work that had gone before and of the general intellectual temper of the Progressive Era:

> We are apt to err in regard to the things to be observed. We are inclined to regard the library as the laboratory of political science, the storehouse of original sources, the collation of ultimate material. . . . But for the most purposes books are no more the original sources for the physiology of politics than they are for geology or astronomy. The main laboratory for the actual working of political institutions is not a library, but the outside world of public life. It is there that phenomena must be sought. It is there that they must be observed at first hand. It is by studying them there that the greatest contributions to the sciences must be expected.[2]

If such is the scientific method of Lowell, it is an admirably flexible thing. The above passage should not suggest that Lowell was indifferent to ideas—far from it; he was in healthy reaction against the type of student who knew his books on *Staatsrecht* and *Staatslehre* but, like Woodrow Wilson at the time he wrote *Congressional Government*, had never even sat for an afternoon in the gallery of the Senate. We may quibble when he says that 'to the scientific mind every phenomenon is a fact that has a *cause*', and we may wish in the social sciences for safety's sake to substitute the historian's concept, 'condition'; but Lowell himself was not likely to sacrifice life to certainty: he was a man of wide culture and deep moral earnestness (as befitted a proper Bostonian). His work on party statistics must be seen in this context.

He was pleased that the Chair he entered into at Harvard in 1900 should be called ' . . . of the Science of Government'.[3] He himself anonymously donated a new lecture hall (from the proceeds of the

---

[1] Lowell, 'The Physiology of Politics', *APSR*, IV (Feb. 1910), 1–16. 'Professor Merriam has recently written an excellent book upon the movement [*Primary Elections* (Chicago: 1908)], marked by a great knowledge of its history, and, what is more rare, by admirable impartiality; but of one hundred and seventy-eight pages of text only sixteen are devoted to actual results' (p. 5).

[2] Lowell, *ibid.*, p. 7.

[3] See Henry Aaron Yeomans, *Life of Abbott Lawrence Lowell* (Cambridge: 1948), pp. 52–8. President Eliot wrote to Lowell in 1900 announcing that he had been elected

carpet looms of *his* model town of Lowell) to seat the unprecedentedly large number of students who took his new introductory Government course. This course, the justly renowned Harvard 'Government I', spent, then as now, half the year on 'political science', as the description of the working of comparative institutions; but the other half on a critical and historical survey of political philosophy from the time of Classical Antiquity. The 'Science of Government' of Lowell, while without doubt more empirical than the concepts of Woolsey, Burgess or W. W. Willoughby, yet embraced a concern for education in the widest and most scholarly sense which only indirectly, but then firmly and well, touched on the practice of politics. But, despite this, political scientists have remembered Lowell not for his happy balance of research into new processes and reiteration of old principles to young men, but for the example of his research alone.[1] *The Influence of Party upon Legislation in England and America* (1902) is hailed as a pioneer work of objective statistical inference in political science, without remembering that Lowell was interested in discovering such facts, not for the advancement of a possible social science, but to provide some evidence, amongst other evidence, for practical judgements. And these judgements must also, Lowell believed, be made in the light of certain moral presuppositions. By 1931 his views had moved so far counter to the spirit of his times that he would sound to many like a pious anachronism when he wrote to Graham Wallas: ' . . . the more I see of it the more I am impressed with the importance of the moral basis as compared with the mechanical contrivances of the organization, that the real test of different forms of government is the stamina that they induce'.[2]

'Professor of the Science of Government': '. . . the term "Science of Government" is the one used by Mr. Eaton, and he seemed to value it because it was used by Washington . . .' (quoted by Yeomans, *ibid.*, p. 60).

Mr. Eaton, who endowed the Chair, was the Dormon B. Eaton whose famous study, *The Civil Service in Great Britain* (1880), was the single work of most powerful influence in the Civil Service reform movements, almost the political bible of liberal Republicans like Charles W. Eliot and A. L. Lowell. It argued that the Republican ideal of America was being jeopardized by a faulty and corrupt public administration, compared to the new professional bureaucracies of England and Prussia.

This lineage between Washington, Eaton and Lowell is more than symbolic of the original closeness between political science and political reform through political education.

[1] See, for example, Charles E. Merriam, 'Political Science in the United States', in the UNESCO *Contemporary Political Science* (Paris: 1950), p. 240: 'The application of psychology to the new politics has gone along with the technical perfection [*sic*] of psychology. . . . The foundation for these studies was laid by LOWELL of Harvard and the most notable advance in this structure was that of LASSWELL.'

But there is a world of difference between Lowell and Lasswell, while Lowell is allowed to speak for himself. Merriam had that generosity of mind that seeks to ignore all hurtful intellectual distinctions that may separate men of even a common profession.

[2] Quoted in Youmans, *Lowell*, p. 400.

Woodrow Wilson, too, is 'a realist', but is more removed from the modern science of politics than even Lowell. 'I do not like the term political science,' he wrote in 1911. 'Human relationships, whether in family or in the state, in the country house or in the factory, are not in any proper sense the subject matter of science.'[1] Charles Beard, also, was eventually to turn in revolt against a science of politics, when he came to see, in the middle 'twenties, how far pure Science and Pragmatism had become separated.[2] Wilson saw the danger—that realism would topple over into scientism—before it occurred; Beard saw it afterwards; but both were powerless to resist the gradual selection from their works by a host of minor men of only those passages that would bear looking at as 'pure facts' and would be the kind of furniture to have around so that one's colleagues in Sociology and Psychology—and even the few one met in the natural sciences—would recognize one as a true scientist.

Wilson's brilliant essay, 'The Study of Administration',[3] has received much attention by students of Public Administration because they could use it to argue the autonomy of Administration from politics, a step that would make more plausible the treatment of Administration as a science.[4] His *Congressional Government* (1885) has often been criticized as an altogether *a priori* condemnation of the actual American system of Government in favour of a remotely possible British Cabinet system. Lowell's *Essays on Government* can cross swords with Wilson on this issue, as any of the typical text-books of the 1940's do later. But Lowell does not deny for a moment that it is the business of the political scientist to propose Constitutional reform, and they were at one in rejecting the Constitution worship inherent in the formal and legalistic approach of their predecessors. Indeed Constitutional reform became almost the touch-stone of respect for the new political scientists; by having some

[1] Woodrow Wilson, 'The Law and the Facts', *APSR*, V (March 1911), pp. 10–11, quoted in David Easton, *The Political System*, *op. cit.*, p. 68, amid some excellent pages on Wilson.

[2] Beard then distinguished between *realism* and *scientism*: 'The method of natural science is applicable only to a very limited degree and, in its pure form, not at all to any fateful issue of politics. What we have, therefore, and can only have is intelligence applied to the political facets of our unbroken social organism.' [Beard, 'Political Science', in *Research in the Social Sciences*, ed. W. Gee (New York: 1929), p. 286.] See generally on the change of viewpoint about a science of politics in Beard, Howard K. Beale, 'Charles Beard: Historian', in *Charles A. Beard: An Appraisal*, ed. Howard K. Beale (University of Kentucky: 1954).

[3] Wilson, 'The Study of Administration', *Political Science Quarterly*, II (June 1887), 197–222.

[4] See Dwight Waldo, *The Administrative State* (New York: 1948), pp. 26–7: 'So far did they advance from the old belief that the problem of good government is the problem of moral men that they arrived at the opposite position: that morality is irrelevant, that proper institutions and expert personnel are determining. The new amorality became almost a requisite for professional respect.'

scheme of reform, small or great, they showed one another that they were in revolt against received opinion, were not 'hidebound by tradition', and were practical men aware of changing circumstances.

The study of Constitutional Law and of American history had originally been vastly stimulated, in both secondary and higher education, by the Civil War. Much of the best work in Burgess illustrates this. But it suffered heavily from an undue legalistic absorption in the questions of war guilt and of the Constitutional status of the ex-Confederate states during Reconstruction. But, by the late 'eighties, there was a definite lack of interest in the formal Constitution as such. Woodrow Wilson by 1887 was urging, at the same time as Oliver Wendell Holmes, Jr., that the student go beyond the letter of the law and become acquainted with the life of the State: he who reads constitutions with lawyers as guides 'must risk knowing only the anatomy of institutions and never learning anything of their biology'.[1]

F. J. Goodnow, A. B. Hart, E. J. James, W. B. Munro, all strengthened the realism of Beard, Lowell and Wilson, but, largely because of an absorption in municipal reform, tended to become more and more narrow in their interests. Yet the more narrow and scattered their interests became, and the more they rebelled against the sweeping generalities of the older books, the broader became the theory of scientific activity that they needed to give meaning and form to their many interests. Science to them was not primarily the framing and testing of general theories, but an undertaking that just set out to describe how any or all political processes worked. When *all* the facts had been gathered, then a theory or a judgement could be risked. Much of their work suffered from the same defects as the contemporary work in sociology: 'American sociologists, it is true, did produce the type of orderly and documented description of their society which contributed in an important way to our self-understanding, but all too often the descriptive passion was *in*discriminate in its objects and in its purposes.'[2] The political scientists, like the sociologists, in many ways 'stood mid-way between the Sociology of the library and learned meditation on one hand, and the increasingly circumspect research techniques of the present day on the other'.[3] They put complete professional faith in more research as the cure for all social ills, but they had a very lively private sense of what were social ills.

---

[1] Woodrow Wilson, 'Of the Study of Politics', *New Princeton Review*, III (1887), 190, quoted by Anna Haddow, *Political Science in American Colleges and Universities 1636–1900* (New York: 1939), p. 240.

[2] Edward Shils, *The Present State of American Sociology*, p. 3.

[3] *Ibid.*, p. 6.

3. The Quest for New Methods

Charles Merriam taught during the 1900's at the University of
Chicago, writing fairly conventional books on American and
European political thought.[1] As a pupil of W. A. Dunning at
Columbia, his notion of academic political thought was to explain
dispassionately the meaning of what political philosophers had
written. His *Primary Elections* of 1908, which Lowell had paused to
praise, was his one venture into contemporary empirical analysis.
These other books followed the methods of the first Johns Hopkins
seminar in history which imported the scientific historiography of
Ranke. They appear, in fact, rather dull and lifeless professional
chores, only remarkable for a growing animus *against* the importance
of political ideas, seeking more and more to find prophecies or
anticipations of the views by which he eventually rose above 'the
subjectivity and uncertainty of political philosophy', those *New
Aspects of Politics* of which he was by 1925 the leading advocate.
But during this period he agreed with the advice of Lord Bryce, who
'told him that at least ten years of practical experience in politics
was useful for the student of government'.[2] From 1909 to 1911 and
1913 to 1917 he was an Alderman in the old Seventh Ward of
Chicago, an active reformer in the raucous days when 'Big Bill'
Thompson ran the city. He ran on the Republican ticket for Mayor
in 1911, going down to a foregone defeat despite the personal en-
dorsement of Theodore Roosevelt. He was an ardent Bull-Mooser
in 1912 and met Harold J. Ickes in Roosevelt's entourage; a generation later he was to bring Merriam to Washington for a while as
part of the corps of advisers to the other Roosevelt's New Deal.
Much of his energy went into a series of Reports on Chicago city
government: detailed and heavily documented investigations which
furnished ammunition for reformers as well as materials for the new
teachers of Municipal Government and Public Administration.

By 1924 he could characterize the 'old historical and empirical'
school, to which his own first academic work belonged, thus:

The outstanding representative of this group was Lord Bryce, who for
two generations carried on a series of practical and theoretical enquiries
into the working of modern political institutions. . . . History and observation combined with practical experience are here most conspicuous, while
philosophy and psychology are subordinated, but by no means excluded.

[1] See: Charles Merriam, *A History of Sovereignty since Rousseau* (Chicago: 1900);
A History of American Political Theories (Chicago: 1903); and *American Political Ideas*
(Chicago: 1920).
[2] Charles E. Merriam, 'The Education of Charles E. Merriam', from the volume of
essays in his honour edited by Leonard E. White, *The Future of Government in the
United States* (Chicago: 1942), p. 4.

Bryce distrusted the past performances of philosophy, but he was not yet assured of the possibilities of the rising science of political psychology.[1]

'The rising science of political psychology'—this tells us more of Merriam than of Bryce. There was little enough reason why anyone should be '*assured* of the possibilities of the rising science of political psychology'. But even before 1920 there was a trend, and Merriam all his life had a good ear for trends. In so far as the early science of politics movement was scientific enough to pass beyond mere description to theory in the attempt to find natural principles of politics, there was a small but rapidly growing body of opinion that saw the superstructure of society as explicable, not in economic terms as Charles Beard or E. A. G. Seligman thought, but in terms of psychological drives. A. L. Lowell could note that modern psychology has taught us 'how small a part of our actions are the result of our own reasoning', and that 'it has become almost a commonplace that the older breed of political and economic philosophers erred in regarding man as a purely rational being'.[2] But it was the English writer, Graham Wallas, Merriam writes, who did most to 'attempt to interpret political phenomena in terms of psychological forces rather than in terms of form and structure'.[3]

Wallas had begun the second part of his *Human Nature in Politics* —called 'Possibilities of Progress'—with a notable claim that was to become widely quoted as almost a programme among many American political scientists:

In the preceding chapters I have argued that the efficacy of political science, its power, that is to say, of forecasting the results of political causes is likely to increase. I based my arguments on two facts, firstly, that modern psychology offers us a conception of human nature much truer, though more complex than that which is associated with the traditional English political philosophy; and, secondly, that under the influence and example of the natural sciences, political thinkers are already beginning to use in their discussions and enquiries quantitative rather than merely qualitative words and methods, and are able, therefore, both to state their problems more fully and to answer them with a greater approximation to accuracy.[4]

This was the testament for political science that Walter Lippmann was eloquently to expound in his *Preface to Politics* of 1913—himself for a year an actual student of Wallas.[5] Lippmann joined Wallas in

[1] Charles E. Merriam and Harry Elmer Barnes, eds., *A History of Political Theories of Recent Times* (New York: 1924), p. 18.

[2] Lowell, *Public Opinion*, p. 16.

[3] Merriam and Barnes, *History of Political Theories*, p. 19.

[4] Graham Wallas, *Human Nature in Politics* (London: 1929), p. 167; first published, 1908.

[5] See Horace M. Kallen, 'Political Science as Psychology', *APSR*, XVII (May 1923). He writes of Wallas and Lippmann that: 'In these latter political science is a new thing, with a new method and a new form.'

attacking what they saw as the twin rationalism of idealism and residuary utilitarianism. Both views had over-stated the rationality of man and borne little relevance to actual politics. What inferences Lippmann wishes to draw from this ancient but oft-forgotten truth were not very clear—the forces 'of our dreams' which Plato clearly recognized but urged man to master by his reason. But he constantly appeals to the authority of 'facts' as against 'reason'. True, he argues that even 'Mr. Wallas's book . . . leaves no doubt that a precise political psychology is far off indeed', but come it will. 'Psychology has not gone far enough . . . it will take time and endless labour,' but a scientific approach can come. One of the difficulties, Lippmann notes, is that Wallas 'works with a psychology that is fairly well superseded'. There is a new school, far more promising: 'The impetus of Freud is perhaps the greatest advance ever made towards the understanding and control of human character.' [1]

In the meantime, Lippmann, like the other realists we have discussed, was interested for university political scientists to turn their interests more to that research which is *directly* related to practical politics. He admired very much the English Fabians: 'Their appetite for the concrete was enormous; their appetite for facts overpowering.' [2] But he noted that even 'Fabian enthusiasm has slackened. One might ascribe it to a growing sense that concrete programs by themselves will not ensure any profound regeneration of society'—which apparently is what everybody wants. What was lacking, he argued, 'is what the traditional political philosophers made the centre of their speculation, a view of human nature. But now this view must be supplied accurately and not speculatively by a scientific psychology.' [3]

Such was the goal of the young Walter Lippmann; it might be said that he was then a short-run pragmatist, long-run scientist. In a later chapter we will have to explore more fully why his introduction of psychology, particularly Freudian psychology, should be of such

[1] Walter Lippmann, *A Preface to Politics* (New York: 1914), pp. 84–5. The title page bears the legend: 'A god wilt thou create for thyself out of thy seven devils.'

[2] Beatrice Webb could quote something that Beatrice Potter had once written: 'We have become pure empiricists, treating each symptom as it appears on the surface of society. And this change has been mainly accomplished by the strong and irrepressible emotion aroused by the narration of the facts.' She notes that such a faith had much in common with the Liberal and Tory reformers of the tradition of Lord Shaftesbury—and we may note its similarity to the 'muckraking' and 'realist' literature in America. But the 'narration of the facts' did not remain alone sufficient for even the Fabian Socialists, once they had found the need for the irrepressible emotion of George Bernard Shaw. But American reformers, by and large, remained at this stage of 'narration'. [See *My Apprenticeship* (London: 1926), Appendix A, p. 417; also Appendix C, 'The Art of Note-Taking', pp. 426–36, is a fascinating parallel, possibly a small influence, to American social science—it is the apotheosis of the doctrine of the 'pure fact'.]

[3] Lippmann, *ibid.*, pp. 71–2.

recurring interest to American political scientists.[1] But on the whole Lippmann's early scientism is more clearly a protest and a criticism against the old, rather than a precise programme for the new:

> Whoever has read the typical book on politics by a professor or reformer will agree, I think, when he [Wallas] adds: 'One feels that many of the more systematic books of politics written by American university professors are useless, just because the writers deal with abstract men, formed on assumptions of which they are unaware and which they have never tested either by experience or by study.[2]

One curious fact remains about the 'influence' of the scientism of Wallas and Lippmann: although Lippmann has made his apostasy notorious, only one American political scientist has ever thought it worthwhile to recall that: 'The history of Wallas's thought on the usefulness of "science" to the methods of the social disciplines is a record of enthusiasm followed by an increasing scepticism, and, in some respects, opposition'—and this not by a member of the scientific school.[3] Wallas is still known for his *Human Nature in Politics* alone, not for his *Social Judgement* or *Our Social Heritage*. This is to go beyond the Progressive Era, but the subsequent failure to refute explicitly the deviations of the early gods makes the suspicion stronger that few such individuals were taken seriously for the whole body of their work; they were only read and remembered in those selected aspects of their work which rendered literate and articulate an existing common sentiment. In other words, we must constantly remember that 'the *average* American . . . has felt an almost limitless confidence in whatever bears the label of Science'[4] —not merely or predominantly the scholarly American.

There is another aspect of the 'new realism' in political science which it is important to notice: the inherent danger that the protest against 'the alien and the formal' would become a mere nationalism, not a way of understanding at all—even if the nationalism of radicals and not of the Federalist tradition. Professor Thomas I. Cook has put this point well (although he exaggerates Beard's influence alone —or perhaps uses him as a symbol):

> The great revolt against the alien and the formal, and for the American and the realistic, was, however, the work of the late Charles A. Beard.

[1] Despite what Lippmann says, it is hard to find any influence of Freudian thought in *Preface to Politics* more precise than the promise of a future importance and influence. It is interesting to find the casual and accidental manner in which Freudianism came to him. See Frederick J. Hoffmann, *Freudianism and the Literary Mind* (New York: 1941), p. 52.

[2] Lippmann, *Preface to Politics*, p. 72.

[3] Dwight Waldo, 'Graham Wallas: Reason and Emotion in Social Change', *Journal of Social Philosophy and Jurisprudence*, VII (Jan. 1942), 149.

[4] Again from Dwight Waldo, *The Administrative State* (New York: 1948), p. 20.

His teaching, which in earlier years led to misguided accusations of irreverence for the American myth, . . . constituted a coherent pattern and served a sustained purpose. It was a plea for realistic analysis of how men actually behave in politics, a search for their motivations and interests. It was an attempt to discover . . . the specifically American political animal and political culture . . . it was a search for an overall sociology of American politics. And, above all, it was an attempt to formulate an American political science . . ., which could be at once hand-maiden and creative critic of American policy for the service of American national interest. *The consequences of Beard's teaching were a somewhat undue emphasis on American government, and an unfortunate separation of it from comparative government; as well as, on the teaching side, especially, a tendency to abandon the study of principles and to subordinate and isolate theory.*[1]

This was the paradox of the emerging political science: as it tried to become more scientific, it in fact became more parochial. In part, this parochialism was pure gain: the pre-eminent part of a political education is, indeed, the understanding of one's own political tradition—and America is a large parish. The Germanophile and Anglophile American teachers had only themselves to blame that they nearly lost all of their achievement, instead of some, when called to a reckoning of relevance to the all-too-human things that went on outside New England colleges. But to understand a national tradition, or to find 'an overall sociology of American politics', there is needed either some perspective such as the study of the national history and its sources will give—not a pragmatic history limited to proving a party point on every immediate political issue; or else there is needed the perspective gained by an intimate knowledge of some other culture.

The 'comparative method' had been the great glory of 'the formalists' and without it no standard of comparison, let alone of judgement, could be established which could save 'the realists' in their reaction to each pressing issue of the times from being blown hither and thither by winds of contingency—the spate of *fashions* in topics and methods which sweep through the American social sciences at almost regular intervals. The strength and brilliance of Beard himself could allow flexibility, but the example of his early days could be treacherous. Ultimately, in him, the nationalist conquered the scientist, and in his isolationist tracts, which sought to defend the American heritage against a disastrous reinvolvement in the affairs of Europe, he had no use at all for a science of politics. From the dangers of international war, he saw that while the objective analysis of the interplay of pressure groups was an important factor to be

[1] Thomas I. Cook, 'The Methods of Political Science, Chiefly in the United States', UNESCO, *Contemporary Political Science* (Paris: 1950), p. 79, my italics.

studied in American politics, it was not the first postulate and far from the main object of political studies.[1] But certainly his early concentration on the American scene was to limit his understanding of international politics and was to leave many of his followers quite unprepared in the dilemmas of America's unsought-for rise to world leadership.

So far the new political scientists whom we have mentioned have been basically pragmatists, pragmatists of the stamp of James or of the practical and reformist aspects of Dewey's social-instrumentalism. They were men who wasted few words on justification, and who, setting an example to the following generation, quickly got down to specific studies. But, unlike their successors, their whole range of studies was orientated by the reformism of the Progressive movement. While many thought that they had avoided any commitment, they were, in fact, caught up in a peculiar phase of American history. By and large, many of the typical attitudes of the Progressive Era were not unhappy ones to be caught up in—while they lasted and appeared to control social happenings. Many, like Lippmann, conscious of the demand for activity, experiment and popular control, knew that to uncover the facts of political party organization, or of 'human nature in politics', was not in practice vain and random, but was done in order to create an arsenal of 'fighting facts' for ready and willing reformers and journalists, who were working in a fairly clear direction with a wide, if unconscious, agreement as to goals—and this was an era when the weekly magazines were practising political journalism of a probity and seriousness that has been unequalled since.

4. The Ambiguous Influence of Lord Bryce

The closeness of Lord Bryce to American political science can serve as both a commentary and a point of comparison to the growing differences between 'realism' and 'scientism'. The 'empiricism' of Bryce appeared to be the same thing as the 'realism' of the Americans, but there were deeper tides of thought, which neither he nor his American audience recognized, that were carrying American political scientists away from this common position and would seem to them a natural development, but would surely have seemed to Bryce a distortion, even a contradiction. His Presidential Address to the American Political Science Association in 1908—no small mark of the esteem in which he was held—aptly called 'The Relations of Political Science to History and Practice', must have fallen easily, perhaps too easily, upon American ears. He began:

In calling politics a science we mean no more than this, that there is a

[1] See Beard's *Giddy Minds and Foreign Quarrels* (New York: 1939), and *The Republic* (New York: 1943).

constancy and uniformity in tendencies of human nature which enables us to regard the acts of men at one time due to the same causes which have governed their acts at previous times ... These tendencies are in so far uniform and permanent that we can lay down general propositions about human nature and can form these propositions into a connected system of knowledge.[1]

This may seem an extreme view, but we can be fairly sure that Bryce was thinking of 'uniform tendencies in human nature' in a manner not very far different, for example, from that of Hamilton and Madison, or passages could be matched from Machiavelli, by no means a 'scientist' in the modern sense, as American political scientists often teach. Bryce probably thought he was uttering an opening platitude, but the audience to whom he spoke could understand him differently. 'Keep close to the facts and never lose yourselves in abstractions', but, he makes clear, political science 'is not a deductive science any more than it is a branch of speculative philosophy'. He gives some admirable *precepts*, craftsman's precepts, for the student of politics—and in the formulation of precepts Bryce had an enviable facility; and then proceeds to give some rather more difficult advice:

You may ask: Are we then to study everything in the light of everything else? And, if so, what limit can be set to the investigation? The answer is: No limit. Every political organism, every political force, must be studied in and cannot be understood apart from the environment out of which it has grown. ... Not all the facts of that environment are relevant, *but till you have examined them, you cannot pronounce any irrelevant*.[2]

There is perhaps a sense in which we may claim—and then only claim—*to understand* a total environment, but to tell us to examine *all* the facts before we know which are relevant, is, when taken literally, impossible nonsense, however much some may try to live up to it.[3]

He continued, or reverts, by sounding a note on the trumpets of Mugwumpery, of which he himself, in American eyes, was almost the greatest example: 'The chief aim of your science is to create in the class which leads a nation the proper temper and attitude towards the questions which from time to time arise in politics.' But most of his audience had founded the Political Science Association

---

[1] *APSR*, III (Feb. 1909), 3.   [2] *Ibid.*, p. 6, my italics.
[3] One ventures to quote Hegel's sensible words on this point: 'Even the average and mediocre historian, who perhaps believes and pretends that he is merely receptive, merely surrendering himself to his data, is not passive in his thinking. He brings his categories with him and sees his data through them. In everything supposed to be scientific, reason must be awake and reflection applied.' [Hegel in *The Philosophy of History*, translated by C. J. Friedrich in his *The Philosophy of Hegel* (New York: 1954), p. 5.]

to get something more definite than a temper of mind; or, from another point of view, they were beginning to admire the temper of mind that was 'truly scientific'. The proper temper and attitude towards politics for Bryce would be scientific in a broad sense, in the common German sense; he did not mean that all questions would or could be solved after the manner of the natural sciences, as was becoming the American sense. Bryce was encouraging the scientific spirit in political science while it operated within a framework, ultimately a tradition, of such clearly defined principles that a method of empirical commonsense could easily apply. But the method of natural science had passed beyond empirical commonsense several centuries before. And the words he was using were beginning to mean radically different things in two increasingly differing traditions. Bryce in the 1900's, perhaps, did not have the measure of his American audience as well as he did in the 1880's. The 'best men' whom he had wanted to enter politics were becoming social scientists instead. The statesman in Bryce would have shied away from the growing belief that the facts themselves would lead to a gradual rationalizing of politics, without any need for the 'arbitrary' element of judgement. But Bryce's own intellectual flaw is shown clearly in his rejection of the work of the one man who seemed to have seen clearly why American democracy threatened to extend political equality into a demand for a method that ensured intellectual equality.

Bryce's criticism of De Tocqueville well illustrates the new temper of mind in political studies, the deliberate breach that took place between political science and political theory:

To De Tocqueville America was primarily a democracy, the ideal democracy, fraught with lessons for Europe, and above all for his own France. What he has given us is not so much a description of the country and the people as a treatise, full of fine observation and elevated thinking, upon democracy, a treatise whose conclusions are illustrated from America, but are founded not so much on an analysis of America phenomena, as on general and somewhat speculative views of democracy. . . . I have striven to avoid the temptation of the deductive method, and to represent simply the facts of the case, arranging and connecting them as best I can, but letting them speak for themselves rather than pressing the conclusions upon the readers.[1]

The significant thing is that American scholars preferred the account of Bryce to that of De Tocqueville; the things that Bryce took for granted were not questioned, nor were the more significant things that he left out of his account entirely. De Tocqueville was remembered as a traveller who had made a few very brilliant remarks, but

[1] Bryce, *The American Commonwealth* (London: 1890), I, 5.

who was 'impressionistic' and who had an aristocratic prejudice against democracy; Bryce was the real student of politics. But the factualist temper of Bryce completely underestimated De Tocqueville's main thesis: that America was the attempted working out of the idea of *democracy*, and was the environment the best fitted to receive with the least danger the furthest extreme tendency of Western civilization towards a democratic-egalitarianism.

Bryce shows here a scepticism about the effect of general ideas, such as democracy, upon history which we now, amid the terrors of ideological politics that have rejected mere 'practice', cannot share, indeed, cannot even share in our interpretation of European and American history since the era of Revolutions. A true 'description of the country and the people' cannot avoid at every step involving a 'treatise . . . upon democracy'. To avoid such is as over-simplified as to write about the government of the U.S.S.R., while ignoring Communist theory; or even of Britain without mention of the content of the political ideas of the two major parties. Asquith recalled in his *Memoirs* having heard William James say that 'to Bryce, all facts are free and equal'. That was a palpable hit. It was precisely this assumption (so closely allied to J. B. Hart's claim that 'the most distinctive American theory of government is not to theorize') that De Tocqueville feared would be the tragic flaw of the hopes of democracy; something that would reduce all literature, art, character and religion to mediocrity and create a mild but utterly enervating tyranny of public opinion. It was in order to reconcile democracy with an active liberty that could maintain ideas of excellence and of right that De Tocqueville tried to fashion his 'new science of politics', a 'science' that would ignore neither the continuities of opinion nor the hierarchies of ideas: 'a science' armed by both sociology and religion.

Bryce, in other words, did not realize what his advice to 'stay close to the facts', and to study scientifically, would mean to an audience who were becoming increasingly possessed by a general idea. The idea of a science of politics, itself immune from scepticism, could reshape his words as he uttered them and refute, for his hearers—in this one respect—his own doubts about the importance of such ideas in politics. The closing paragraph of a long and generous obituary of Bryce in the *American Political Science Review* shows clearly the transformation of thought that was taking place from the more flexible empirical or pragmatic outlook towards the more rigid positivistic idea of scientific method:

Bryce's contributions to political science form a prominent landmark in the development of this important branch of knowledge. . . . His work was that of a keen-sighted observer, with a well trained mind and a broad knowledge of history, law and the physical facts of the world; and his studies were much more comprehensive than those of Darwin [*sic*] in collecting and analyzing the materials for his scientific discoveries. If these studies have led to no such fundamental principle as that of natural selection, this may be due to the more extensive scope or the greater complexity of the enquiry; or perhaps the student of politics has been more cautiously scientific than the biologist, in not committing himself to a hypothesis which later investigations might require to be subject to substantial modifications.[1]

Almost everything about the origins, conditions and consequences of the scientific school of political science could be based on a commentary on those sentences, both in their element of aptness to Bryce and in their larger element of unconscious distortion.

[1] Anonymous, *APSR*, XVI (May 1922), 311.

VII

THE SCIENCE OF THE GROUP
PROCESS OF POLITICS: A. F. BENTLEY

> When the groups are adequately stated, everything is stated. When
> I say everything I mean everything. The complete description will
> mean the complete science. . . .
>
> A. F. BENTLEY, *The Process of Government*

> The Sophists . . . have conceived it be 'an easy matter to legislate
> simply by collecting such laws as are made famous because, of course,
> one could select the best', as though the selection were not a matter
> of skill, and judging aright a very great matter, as in Music. . . .
>
> ARISTOTLE, *Nichomachean Ethics*

1. The Contemporary Importance of Bentley

'THERE ARE few fields which American political scientists have
cultivated as intensively and profitably', Professor Merle Fainsod
has written, 'as the analysis of the dynamic interplay of interest
groups as they give shape to public policy at almost all governmental levels. The interest group is almost a unique characteristic of
American political science.' [1] By the 1900's the unity of American
experience and the stress on tactical considerations of politics in a
Federal system gave a meaning to politics that was radically unlike
the ideological and doctrinal struggles of Europe. Progressive reformers might still try to hold fast to the ultra-individualism of
direct democracy, but the new political scientists began to see politics
as a contest for marginal privilege by a great many pressure groups,
mostly regional and economic rather than primarily ideological and
doctrinal. To the student these could all appear as very much equal
in their claims. They all operated broadly within the same assumption of the one liberal-democratic tradition. They made it easy for
the student of politics to think of himself as just the dispassionate

---

[1] Merle Fainsod, 'The Study of Government and Economic Life in the United
States', in UNESCO, *Contemporary Political Science* (Paris: 1950), p. 473.

observer of 'the democratic plurality of pressure groups'. There was only the need for a methodological discussion of how best to study these groups and for the *primum mobile* of the system to be seen as 'power' or 'interest'. There was felt to be no need for the kind of constant critical recourse to philosophy and history that the European student of politics had to make. Where evaluation did arise, it was in the form of deciding whether the competing pressure groups and interests were keeping to the letter of the Constitution and to the spirit of the ingrained laws. Where arguments for institutional reform did arise, they took the form of seeing how a pre-existent harmony of popular sentiment could be more clearly represented. Indeed, politics became viewed not as the crisis and adjustment of rival ideas and disparate institutions, but as *process*, a continuous functional relationship of indivisible parts.

During the 1900's the twin claims first clearly arose that the true level of reality for political understanding and investigation was *the group* and that politics was only 'real' when it could be viewed as *process*. The old 'formalism' was to be replaced by the non-ethical study of social groups as *functions* of particular interests and of their actual dynamic *activity* in the *process* of group relationships and conflicts, which was the new definition of politics.

The great synthesis of these tendencies was Arthur Fisher Bentley's *The Process of Government* (1908). Until the last decade the question of its direct influence was obscure. Bertram Gross, of the Council of Economic Advisers, reviewed in 1950 only the second reprint of Bentley's book and could draw attention to how greatly it had been neglected and how surprised its by then numerous rediscoverers were to find their own methodology anticipated. 'If someone were compiling a list of the most important books on government ever written in America,' began Gross, 'this reviewer would heartily recommend the *Process of Government* for inclusion. If a list were made of the most important books on government to have been written in any country, this book would be on that list also.' [1] The strength of such a claim contrasts sharply, as Mr. Gross himself points out, to its brusque and uninterested original review.[2] Something of this neglect can easily be explained. Bentley certainly gave himself 'all the penalties of laborious authors' and, furthermore, unlike Charles Beard (who was to introduce Bentley's books to his graduate students), he actively avoided both teaching and public affairs. And

[1] This is a long leading review in *APSR*, XLIV (March 1950), 742–8.

[2] James W. Garner then commented in a mere 'Note', not even a full review: 'A hasty reading of some of these chapters fails to impress the reviewer with their value as a contribution to the literature of political science, though the work as a whole will doubtless interest students of social institutions. It bears evidence of wide and careful reading. . . .' [*APSR*, II (May 1908), 457.]

he soon turned his energies in other directions, making a modest reputation as a philosophical writer, developing the methodological interests of *The Process of Government* until he became the purest logician among the pragmatists since Charles Sanders Peirce himself, achieving the recognition of collaboration with Dewey.[1] But the opinion of Mr. Gross, that *The Process of Government* is 'one of the most important' books on government in 'any land', is by no means eccentric; it is now shared by many writers.[2]

2. A Tool to Reveal a Process

Bentley inscribed the fly-leaf of his book: 'This book is an attempt to fashion a tool', and as a tool of investigation, not as a theory of political change or as a descriptive work of politics, it has been mainly received. But a particular methodology becomes a way of stating what is alone thought to be significant political experience. Bentley exhibits both the group-conscious pluralism that stemmed from pragmatism and its faith in methods of natural science. 'There is no idea', he says, 'which is not a reflection of social activity'—a proposition that goes at once to the heart of the logic of pragmatism and to the heart of its own social ambiguity.

Bentley saw himself as in revolt against 'much of the traditional word-burden of learning', as Harold Lasswell was later to write in praise of Charles Merriam.[3] He argued with great force that *all* previous theories of politics had been based on a type of explanation that was itself inexplicable. Metaphysical propositions had been used

[1] His subsequent works are: *Relativity in Man and Society* (New York: 1926); *Linguistic Analysis of Mathematics* (Bloomington, Ind.: 1932); *Behaviour, Knowledge and Facts* (Bloomington, Ind.: 1935); and, with John Dewey, *Knowing and the Known* (Boston: 1948).

[2] See, for example: Earl Latham, *The Group Basis of Politics* (New York: 1952), p. 10; Harry Elmer Barnes, 'Some Contributions of Sociology to Modern Political Theory', in *A History of Political Theories in Recent Times*, ed. Charles E. Merriam (New York: 1924), 'A. F. Bentley has shown that the essence of all governments is the struggle of interest groups with each other . . .' (p. 377); Merriam himself wrote that *The Process of Government* 'is regarded by many penetrating critics as the most notable American contribution to political theory' (p. 363; see also p. 377); Merle Curti, *The Growth of American Thought* (New York: 1943), p. 573; David Easton, *The Political System* (Chicago: 1954), *passim*; the UNESCO symposium, *Contemporary Political Science*, has several claims for Bentley's importance, among them Benjamin E. Lippincott's on p. 212; Herbert W. Schneider's *A History of American Philosophy* (New York: 1946), pp. 568 and 586; W. Y. Elliott's anthology and essays in political philosophy, *Western Political Heritage* (New York: 1949), has two pages strongly critical of Bentley, but this in itself is testimony to his conventional importance; Margaret Spahr prints a long extract from Bentley in a chapter called 'The New Psychological Approach' in her widely used *Readings in Recent Political Philosophies* (New York: 1948); David Truman's much read *The Governmental Process* (New York: 1951), is an explicit attempt simply to bring Bentley's analysis up-to-date and Avery Leiserson's review of this book is a useful summary of the views of the Bentley-Truman school, *APSR*, XLV (Dec. 1951), 1192.

[3] UNESCO, *op. cit.*, p. 536.

to explain where they could only vainly command. Such 'soul-stuff' explanations—his own ironic phrase—he saw, in the manner of Thorstein Veblen, as anthropological survivals, antipathetic to scientific explanation. Where there had not been metaphysics there had been mere classifications, sterile and arbitrary, that:

> . . . lose all sight of the content of the process in some trick about the form.
>
> When it is necessary to touch up this barren formalism with a glow of humanity, an injection of metaphysics is used. There will be a good deal to say about civic virtue or ideals of civilization. It makes a very pleasant addition to the work, but the two parts have no organic unity, not even in the hands of a Bluntschli.
>
> After compounding the formalism and the metaphysics, political science adds works on practical problems of the day or on the higher politics to suit the taste. These works are sufficiently detached to be capable of preparation in almost any form, and they can be manufactured as well by rank outsiders as by the experts of the science to which they are supposed to belong.[1]

It is sometimes helpful to look at politics as the adjustment of docrines to institutions. Bentley warns us that we do so at the peril of seeing double: ideas in ghostly contrast to concrete institutions. His notion of a direct study of the activity and *process* of politics subsumes both categories, as indeed they must be subsumed in the essential unity of any true judgement. He enters his own plea for both a 'commonsense' level of judgement and for measurement. But, in fact, measurement soon begins to swallow commonsense. For Bentley only the measurable becomes significant: 'It is impossible to attain scientific treatment of material that will not submit itself to measurement in some form. Measure conquers chaos.'[2] If the material is not measurable, so much the worse for it. 'Process' and 'activity', 'function and 'relationship', may be claimed to supplant as well as bridge 'idea' and 'form', yet his stress on measurement is surprising for someone who appears in part to be attacking the rigid dualism of 'fact' and 'value':

> If we can get our social life stated in terms of activity and of nothing else, we have not indeed succeeded in measuring it, but we have at least reached a foundation upon which a coherent system of measurement can be built up . . . we shall cease to be blocked by the intrusion of immeasurable elements, which claim to be themselves the real causes of all that is happening, and which by their spook-like arbitrariness make impossible any progress towards dependable knowledge.[3]

From the world of absolute but empty idealism—'soul-stuff'—we

---

[1] *Process of Government*, p. 162.   [2] *Ibid.*, p. 200.   [3] *Ibid.*, p. 202.

seem to topple into a world of brute facts, all equally significant and with no principle for organizing them and determining their relative significance.

He talks endlessly of 'measurable uniformities' without in any way showing us what to measure and how. He admits, of course, the need for classification, but contents himself with shrewd, sprightly attacks on existing classifications and with stressing the *ad hoc* nature of any scheme of classification: 'A classification into farmers, artisans, merchants, etc., will answer some purposes in studying our population, but not others.' [1] And then, though this is surprising, he ignores all discussion of 'purpose' and of the differing purposes of groups as the guide and aim of their classification. Presumably because politics is now to be seen as a 'process', any firm distinction between the importance of any parts of the total process is unnecessary or dangerous. Bentley seems so frightened of drawing distinctions that might appear to land him back in the world of politics as an interplay between ideas and structure, that he fails to discriminate at all, dissolving all distinctions away into 'process'. At this point in his argument, then, instead of discussing the criteria of classification *within* the total process, he merely goes on to reiterate the obvious importance of 'the group' in analysing 'any form' of social life:

> The great task in the study of any form of social life is the analysis of these groups. It is much more than classification, as that term is ordinarily used. When the groups are adequately stated, everything is stated. When I say everything I mean everything. *The complete description will mean the complete science*, in the study of social phenomena, as in any other field. There will be no more room for animistic 'causes' here than there.[2]

We are offered the hope of a 'complete description' but are given no possible guide for action in that long-drawn-out realm of imperfection before politics between groups is replaced by 'the complete science'. Groups are then defined in terms of 'interests', measurable interests, of course. 'There is no group without its interest. An interest . . . is the equivalent of a group.'

An obvious objection to the above argument is that *governmental agencies* by their nature and intention often frame their policies in light of some calculation of the national interest, not just in their interest as an interest group amongst others. Something more than a descriptive analysis of pressure groups is needed to explain their function. Central government agencies, indeed, do exercise 'a certain amount of independent power' to change their environment, as Professor Merle Fainsod has well said in a rare and specific criticism of

---

[1] *Process of Government*, p. 208.
[2] *Ibid.*, pp. 208–9, my italics.

Bentley.[1] The nearer governmental agencies approach to the indiscriminate world of Bentley's competing interest groups, the nearer many political scientists are to seeing this as a dilemma which some favoured branch of the Government must resolve by leadership in the national interest.[2] (Despite the title of Bentley's book, there is a great deal about *politics* in it, but very little about *government*.)

How could Bentley leave undefined, uncriticized and undiscussed both the 'purpose of groups' and the precise meaning of his appeal to 'return to the facts'? Obviously, for him facts had an implicit meaning that he never even made clear to himself. Not merely must the warm zeal of his appeal to 'facts' against 'soul-stuff' be explained, but also, flowing from this, his obvious optimism that political problems could be solved by mere investigation. His meaning is not logically or intellectually derived, but is derived from an almost symbolic part of the atmosphere of the Progressive Era. A journalist himself for several years, he must, at heart, have shared the belief of actual journalists like Tarbell and Steffens, municipal reformers like Munro and Merriam, sociologists like Park and Thomas, and jacks-of-all-good-trades like Beard and Dewey, that in America the original and natural democratic virtue was being corrupted; this was due to the vast speed and complexity of industrial and urban growth, and could only be cured by getting more of 'the facts' before the people and more government under popular control. Facts will expose corruption and facts will expose the problems to be solved—of non-voting, gerrymandering, municipal corruption, even crime, disease and poverty. . . . Only in such a light 'the complete description will mean the complete science'.

We have a telling example of this style of thought when Lincoln Steffens recalled his first employment of the young Walter Lippmann on *Everybody's*—Lippmann, who had come straight from the feet of William James at Harvard and a year's association with Graham Wallas:

My view that our work was scientific and that I should be able to predict the facts he went forth to find, he heard with a canny doubt. To put it to the test we picked out a little, lively business community in south Jersey where there was a big business, a packing house centre. I had never been

---

[1] Merle Fainsod, 'Some Reflections on the Nature of the Regulatory Process', *Public Policy*, I (1940), 229.

[2] Professor R. M. MacIver, in his *The Web of Government* (New York: 1947) echoes Fainsod's criticism of Bentley in a chapter called, 'Government as Equilibrium of Interests': 'Politics became, with far less qualification than in many countries, the jockeying of organized groups for relative advantage. This situation has been reflected in the view of many American students of politics such as Bentley, Munro. Beard and Robinson. To Bentley, for example, a legislative act is always the calculable resultant of a struggle between pressure groups, never a decision between opposing conceptions of national welfare' (p. 454).

there, but I described the system of politics as it must exist there if our picture of Wall Street and government was right. He took a train, investigated the town, and brought back a report which met the prediction.[1]

Steffen's work was 'pragmatic', but even a modern publicist of scientism like Mr. Stuart Chase would scarcely call it 'scientific'.

But at least Steffens offers us an example of scientific procedure and verification in politics; Bentley never does. In practice Bentley was the least pragmatic of pragmatists, never coming down to cases, problems or precise examples. But the important facts of politics were to him clearly those about interest and pressure groups, the same focus of interest as to Steffens and the muckrakers and the Municipal Reform leagues. Steffens was overtly reformist, practising a 'tough-minded' understanding as the direct bridge to reform. Bentley was overtly a-moral, advocating a tough-minded understanding of actualities, 'not in terms . . . of a morality projected to ideality from any given point of view, but in terms of the adjustment needs of actual strengths in a given society'.[2] But Bentley's 'tough-mindedness' really showed a great optimism and tender-heartedness about the long-run problems of society. He did not for a moment question that the clash of pressure groups will lead not merely to balance but also to harmony; to not just a possible static equilibrium, but to the optimum dynamic equilibrium.

'Facts' were a part of a homogeneous 'political process' in which government was a 'seamless web'—a phrase of which Bentley made much use. Indeed, it explains more about how his system appeared coherent and persuasive to see that 'the facts' were taken not just as part of a political *process*, but as a part of social *progress*. Bentley is in the tradition of the Social-Darwinists, although by his time such a view had become a tacit assumption; it no longer needed to be an explicit argument. He creates a theory for political science out of the same climate of opinion in which Lester Frank Ward had tried to create a scientific sociology. He does not argue for Ward's 'sociocrat' to ensure—in Ward's words—'the artificial means of accelerating the spontaneous processes of nature', but implicit in his view is the belief that the same results can be gained by the social scientist just— again in Ward's words—'furnishing the largest amount of the most important knowledge, letting the beliefs take care of themselves'. If we merely describe society as it is, and diagnose the ills that society has brought upon itself by a lack of reality in its self-understanding, progress is assured. Bentley clearly accepts the whole climate of democratic idealism and optimism of his time. He is a clear example of the pragmatist who treats as 'self-evident' and 'natural' the par-

[1] *The Autobiography of Lincoln Steffens* (New York: 1931), p. 594.
[2] *Process of Government*, p. 458.

ticular beliefs of a particular era of American life. He argues for a strictly 'factual' analysis with a rigidly preconceived belief in a progressive harmony—the process of politics.

The result that this had for Bentley's explicit methodology, as for most of the pragmatists, was an ambivalence in his concept of the proper model for scientific procedure. His constant use of the words 'process', 'function', 'activity', 'adjustment', and 'environment', are part and parcel of the biological metaphors and inferences of the Social-Darwinists. On the other hand, Bentley, and often Dewey, can appear to take Physics (as it was then popularly conceived) as their model of scientific method. Description then becomes an end in itself: 'the complete description will mean the complete science'. The illegitimately concealed 'purpose' of biological metaphor is formally ostracized. There is then a belief in a natural harmony, a system of inbuilt checks and balances, 'government as the equilibrium of interests', as MacIver called Bentley's doctrine. Some perverse forces may temporarily spoil this balance, but the minimum of regulation can restore the small group competitive harmony—indeed, such became exactly the doctrine of Woodrow Wilson's 'New Freedom' in the campaign of 1912. But the problem of studying the conditions of long-run change in political systems was lost in the praise of short-term mechanical harmony.

The reasons for the change and survival of institutions through time are clearly one of the foremost interests of the student of politics. This is why even Professor Woodrow Wilson once claimed that Darwinism in political thought was a clear advance over Newtonianism. At least it threw the problems of politics into an historical context. But, despite this, Bentley saw only a slender and marginal use for historical knowledge. From biology he certainly recognized that there was some *pragmatic* value in knowing the history of a species, form or group; but, again, the biology of his day was inherently teleological, assuming that there was a process of spontaneous progressive harmony—whatever had evolved was best and would be better. Unlike modern biology, it had no sense that evolution is not necessarily progressive: that devolution and catastrophe are also typical processes—one might add, especially in the life of nations. And, from a naïve view of physics, the analogy of interacting force and friction is applied to pressure groups, with human interests regarded as mechanical forces in society; prediction is stressed above all else, supplanting, in this time-free conceptualization, all need for history and tradition as important guides for human action.[1] Furthermore, the pressing political need for criteria of

[1] Bentley can say: 'I see no reason for offering definitions of the terms reflect, represent, mediate, which I shall use freely through this work. They indicate certain

relative importance becomes swallowed in the limitless opportunities for research.

This confusion in Bentley vastly limits his genuine achievement. There is both practical and philosophic value in his protest against the tendency for the abstractions of 'structure' and 'soul-stuff', as he says, to split the study of politics into either ethics or jurisprudence. He argues that 'the "feelings", "faculties", "ideas", and "ideals", are not definite "things" in or behind society' that operate as causes, but that 'they are society itself, stated in a very clumsy and inadequate way'.[1] He denies 'that the separation of feelings and ideas, looked on as individual psychic content, from society . . . or from social activity, is a legitimate procedure in a scientific investigation of society'. And he 'admits' with the sweeping concealed claim of the pragmatists, that the point of view he is taking is not novel, except in 'presentment and emphasis', but that 'I conceive that every advance step that is taken in analysis or understanding of society, whether in history, in ethnology, or in sociology, involves, tacitly at least, this point of view'. Bentley does, at least in his biological mood, attempt to grasp experience as a whole and to reject the stark and silly contrast between politics as metaphysics and politics as methodology. But in his physical science mood he then arbitrarily limits significant experience to the measurable. Despite his rejection of false identifications, he is finally unwilling just to treat politics as politics; instead, he tries to reduce it to behaviouristic sociology. He becomes Pavlov in a world where even dogs have character.

3. Interest in Politics

Bentley's chapter, 'The Pressure of Interests in the Judiciary', shows well both the strength and weakness of his method. He attacks the idea of the pure impartial judicial decision made upon the unambiguous and timeless text of statute and precedent. He has somewhat the same shrewd realism as Justice Holmes. He says of the Supreme Court that:

. . . so far from being a sort of legal machine, they are a functioning part of this government, responsive to group pressures within it, representative of all sorts of pressures, and using their representative judgement to bring these pressures to balance, not indeed in just the same way, but on just the same basis, that any other agency of government does. . . .[2]

Such a sociological view of the Court was in principle no more

facts that appear directly in the analysis of social activity; the very facts indeed that I am especially studying. My epistemological point of view is admittedly naïve, as naïve, I hope, as the point of view of the physical sciences . . .' (*Process of Government*, p. 177).

A naïve man could scarcely make much of the methodological literature of modern physics.

[1] *Process of Government*, p. 165.   [2] *Ibid.*, p. 393.

extreme than the growing school of 'the new jurisprudence' who were following the paths set by Oliver Wendell Holmes in his great treatise of 1881, *The Common Law*: Louis Brandeis, Roscoe Pound, Benjamin Cardozo. . . . It was a view more likely to be fruitful than that of the celebrated Justice who once said, 'The Constitution is exactly the same as in 1787, except for the Amendments. We know more about it, that's all.' But not even the most extreme followers of the judicial positivism of Mr. Justice Holmes, including the Justice himself, would have said that the Supreme Court operated '. . . on just the same basis that any other agency of government does. . . .'

There is a lack of discrimination in Bentley amounting here to plain error—the 'web of government' is not really seamless, it only looks that way when, in a Federal system, the Supreme Court stitches firmly and discreetly. Any elementary textbook on the Federal system would ascribe a role to the Supreme Court in American politics that makes Bentley's statement an absurdity. It may be said that all he meant was that the Court is subject to pressure groups and is in some manner one itself, and acts accordingly: that we should look at the politics of the country at large as well as at legal principle when trying to understand how a decision is made. This is often true, but the objection still remains that he must offer us some criteria to separate the Court's functions from those of other governmental agencies, otherwise the whole theory of pressure groups may look like a tautology: that all political activity involves the clash and adjustment of interests and groups—that is what we mean by politics. But this is to swallow all questions of content in a stress on process and progress. It is sheer obscurantism for the function of the Supreme Court to be seen on the same level as any and every other institution—and the same argument holds, *a fortiori*, for his treatment of the Presidency and of Congress. A balance in understanding at the time may have been restored partly by Bentley's extreme position. But the later uncritical acceptance of it has helped lead either to pure methodology or to purely unselective research. To say that the Court must be seen as an arm of political government is a proposition that few now would deny. But to say that it functions on 'just the same basis' as 'any other agency of government' is only meaningful when already, in his system, all agencies of government have been reduced purely to pressure groups of their particular interest. When Holmes argued that the law must adjust itself 'to the felt necessities of the time' he was in direct political terms appealing to a wider 'interest' of educated opinion than to the particular pressure groups of Bentley's world, and was in historical terms stressing the need for a constant study of the historical origins of legal concepts in relation to the history of institutions and sentiments: 'The law embodies the story of a nation's development through many centuries, and it cannot be dealt with as if it contained only the axioms and corollaries of a book of mathematics.' [1] It is this historical discipline that Bentley so glaringly lacks. And it is the existence of Constitutional Law and convention that is one of the greatest stumbling-blocks to that view which seeks to understand politics purely as process.

Now, of course, pressure groups are more important in the United States in relation to politics than in any other country. But this is not the point. Bentley does not spend four hundred and ninety-four pages asserting this. He views his method as completely general. The actual importance of pressure groups in American life may help explain genetically why he frames such a general theory, but it cannot explain why he thinks it completely general and how he thinks it differentiates between groups. Many are more apt to think it a dilemma than a scientific law. Furthermore, there is no apparent reason why a politics compounded of pressure groups necessarily 'forms' a 'process'. True, we may find an explanation in American social and political history of why in the 1900's politics could plausibly seem like a 'seamless web', a process of harmoniously interrelated parts. But this is not true of European politics or even of Canadian politics, and seems scarcely helpful in understanding American politics in the 1850's and 1930's, and even as affected by external tensions, in the 1950's. Politics as a group process is a type of ideal category more than an actual one, or perhaps the obvious organic implications of 'process' show that Bentley, as has often been said of Dewey, had absorbed a good deal of the Hegelianism that he attacked; if not the ethical theory of the State, yet certainly the organic view of society.

Bentley's pragmatic realism looks at first helpful, as in his treatment of the Supreme Court, but soon proves misleading. When he then asserts that 'the only reality of the ideas is their reflection of the groups, only that and nothing more', he immediately adds that though the 'habit background' may usefully be considered, 'as summing up a lot of conditions under which groups operate', yet there is in this a tendency towards 'unnecessary mysticism. . . . By appealing to the habit background we must not hope to get away from the present in our interpretations.' [2] He warns us that 'just as ideas and ideals are apt to give us a false whirl into the future', so in somewhat the same way the 'habit background' or 'tradition' is apt 'to carry us back into the past and away from our new material . . . indeed if the idea of tradition is anything at all, it is an affair of the

---

[1] Holmes, *The Common Law* (Boston: 1881), p. 35.
[2] *Process of Government*, p. 206.

present'.[1] But if 'tradition . . . is an affair of the present', as indeed it is, surely this cuts against measurement of the strength of interests at this moment as the sole meaningful activity and the whole study of politics? Surely this tradition must then be studied and understood? How can we understand the significance of the present except through an understanding of the outcome of history that it represents? The pure present of Bentley is a purely arbitrary arrest of a wider experience of mind: the now as soon as uttered becomes the nevermore, or can be seen as but a part of a total and continuing argument and dilemma, not as a resting point. The present that is both rootless and bereaved of purpose soon becomes the mere fashion of yesterday. The doctrine that everything is merely present interest would lead logically to a completely patternless empiricism: activity without pattern or plan, politics without statesmanship. If everything is just 'in the present' and just 'an interest' can we not have an interest in another theory, in a broader understanding of the long-term conditions of political stability that is so much of the activity of the true student of politics; and also have an interest in the attempt to rationalize a sense of relevance to nature that is the germ of metaphysics?

When, for instance, David Easton praises Bentley for the 'crucial insight' that analysis of 'feelings' and 'situation' can be reduced to description of the 'activity' that ensues from their merging,[2] he forgets that the very concepts he talks about would be unintelligible and would have no richness of content apart from a rigorous historical understanding of what they came to mean. The meaning and importance of any concept or institution for any problem of politics implies an understanding of its place in a common historical tradition. *The purely contemporary is philosophically, pure contingency; and practically, pure journalism.* One need have no quarrel with Bentley or Easton on the score of the importance of the present, but only that they fail to explore and to think worth exploring, in any sense of the terms, whether the present is rational and just. Bentley was no immoralist nor one who thought the 'ought' can only be the 'is'. Like most who deny the importance of tradition and doctrine in the practical study and practice of politics, his thought rests upon vast hidden assumptions about what is natural or self-evident. Happy the optimism, happy the unity of doctrine, happy the victories of technology, happy the half-conscious belief in the limitations on politics of 'natural law', all of which progressive America of the 1900's had in large but unique and fragile measure. But circumstances and doctrines have changed, internally and externally, and the science of politics of Arthur Fisher Bentley surely appears in those who still

---

[1] *Ibid.*, pp. 218–19.   [2] Easton, *The Political System, op. cit.*, p. 216.

hold it so strongly less as a science and more as an uniquely American political doctrine, a doctrine based more on faith and on a particular part of a tradition than on continuing empirical evidence, a doctrine become doctrinaire rather than pragmatic in relation to the dilemmas of present-day politics. If, as Bentley and his followers claim, *all* ideas are 'a reflection of social activity' (which is the academic or passive theory of 'ideology'), then they can have no possible grounds for criticism of the modern active and tyrannic ideologies that spring from this same claim. In fact, of course, as we have shown, the manner in which American political scientists held such theories contradicted their literal content. Bentley's belief in the total dominance of society and of social groups over all ideas of intrinsic worth is not a prelude to totalitarianism, but merely a symptom of or a prelude to a growing intellectual confusion within American liberalism.

The *Process of Government* assumes a harmony and a single calculable natural order of society, the lack of which, we may agree with the first political scientist, is the very reason for the existence of government and politics.

PART THREE
Consequences

VIII

CHARLES MERRIAM AND THE NEW ASPECTS OF POLITICS

The only safety for democracy, faced as it is with sudden crisis, is to arm itself with facts as definitely as with navies and armies. . . . If there is to be intelligent foresight in national questions, we must get rid of our careless habits of 'muddling through' and give up working our governments by rule of thumb. In short, we must apply scientific methods to the management of society as we have been learning to apply them in the natural world. . . . We are in the political sciences where the natural sciences were two hundred years ago.

JAMES T. SHOTWELL, *Intelligence and Politics* (1921)

Who will deny that the perfection of social science is indispensable to the very preservation of this . . . civilization?

CHARLES MERRIAM

A prophet is a man who foresees trouble.

MR. DOOLEY, also of Chicago

1. The Crisis of the Closed System

BY 1928 Professor Raymond G. Gettell's *History of American Political Thought*[1] could set forth a fairly orthodox 'Progressive' account of American politics—a dialectic struggle between the Federalist and the Jeffersonian—but could also include a final chapter, 'New Influences on Political Thought', that mirrored the rise of the Social Science on the campuses. 'By the opening of the twentieth century', he wrote, 'political thought began to be influenced by progress made in many other phases of intellectual inquiry'; biology and anthropology had given 'a stimulus to the methods of scientific research, rather than of abstract speculation. They emphasized the evolutionary point of view.' This evolutionary point of view, Gettell said, 'denied the sacredness of the past . . . and

[1] (New York: 1928), one of the Century Political Science books, a leading series written by acknowledged authorities.

133

supported the liberal doctrines of change and reform'.[1] These liberal doctrines, further, could now be better implemented due to the 'improvement in the methods of quantitative measurement [of?] facts'. Therefore, he sums up: 'In contrast to the *a priori* and deductive methods of politics prior to 1850, and to the historical and comparative method, which was dominant in the latter half of the nineteenth century, the modern method shows a distinct tendency towards observation, survey and measurement.'[2] Thus Gettell looked forward to a science of politics as the *culmination* of American political thought, not as an alternative activity. And his tripartite division of the history of political theory was a paraphrase from Charles Merriam's writings, whom he quoted in his penultimate paragraph: ' "There can be little doubt that we are on the verge of fundamental changes in the study of government, the precise nature of which not even the hardiest ventures to forecast." '[3]

It was apt to quote Merriam. For he had become the acknowledged leading advocate of 'fundamental changes':

the ways that were adequate one hundred years ago are no longer adapted to many phases of human life. . . . Have we not reached the time when it is necessary . . . to apply the categories of science to the vastly important forces of political and social control? . . . What advantages shall we reap if science conquers the whole world except the world's government, and then turns its titanic forces over to a government of ignorance and prejudice, with laboratory science in the hands of jungle governors?[4]

But by the time he wrote this, in 1924, Merriam had withdrawn from direct political activities, like so many of the previous 'generation of reform' who had once preached so eloquently the duty of personal participation. For the total defeat of Woodrow Wilson, *the* political scholar in politics, and the election of Warren Gamaliel Harding were more than symbolic of the passing of the ethos of the Progressive Era. The Progressives had worked to return politics to the people, and the people had returned Harding. These events, together with the 'Red Scare' of 1919 and the fierce anti-intellectualism of the popular press in the early 'twenties, must have convinced men like Merriam that they were only burning their fingers in practical politics: they would do better to construct a genuine science of politics that would make such 'jungle' politics impossible. So far from entering politics themselves, leaders of opinion in the univer-

---

[1] Gettell, *History of American Political Thought*, p. 611.
[2] *Ibid.*, pp. 615–16.   [3] *Ibid.*, quoted on p. 620.
[4] Charles Merriam, *New Aspects of Politics* (Chicago: 1925), pp. v and xi. There was a Second Edition in 1931. It has been one of the most widely read books in modern American political science.

sities came more and more to hope that social science could, as it were, take the politics out of politics.[1]

'Charles Merriam', wrote Harold Lasswell, his former student, 'was trained in the history of political doctrine, but possessing a vigorous and impressive personality, he was impelled toward the life of action. Few men have sensed the sterility of much of the traditional word burden of learning more fully than Merriam, or sought more continually to invent operational contacts between theory and fact.'[2]

Merriam was blessed with a long and an active life. He died in 1953 at the age of seventy-eight, the acknowledged *doyen* of American political science, having been active in academic and public affairs from 1900 until two or three years before his death. As Lieber and Burgess had established political science as an academic discipline, so Merriam, more than any other, established it as a social science.[3] He took his doctorate at Columbia in 1900 under Professor William A. Dunning. Earlier, we remarked on the conventional, dryly factual histories of American political thought that he wrote during the Progressive Era, and also his first essay into empirical contemporary research. He went to the University of Chicago as an Instructor in 1903, where among his close colleagues were Dewey and Tufts. Until 1920 he was active in Chicago politics, running, unsuccessfully, for Mayor on a 'Bull-Moose' Progressive-Republican ticket. He

[1] Professor Francis Wilson has noted this well: 'When Charles Merriam published his *New Aspects of Politics* . . . he was expressing . . . the escapist, the hopeful tone of American social science. . . . It was an atmosphere in which the chastened Progressivism and reformism of a previous generation had come to rest in the academic chair. Intelligence, reason and scientific method in the social sciences could solve the problems facing society' [*The American Political Mind* (New York: 1949), pp. 414–15]; there is also a brilliant interpretation of the same theme in Professor Arthur E. Murphy's essay, 'Philosophical Scholarship', in *American Scholarship in the Twentieth Century*, ed. Merle Curti (Cambridge, Mass.: 1953), pp. 185–8.

[2] Lasswell, 'Psychology and Political Science in the U.S.A.', in UNESCO, *Contemporary Political Science* (Paris: 1950), p. 536.

[3] Among many recent witnesses to the influence of Merriam are: Lasswell's writings throughout, for example: Lasswell and Kaplan, *Power and Society: a Framework for Political Enquiry* (New Haven: 1950), p. xi; one of the strongest cases for 'behaviourism', 'Research in Political Behaviour', *APSR*, XLVI (Dec. 1952), 1005; David Easton, *The Political System* (New York: 1953), pp. 64, 171, and 297–300; UNESCO, *Contemporary Political Science*, throughout the American contributions, especially pp. 366 and 467 [a 'word count' in the 'Index of Names Mentioned' reveals, for what it is worth, among English-speaking political scientists, the first four as: Merriam (33), Lasswell (20), Laski (19) and Bryce (16)]; V. O. Key's excellent *Politics, Parties, and Pressure Groups*, 3rd ed. (New York: 1952), pp. 4, 12, and 13; and the recent attempt at a definitive bibliography of a scientific politics, Jean M. Driscoll and Charles S. Hyneman, 'Methodology for Political Scientists: Perspectives for Study', *APSR*, XLIX (March 1955), 215. I have benefited in estimating Merriam's contemporary importance from reading Dr. Tang Tsou's unpublished Ph.D. thesis, 'A Study of the Development of the Scientific Approach in Political Studies in the United States . . . with particular emphasis on the methodological aspects of Charles E. Merriam and Harold D. Lasswell' (University of Chicago: 1951)—part of this has appeared as 'Fact and Value in Charles E. Merriam', *Southwestern Social Science Quarterly*, XXXVI (June 1955), 9–26.

served as a City Alderman and produced a series of Fabian-like reports on Chicago City government which earned him, he tells us, invitations from Taft and then Wilson to fill quite important Federal posts, all of which he declined.[1]

But, as he himself wrote, the end of the World War marked a new phase in his activities. His *The American Party System* (1922) was a straightforward piece of descriptive analysis, though covering the topic more fully and impartially than any previous book. And, 'reverting to an earlier type', as he said, he completed in 1920 his *American Political Ideas: 1865–1917*, supplementing his *American Political Theories* of 1903. The volume he edited jointly with Harry Elmer Barnes, *A History of Political Theories: Recent Times* (1924), was a fairly conventional account, though marked by a strong impatience with the utility of most of the materials that they described. In his own words, 'He was once more headed toward a five foot shelf of political erudition and might presumably have lived happily ever afterward upon the fruits of such undertakings.'[2] The mere cataloguing of political ideas and placing them in their historical context—the kind of approach which he had learned from Dunning, which Dunning had learned from the German school of scientific history, and which Sabine has continued—quite rightly did not satisfy Merriam.

But in reacting against 'political ideas' and Dunning, it is important to see how much of Dunning's general attitude Merriam in fact carried over. In 1927, he wrote of Dunning that 'he seemed to have had two aversions, one to contact with political affairs, and the other to the development of systematic or dogmatic political philosophy'. The second of these Merriam emphatically shared throughout the 'twenties and early 'thirties; he rejected the body of Dunning's work because of its irrelevance to the first 'aversion', not because of its method. Merriam spoke approvingly of Dunning's 'unwillingness to dogmatize', which 'has of course always been the despair of those who believe that historical writing consists in the free interpretation of events for purposes of such local application as the writer regards as appropriate'. Such men were, presumably— according to this line of argument—those who had taught 'systematic or dogmatic political philosophy' (though he names us no names). 'Dunning considered his own method as a departure from personal

---

[1] See his autobiographical essay, 'The Education of Charles Merriam', *passim*, in the volume of essays in his honour edited by Leonard D. White, *The Future of Government in the United States* (Chicago: 1942); also *The New York Times* Obituary notice, Jan. 9th, 1953, p. 20.

[2] *Ibid.*, pp. 9–10. This autobiographical essay, 'The Education of Charles Merriam', is written in the third person. It presumably challenges comparison with a lengthier work by Henry Adams.

opinion and an approach to objectivity.' [1] Now, Merriam clearly admired Dunning's objectivity of approach, even though he thought that his choice of subject matter was largely a waste of time. It is important to realize, as we now come to hear Merriam rejecting the 'traditional approach to politics', that it was *Dunning's* method and topics with which he was the most acquainted when he made his break with the past—a purely classificatory, unphilosophical type of thought.[2]

Merriam, however, did not seek to reconstruct political philosophy, he sought to avoid the 'five foot shelf of erudition' by improving the methods of political research:

But, alas, by this time he was profoundly dissatisfied with the basic methods of observation and analysis in political science. Systematic politics was again delayed in the search for firmer ground upon which to proceed. One of Merriam's first efforts was directed toward improvement in the machinery for research. He had gone to a high official of the University and asked for a stenographer and other assistance in the conduct of an enquiry . . . the reply was that 'the University could not possibly afford to aid all its Professors in writing their books'. The old methods seemed a little stuffy! The answer was the Social Science Research Building . . . and . . . the Public Administration Centre.[3]

From that time on, Merriam became as much a promoter of research as an author in his own right. Within the American Political Science Association he organized and led a 'Committee on Political Research' and a 'National Conference on the Science of Politics'. 'These', he said, 'opened the way to an advance in the direction of more adequate techniques.' Largely by his efforts the Social Science Research Council was founded in 1923. He was its first Chairman. It was dedicated to the unification of the social sciences and to the raising and administering of financial aid for scientific social research. It was soon to become the greatest single patron or clearing house of patronage for the social sciences, liberally aided by the philanthropy of the Rockefeller Foundation.[4] Lasswell paid Merriam the generous tribute

[1] Merriam, 'William Archibald Dunning', in Howard W. Odum's *American Masters of Social Science, An Approach to the Study of the Social Sciences Through a Neglected Field of Biography* (New York: 1927), pp. 136-7.

[2] I thank Professor Norman Jacobson, of the University of California, for drawing my attention to this point. Beard can also show clearly how Dunning's methods came to furnish the case for the destruction of his own subject matter: 'He [the social scientist] is convinced of what Professor Dunning has so amply and admirably demonstrated, that political philosophy is the product of the surrounding political system rather than of pure reason.' ['Politics', in *Lectures on Science, Philosophy and Art* (New York: 1908), p. 10.] In that sentence we are again on the threshold of the intellectual reduction of all politics to ideology.

[3] Merriam, 'The Education of Charles Merriam', *loc. cit.* It may be pardonable to quote laboriously from Merriam because of his eye for the significant detail.

[4] *Ibid.*, p. 10, *et passim*; also, Social Science Research Council, *Decennial Report, 1923-1933* (New York: 1933).

that it was he who 'first saw the importance of psychology for politics'; certainly Lasswell's own essays in political-psychology sprung from Merriam's suggestions.[1] 'Co-operative research' and 'collaborative effort' were things that Merriam strove to stimulate on every side. The content of such research is often elusive, but certainly 'the studies in non-voting and quantitative methods [of studying electoral behaviour] with Dr. Gosnell and others' were solid pioneering, apart from A. L. Lowell's work, in a now much occupied field.[2] Paradoxically, Merriam's own steady stream of writings grew more and more hortatory and less and less descriptive or analytical. Most of his writings simply urge the creation of a science of politics; it is hard even to class them, like the bulk of Lasswell's subsequent work, as 'methodology'. But the manner in which they do so is what interests us here, and must be looked at in some detail.

In presenting the report of the A.P.S.R. 'Committee on Political Research' he asks:

> Is politics making use of all the advances in human intelligence which the social and natural sciences have brought into the world in the last few generations? Astronomy, chemistry, physics, biology, and, in later days, psychology, have made rapid progress. . . . Of especial interest and value are the ways in which instruments for precise measurement have been devised by human intelligence and applied to the needs of various arts and sciences.[3]

The same theme is repeated when he writes the report of the 'National Conference on the Science of Politics':

> Those who have been following the work of the committee on political research cannot escape the conclusion that the great need of this hour is the development of a scientific technique and methodology for political science. When one considers the number of pressing problems in the field of politics and administration, and the scarcity of scientifically gathered data . . ., the seriousness of the situation becomes apparent. Moreover, most of these problems require immediate action. . . . Consequently, it is small wonder that legislative and administrative action is too frequently the result of guess work and speculation rather than of precise knowledge and scientifically determined principle.[4]

The only trouble is that in 'following the work of the committee' we cannot escape the conclusion that most of what they did was either to write like that, or else, in their customary work, carry on with the same kind of 'realistic' studies that the writings of Lowell and Bryce

---

[1] Lasswell, UNESCO, *loc. cit.*; Merriam, 'The Significance of Psychology for the Study of Politics', *APSR*, XVIII (Aug. 1924), 469–88.
[2] C. E. Merriam and Harold Gosnell, *Non-Voting* (Chicago: 1924).
[3] *APSR*, XVI (May 1922), pp. 317 and 319.
[4] *APSR*, XVIII (Feb. 1924), p. 119.

had typified. Merriam speaks of 'the urgent need . . . of minute, thorough, patient, intensive studies of the details of political phenomena', but he offers no example of such work himself. He is obviously far more interested in using 'science' as a concept of a general political theory than in being scientific himself (even though the conference took the meaning of 'science' for granted, *never once* discussing 'the philosophy of science', presumably their basic premise). There clearly was a need for a great deal more knowledge about American government and politics; there were any number of administrative problems on which academic knowledge could come to bear. But Merriam uses the common realization of this need, not to point out particular problems for research in some order of priority, but to point to the need for a general 'science of politics'. His own attitude to research in Chicago City politics, for instance, was pragmatic; but when he writes for political scientists, it is positivistic. Merriam becomes the first clear example of that frequent type whose 'private' political experience is a far richer source of knowledge than his 'public' political theory, only the particular theory he held inhibited the expression of his experience.

Merriam expressed his faith in a science of politics endlessly. His argument is always basically quite simple: 'the marvellous techniques' of the physical sciences have 'proved an incalculable benefit to civilization'—simple, at least so far—'but who will deny that the perfection of social science is indispensable to the very preservation of this same civilization?' This last is a remarkable claim which, when all allowance is made for sheer rhetoric, the prestige-building of a new discipline, and the general common authority of 'science' which we have seen steadily growing, is still hard to understand. It is a theme to which he returns far too often to be thoughtless rhetoric:

The world will not put new wine into old bottles, politically or otherwise. Jungle politics and laboratory science are incompatible, and they cannot live in the same world. The jungle will seize and use the laboratory, as in the last great war, when the propagandist conscripted the physicist; or the laboratory will master the jungle of human nature and turn its vast, seeming futility to the higher uses of mankind.[1]

One might wonder what this 'jungle' was if Merriam had not mentioned 'the last great war'. We in Europe must never under-estimate the terrible impact of the First World War upon American liberals. Once the drums and the trumpets of the last fighting had ceased, a vast revulsion away from the War, away from Europe, and away from 'entangling alliances', seized nearly all Americans. Both elements of the strange and exceptional alliance between Rooseveltian

---

[1] *New Aspects of Politics*, p. 247.

jingoism and Wilsonian internationalism went down to defeat. For it was *in fact widely understood* that the uniqueness of American liberalism had depended in large measure upon her isolation, had followed from her great founding act, recreated in the experience of every immigrant, of repudiating the world of power politics that was their dominant image of Europe. 'Kindly separated by nature and a wide ocean', Jefferson had said in his First Inaugural Address, 'from the exterminating havoc of one quarter of the globe. . . .' (It was a noble dream, for the rough awakening from which it is a wonder that ordinary Americans do not blame Europe more harshly.)

> The War had threatened her blessed isolation, her 'Providential Dispensation', and there was doubt whether or not it could be regained. It was certainly reaffirmed as a faith, but the objective conditions for the uncritical transmission of a traditional liberalism were now thrown into doubt. The 'urgency' of political science to Merriam must have been a reflection of this tragedy or doubt: a massive attempt *to preserve* American liberalism by arming it with science, or, objectively, the creation of a defensive ideology that would insure a belief in Progress against external intrusions. Indeed, throughout the Western World, the First World War marked the end of the classic era of liberalism, an era in which the limitation, or the isolation, of certain areas of experience from political control or destruction could be widely taken for granted. In large areas of Europe there grew an attempt to master the new uncertainties and to restore a shattered sense of belonging, by both intellectuals and the masses; it had a totalitarian character, based on the understanding and the programme of a total ideology. Politics was rejected for ideology. The Americans were never tried so hard, but the end of isolationism as a national goal and reality was sufficient to lead many of the old Progressives, like Merriam, to seek still harder to transcend the vicissitudes of politics. They sought to transcend politics, not in a philosophic sense, by seeking to understand the limits on politics that follow from a belief in the moral structure of human reality, but in a scientific sense, although, palpably, and happily, they remained as liberal at heart as before. There came a widespread attempt to substitute political science for political thought, in the sense of political thought that is always, in some manner, knowingly or unknowingly, concerned with the problem of legitimacy. A science of politics would give a total explanation that would restore the sense of shattered 'givenness', a movement in the plane of abstract thought parallel to the totalitarian movements of European politics in the plane of action. (Both totalitarianism and modern social science, throughout the West, have a common intellectual beginning in the claim made by Marx and Engels in the essay on *Ideology and*

the German Philosophy, that consciousness is *solely* a product of social structure.)[1]

It should not be thought, however, that American liberalism in fact depended so simply upon an isolated environment. As we have already argued against the 'frontier thesis' of Turner, the idea in fact preceded the circumstances that were so favourable for its unchanged continuance. The idea—and no nation is more the nation of an idea than the United States—has continued, has survived the ending of the assumptions of a 'closed system', even in those who have not fortified this belief by the creation of a scientific ideology or methodology. Yet, it is interesting to recall that several of the leading proponents of the scientific school like Charles Beard, Harry Elmer Barnes, and, in sociology, George Lundberg, became, in the 'thirties, passionate isolationists.[2] Such a move is not hard to understand; it might seem the most natural thing in the world, if thought did not always have some element of transcendence over social and natural environment. And there was another solution to the same problem, equally thoroughgoing, though politically the converse: Merriam, as part of his science of politics, constantly reiterated the need for an eventual 'World Government' or, at least, 'a world *Jural* order'. He tried to make *the world* the closed system fit for science: a science of politics must either be self-contained, or else it must be totally embracive.

The restrictive Immigration Acts of 1917, 1921 and 1924 were also symptoms of a widespread belief among Americans that their way of life could best be preserved by isolation. In many ways the Immigration laws, like the idea of a science of politics, deny the very

[1] This appears strikingly in a passage from Lasswell: 'The emphasis which is here put upon the importance of appraising the total meaning of the developing situation for social values is in many respects parallel to the viewpoint introduced by Marx and Engels into modern social theory. They may be said to have marked the recovery of the political standpoint; they vigorously applied the political perspective to certain features of modern society that had been tacitly exempted from such consideration. . . . Their work was not political-particularistic, in the sense that they restricted themselves to describing patterns of 'government'; their perspective was political-totalistic, for they sought to assess the meaning of every detail of the total situation for preserving or demolishing particular value pyramids.' [*World Politics and Personal Insecurity* (Chicago: 1934), pp. 22–4.] Lasswell, of course, is *only* accepting the methodology of Marx and Engels. But surely the main purpose of 'political' thought in the West was to 'tacitly exempt' certain areas. Aristotle set *the use* for the concept of 'the political' when he denied that omni-competent governments, tyrannies, extreme democracies, or speculative utopias, were *political* forms at all.

[2] See Beard's later writings, noted above, p. 113; and recently, Harry Elmer Barnes, ed., *Perpetual War for Perpetual Peace: a critical examination of the foreign policy of Franklin Delano Roosevelt and its aftermath* (University of Idaho: 1953); the contributors included George A. Lundberg, William Neumann, George Morgenstern, Frederick Sanborn and William Chamberlain. This is no work of eccentricity; it has all the size, weight, format, notes and apparatus of scholarship of the 'revisionist' works which it attacks, such as Langer and Gleason's *Challenge to Isolationism* (New York: 1952).

things that their proponents are trying to preserve because they have no historical sense with which to understand its content. The belief in Progress, whether through racial or through scientific purity, could carry forward a liberalism that became increasingly vague as the importance of an historical and philosophical understanding of its roots was more and more denied. Both restrictive Immigration laws and the idea of a science of politics have in common a hope for the progressive elimination of conflict if given a 'closed system': there must, as in a popular understanding of the grounds for scientific theory, be a system in which the number of variables is finite and at least theoretically calculable, and in which no external factors can intrude to upset expectations about the future.

The greatest 'external' factor that can spoil a calculable harmony, and the greatest of evils that faces man as a social animal, is, of course, war. And Merriam returns again and again to the problem of war:

> The problem of war itself has never been scientifically studied. It has been attacked religiously and emotionally, but not with the systematic thoroughness of science. . . . It is possible to visualize a systematic enquiry into the causes of war, objective and scientific, out of which might come constructive suggestions as to ways and means of abolishing or ameliorating the worst aspects of war.[1]

He never attempted such an enquiry, although he often would 'visualize' it. One cannot tell whether the fear of disaster and the sense of urgency that runs through his addresses is primarily an exaggeration of the impact of the First World War upon American liberalism, or primarily a theoretical forecast of the shape of things to come in the world politics of our generation. His solution is wrong and, we have hinted, closer to what he sought to avoid than he himself ever realized; but his intuitive imagination is greater than he, as social scientist, would give even himself credit for.

2. The Claims of Charles Merriam

Merriam's *New Aspects of Politics* drew together the ideas he had been advocating in the various Research Committees that he founded. The argument of the body of the book is now familiar. The recent 'history of political thinking' was briefly discussed—its chief feature was held to be 'the development of methods of enquiry in recent years in the field of political science and the related social sciences'.[2] The relation of psychology to politics, the use of quantitative method in political enquiry, the relation of politics to the study of environment and biology, 'the organization of political prudence',

[1] *New Aspects of Politics*, pp. 156–7.　　[2] *Ibid.*, p. 24.

all these are discussed 'in the hope that others more competent might be stimulated to contribute to the new politics which is to emerge in the new world: that of the conscious control of evolution toward which intelligence steadily moves in every domain of human life.'[1]

The importance of Science and of Progress are thus warmly re-iterated, and actual research is urged or promised. He does list in the preface to the second edition of *New Aspects of Politics* (1931) several research projects which have gotten under way since 1924. But they are all sadly out of proportion to his vision, and his list is actually composed more of 'go research!' and 'how to research' books than of actual research.[2] In the second edition he also noted that John Dewey 'has continued the application of pragmatism to social and political problems, notably in his *Public and Its Problems*' and also '[T.V.] Smith in his *Democratic Way of Life*'.[3]

His stress on research and on methodology always has an air of urgency by being developed alongside a presentiment of disaster: 'Political maladjustments of the most formidable and menacing kind threaten modern civilization at various points, and he would be a rash prophet who would promise the speedy and the certain cure of all the ills the body politic is heir to. These are signs of still greater cataclysms than those the race has yet experienced. . . .' But immediately after this warning he himself becomes 'the rash prophet' and sees signs—'though temperament perhaps determines', he says, 'which view one takes'—of the emergence 'of a higher type of political and social science through which human behaviour may be more finely adjusted and its deeper values more perfectly unfolded, as the arts and sciences of human living progressively develop their fuller possibilities'.[4] In these last words there is a striking, if simple, idealism revealed, a concept of the historical immanence of the ideal whose grounds, unfortunately, Merriam never pauses to discuss. We have already seen, in our discussion of the pragmatists, how obviously their science and logic depend on their prior and tacit agreement about the basic values of American life—or rather, that they acted as if there were basic values of the kind of the natural law of Locke and Jefferson.

[1] *Ibid.*, pp. xv–xvi; see also 'Education of Charles Merriam', p. 11 *et passim*; and UNESCO, pp. 233–43.
[2] He cites Gosnell's *Getting Out the Vote* (Chicago: 1927) and *Why Europe Votes* (Chicago: 1930), of which the first certainly employed new and refined technique for studying the motivation of voters and the reasons for non-voting. But then he cites the Stuart Rice symposium, *Quantitative Methods in Politics* (New York: 1928) (which as methodology we will discuss in detail in the next chapter). And, in the same category of 'important developments in the study of the political process', he cites Professor George Catlin's *Science and Method in Politics: Principles of Politics* (New York: 1927).
[3] *Ibid.*, p. xxv. Professor T. V. Smith's thought will be considered in Chapter IX.
[4] *Ibid.*, pp. xxxi–xxxii.

It is no accident, then, that there occurred in Departments of Political Science an almost exclusive concentration on American themes at the same time as the idea of a precise science of politics gained ground. Just as Marx could say that the Classical Liberal Political Economy was genuinely scientific as long as the super-structure of bourgeois society remained intact, so there is a sense in which American political science could appear genuinely scientific as long as the superstructure of traditional American society remained intact. The scientific 'idealism' of Merriam seems most easily understood as an attempt to maintain belief by, as it were, 'freezing', not rethinking, the traditional values, and by holding out the hope of a manipulative science that could alter social structure so as to reflect again those values. It was the fate of Merriam that the things he took for granted were more real than the things he hoped to achieve.

Not merely is Merriam uncompromisingly vague about the nature of the 'deeper values' that will 'progressively develop', but also, more surprisingly, in his concept of scientific method. When it comes to the point, just as in A. F. Bentley's *The Process of Government*, there is *no* proper discussion of the logic of the natural sciences. There is only an iteration and reiteration of the need for more description and measurement, placed alongside the constant use of biological metaphors of evolution. He notes that sociology has had a profound effect on political science, praises its descriptive techniques and notices the importance of Lester Frank Ward as the pioneer of American sociology;[1] but Merriam is no more able than Ward rationally to connect his faith in Progress with his advocacy of detailed statistical measurement. In his references to measurement there is no discussion of rules of inference as distinct from rules of description. (What can it tell us when his pupil, Harold Gosnell, finds that there are seventy-two informal 'prestige ratings' in the Chicago Civil Service? We may be elated that there is a way for differentiated merit to be recognized, or embittered that the class-lessness of American life is shown to be a sham.) He has two approving references to Karl Pearson's *The Grammar of Science* (1892), the *only* genuine work on scientific methodology cited in the *New Aspects of Politics*—a work that was a standard text for a generation, until the fallacies of its crude Baconianism became too apparent.[2] Merriam

---

[1] *New Aspects of Politics*, p. 63.

[2] See Karl Pearson, *The Grammar of Science* (London: 1892), cited by Merriam, *ibid.*, pp. 111 and 116. See especially, Sec. 12, 'The Method of Science Illustrated', when Pearson takes Stanley Jevons to task for stressing—surely correctly?—the primacy of theory over classification in scientific discovery (pp. 39–45). Pearson quotes with approval from a letter of Darwin's the fantastic statement: 'I worked on true Baconian principles, and, without any theory, collected facts on a wholesale scale . . .'

never stops to explain what he means by 'science', nor what is this 'science' that had done so much for man and can do more if applied to the study of politics and society. He seems to take the meaning of the concept completely for granted. We can only deduce, as we did when faced with the same difficulty in understanding what A. F. Bentley meant, that Merriam confused the philosophy of science with a sociological understanding of the genius of Americans in technocracy.

At times Merriam does show some awareness of the major problems raised in his claim. He could warn against 'a rush into the collection and quantitative measurement of facts without preliminary consideration of what we call the problem', and stressed that ' "hunches" or insights' would prove fruitful.[1] But there is no consideration of how we reason about the order of priorities of 'problems' to be solved and of what we may count as 'problems'. He assumes that these 'problems' can be stated in such a way that the social scientist 'can verify by quantitative measurement, and, if possible, by controlled experiment' the solutions to them. A truly sceptical positivist could point out that to speak in such a way is to confuse 'problems' with 'puzzles', which by definition are capable of physical or numerical solution. One can be sure, however, that Merriam's own 'private' experience in public life would have led him to approach problems that the most active minds of his time regarded as significant, if he had actually given his main energies to the study of problems. There was little or no middle ground between Merriam's commitments to the high generalities of his science of politics, and the precise, but necessarily untheoretical, usefulness of his public service in Chicago and Washington.

A specific claim of Merriam's in the *New Aspects of Politics* was 'the large possibilities in the co-ordination of Medicine, Psychiatry, Psychology and Political Science'.[2] He devotes a whole chapter to 'Politics and Psychology', arguing that 'to understand the role of the instinctive, the habitual, the subconscious in political action is not to diminish the role of intelligence in controlling them. Quite the contrary . . . as Bacon said, we obey nature in order to control her.' But the general claim to base the science of politics upon psychology is best discussed later in relation to the doctrines of his pupil, Harold Lasswell (in Chapter XI)—for Lasswell's *Psychopathology and Politics* (1928) had the greatest subsequent influence.

(p. 39). This self-deception of Darwin's has been a common one among social scientists, often obsessed with the problem which they call 'observer bias' to the point of intellectual suicide.

[1] *New Aspects*, pp. 132–3.

[2] *Ibid.*, p. 84 *et passim* . . . and Eugenics, too (pp. 145 ff.), but life is short. He points out that in this field Plato was, indeed, a pioneer.

They share the belief that politics and psychology exist to eliminate, not to regulate, *conflict* (a belief that was also becoming, interestingly enough, the growing orthodoxy of the 'progressive education' in the new and powerful Teachers' Colleges).

We have seen that Merriam could concede that speculation about problems must come before research and that his hopes for research were grounded in what was, in effect, a metaphysical belief about the eventual self-realization of man at his best, which could be gained by way of social and political controls—at times he has an almost Millenarian fervour. At the same time as he was a pragmatist, he had an almost cosmic teleology; at the same time as he wished to reduce politics to science, he spoke of moral ends. In his article on 'Political Science in the United States' in the UNESCO symposium of 1950, a strange eclecticism arises out of these contradictions: scientific method stretches and contracts its meaning almost at will. Towards the end of his life he clearly became less sure that 'quantification' was the only route towards the new age of reason; but he did not abandon his earlier positions, he merely benevolently made them lie down side by side with their old enemies. Referring to the growth of American political science, he wrote:

Using observation and experience as a basis, Merriam undertook the formulation of new concepts in terms of philosophy, as well as science (including atomic science) as a basis for further observation and experiment, directed towards clearer insight into meaning of political phenomena and toward the closer inter-relationship of value systems with philosophical and scientific conclusions. For many American students interest in general philosophy had been implicit rather than explicit, and broadly speaking the tendency has been in the direction of applied philosophy rather than creative philosophy. There is every reason to believe that these techniques will continue to be used and even in broader measure than heretofore. New development will inevitably be found on the borderline of philosophy, ethics, and politics rather than in the narrower confines of any disciplines of social science.[1]

Merriam liked to see expansion in any sphere and seemed aware that the old narrowly 'scientific' promises had been felt by some to be hollow, and so, with typical generosity of spirit, he added more. Something of this generosity had been apparent earlier. In the second edition of the *New Aspects* he noted that a 'dissenting opinion' has been filed by Harold Laski, and even, by then, by Charles Beard, 'on the newer types of political research. . . .' 'But,' he continued, 'it would be unfair to conclude that either of these writers wishes to do more than file a caveat regarding undue emphasis on methodology

---

[1] UNESCO, p. 240. He adds a footnote referring to the *New Aspects*; he must have thought it still quite compatible with this later essay.

as against creative intelligence, and materials to the exclusion of values.' [1] But almost any other reader of Laski's biting essay could not have regarded it as a mere 'caveat'. It denied root and branch the competence of the Court of Science to try the cases of Politics at all, and held the Social Science Research Council up to an especial scorn.[2] And then Merriam, in the very next paragraph, refers to W. Y. Elliott's *Pragmatic Revolt in Politics* (1928) as being a 'trenchant criticism of Laski'. So it was; but of Laski's pluralism, not of his anti-scientism. Indeed, Elliott's book was itself the harshest and strongest criticism of the whole pragmatic and scientific school in politics to be written in the 'twenties. (On this score Laski and Elliott were, for once, as one.) Why did Merriam ignore such differences and never state clearly, and seek to refute, the obvious objections to his 'new aspects of politics'? Merriam appears to have been that kind of openhearted liberal who hated all intellectual contention and wished hospitably for all opinions to find a place within his conceptual world. He would not take intellectual differences seriously, as if he feared that to make a theoretical distinction would involve a social or political discrimination. He was that type, at once so amiable, humble and earnest of manner, and yet so sweepingly ambitious and vague in thought, whom it is almost impossible to offend or hurt —as hurt we must at times when men, as they must, build nuances of mental discrimination into the pattern of their lives, personally and passionately. At times he appears to make a concession—not on any particular assertion, but on his general optimism—but then he will immediately gather up any stumbling block or foolishness and touch it with the spirit of Progress.

He did become acutely worried in the late 'thirties at the rise of Naziism and the growing darkness of the world scene. There then came a marked tendency for his writings to concentrate less on urging the discovery of specific techniques of investigation than on affirming passionately the spirit of Progress itself:

In a moment when exaggerated tribalism sweeps all before it, I seem to see thrusting upwards from below a new world order.

In a moment of cruel race antipathy and incredible brutality among civilized people, I seem to see the rising figure of the brotherhood of man. . . .

In a moment of widespread treason to reason, I seem to see the inexorable and inevitable triumph of intelligence over ignorance and error.

In a moment of values measured by standards of pecuniary order, I

[1] *New Aspects*, p. xxiv.
[2] See 'Foundations, Universities and Research' in Laski's *The Dangers of Obedience* (New York: 1930). 'It seems fated', it began, 'that the social sciences should take over their methodology from sister-disciplines which aim at, and achieve results which are not open to those who study human relations.'

seem to see a rising scale of human values richer than riches in a régime of social justice.

I see the stately structure of the new commonwealth, a temple of our common justice, a centre of our common interest, a symbol of our common hope.

I do not know this. But you asked me what I saw, or seemed to see; and I am answering, through the storm and fog, as best I can.

'Brave words, Professor,' you may say, if we meet in a concentration camp or in an army hospital. But then my answer would be, 'Patience.' [1]

In the face of such 'Scientific Revivalism' and synthesizing genius, it became extraordinarily hard to pin Merriam down in his last years to any specific view at all.

Merriam tells us in his autobiographical essay that all his days he hoped to complete a contribution to 'systematic political theory'. At times he seemed well aware that he was only pointing a road, not showing whether it could be built. His *Prologue to Politics* (1939) is a prologue to this constantly delayed enterprise. He sought for a single concept, like Beard's early stress on 'economic motivation', that would 'explain the political process'. In 1932 he made his first attempt, wisely seeking to give himself the leisure to think and write. He wrote frankly of this: 'Overwhelmed, in a way, by the huge mechanism of research he had helped to develop in Chicago and elsewhere, he was impelled to flee from it for a time.' 'Power' was the concept he chose and the Isle of Sylt was to be the place of leisure. A. F. Bentley had already treated 'interest' as the whole of politics and as almost a synonym for 'power'; the concept was implicit in most of the older 'tough-minded' realists. The notion of power in politics as the equivalent of 'mass' and 'energy' in physics is, perhaps, if we follow the logic of Hobbes, implicit in the whole trend of Western thought that has seen politics as a part of natural science. Merriam was the first in America to see clearly this inner consistency of the whole claim. Lasswell's *Politics: Who Gets What, When, How* (1936) is better known than Merriam's *Political Power* (1934), but it is confessedly derived from Merriam's notion. But circumstances, as De Tocqueville remarks in his *Memoirs*, shape even the most general ideas, and, furthermore, style, as even Marx comments in his essay on *The Prussian Censorship*, is the man:

However . . ., the Isle of Sylt was no place to write a study of political power while a terrific battle was raging in Berlin. . . . Settling in the Hotel Bristol, Unter den Linden, in a room adjoining Professor Samuel Harper's, without a book, in six weeks he pounded out the political essay published

[1] *Prologue to Politics* (Chicago: 1939), pp. 74–5, quoted by himself in 'The Education . . .', pp. 19–20. (This seems to be the 'patience' of the Anabaptist calmly expecting the *Parusia* as the Imperial troops batter down his gates.)

under the title of *Political Power: Its Composition and Incidence* (1934). . . .
He worked again in the midst of a furious struggle for the possession of the
symbols and substance of political power. In the mornings, he wrote;
in the afternoons he and Professor Harper became observers and students
of Hitler, Bruening, of Reds and Whites from Russia, of all manner of
folk who came streaming through the town and stopped for a glass of
lemonade with Harper and Merriam. He saw Lasswell, a little pale that
night, setting sail for Moscow. He saw President Gideonese roaming the
streets in search of data. Most of all, he saw the genial and sophisticated
Edgar Mowrer, representative of the *Chicago Daily News*.[1]

In the resulting book he undertook to show:

. . . the situation in which power comes into being; the plurality of competing loyalties; the shame of power and some of the credenda, miranda,
and agenda of authority; some of the techniques of power holders who
survive; and some of the defence mechanisms of those upon whom power
is exercised; the poverty of power; the disintegration, decline and over-
throw of authority; the emerging trends of power in our time.[2]

But, unfortunately, it is clear to anyone who reads the book that
the promise is again greater than the fulfilment. There are remarkably
few illustrations or examples of the topics to which he refers, such
as the older works of the 'Comparative institutional school' would
have contained; there is no detailed empirical analysis, such as was
beginning to be applied to American voting behaviour; there are
some solid facts and timely warnings on the last topic he mentions
alone—'the emerging trends of power in our time'; but the book is
mainly a wind of inflated concepts, stated and then restated in new
words, repeated again and again as synonyms, as if agile repetition
were empirical proof of abstract concepts. It ends, as ever, by pulling
all the threads together in a blazing fuse of promise: 'The future
belongs to those who fuse intelligence with faith, and who with
courage and determination grope their way forward from chance to
choice, from blind adaptation to creative evolution.' [3]

These naïve and rhetorical passages characterize the defects of the
whole Chicago school that sprang from Merriam. They spoke as if
their predecessors had sat too long in libraries reading the Greeks
and had lacked that knowledge of mores and folkways which, say,
Matthew Arnold's Scholar Gipsy would have had at his finger-tips.
There is an almost romping excitement to be frank about power,
brutally frank, about the oldest facts in politics. Their defects are
the same defects as of the aggressively naturalistic novel of the time,
whether of the Dreiser or the Scott Fitzgerald kind (they have none of
the sense of the interplay of personality with time that is the genius

---

[1] 'The Education . . .', pp. 12–13.
[2] *Political Power* (New York: 1934), p. 4.   [3] *Ibid.*, p. 326.

of Faulkner). But, as in the generation before, there is a belief that, just by exposing these facts, things will get better and better. So much do they presume to know what the better and better is or will be that they are, too speak mildly, no Hobbists. There is the most flagrant contradiction between their actual experience, their apparent worries and their formal written theories.

The weakness of Merriam's essay on Power is that he does not draw any distinction between *power* and *authority*.[1] He uses the two terms synonymously, whereas the tradition of their use enshrines a real distinction. Power is an instrument of coercion, a physical effect; authority is a condition of either justice or consent—at the best, as when we speak of 'legitimate authority', of both. 'However strong a man,' said Rousseau, 'he is never strong enough to remain master always, unless he transforms his Might into Right [or Law], and Obedience into Duty.' It should be said that it is precisely this confusion that has hindered both popular and academic understanding in the United States of the nature of totalitarian régimes: the myth is perpetuated still in some respectable academic quarters that power, 'naked' power, in the hands of a few men alone keep down the Russian, the Chinese and once the German masses. Obviously there are many political and social institutions that exercise a great authority but have little power apart from consent. Power may always be a potential, but it makes the distinction between Tyranny and Democracy whether it has to be exercised habitually or not; and it makes the further distinction between Totalitarian-Democracy and Constitutional-Democracy whether it is done so legitimately. And what is meant by legitimacy or legitimate authority? That is the master question of politics that the scientific school ever seeks to avoid. A parent, for example, has absolute power over a young child; but its upbringing and education are a process of transmuting power into authority until fit for freedom. The authority of a teacher, a judge or a statesman is respected because they fulfil an agreed need and because they are recognized to be more expert or experienced within the constituted boundaries of their function: but we obey the power of the sword because we have to, or fear worse if not. Clearly, authority depends upon a varying complexity of competence, character, notions of rights and duties—ethical, legal and conventional— almost all of which the bare concept of 'power' evades, while its advocates, such as Bentley and Merriam, deny the empirical existence of authority in 'the political process' at all.

[1] I thank Professor C. J. Friedrich for first pointing this out to me in relation to Merriam. See further, his 'A Sketch of the Scope and Method of Political Science', Chapter XXV in his *Constitutional Government and Politics* (London and New York: 1937), pp. 583 ff., and published separately as a supplement to the revised edition, *Constitutional Government and Democracy* (Boston: 1946).

Merriam's burning democratic liberalism makes this 'power' view of politics an exercise in morbidity more than in aggression. All power, his argument presumes, being only power and dangerously power, must be distributed as widely as possible; therefore, all power of ultimate decision should be in the hands of the people. This view of democracy may be a realistic description of some régimes—though fortunately not of actual American politics; but power would still then remain a force, a dilemma, not a *political* solution to a problem. At least the distinction was enshrined in Cicero's descriptive formula: '*Potestas in populo, auctoritas in Senatu.*' The Chicago School was, however, fully self-conscious in trying to get away from the 'subjective' element in 'authority'. There is a common feeling among American liberals that for some individuals to have 'authority', especially over others, is something inherently undemocratic.

3. The Stature of Merriam

Perhaps it is unfair to Merriam to judge him as a contributor to knowledge. It is as a promoter of political science that he may best stake a lasting claim for gratitude. Some who heard him in the 'twenties admit that they grew bored with hearing his habitual address at meetings and conventions on the need for more scientific method. But each fresh crop of students and instructors, hearing him for the first time, obviously caught a contagious enthusiasm. An enthusiasm for what? In the most general sense, for the sense of the importance of political studies at all and for the assurance that political science was no longer a hang-dog, second-class citizen upon the campuses. We are far from arguing that this was not a worthwhile achievement.

Merriam did write two very good books. His *Chicago: A More Intimate Study of Urban Politics*, published in 1929, though written five or six years earlier, was the fruit of the practical experience of a man highly intelligent in actual matters of civic administration and, after all, not unversed in the tradition of political scholarship. It is the best kind of fruit of an unreflective pragmatism applied to the very kind of circumstances that pragmatism explains so well; it is unencumbered by the flights of pseudo-scientific rhetoric that ruined the works he himself valued more highly. Its scope is more modest than his attempts at systematic political theory, but is far more valuable, both as a contribution to urban government and as an example of political understanding; it is an easy blend of experience, research and criticism. The Henry Ward Beecher lectures he gave at Amherst College in 1926, printed as *Four American Party Leaders* (1926), were a splendid evocation of the American political mind by one who knew American national leaders of his day and also the formal literature of American political thought. The pity of it was that he did not regard this kind of thing as 'science'. One gathers that his ordinary lectures on 'American Politics' were far richer than his writings on political science. When he wrote his *American Political Theories* he was still too much under the influence of Dunning's dry factualism, and later he was too enthusiastic about the social science of the future to think that the past was important at all.

The changed political atmosphere following the Depression of 1929 did bring Merriam back to Washington for a large part of his time. It would be churlish, having written so harshly of his political theory, not to pay tribute to his public service. He was Vice-Chairman of President Hoover's Committee on Recent Social Trends (1929–32). Under the Roosevelt Administration he served on the Public Service Personnel Commission (1935); the Commission on the Social Studies (1932–5); the National Resources Planning Board (1933–43); and the Committee on Administrative Management (1935–7). He still was a leader in organizing research projects in the American Political Science Association, the Social Science Research Council and other *ad hoc* bodies. In 1940 he became an able Chairman of the Chicago Plan Commission, a body of considerable importance. But the drain on his time made his theoretical writings shallower and, alas, even wider.

As we have already said, he was clearly deeply affected by the rise of Naziism and the growing international crisis. His *Prologue to Politics* of 1939 is filled with an almost desperate reiteration of a faith in Progress rather than with the old advocacies of detailed quantitative research. When the cards were down, the order of priorities became more clear:

The greatest of all revolutions in the history of mankind is the acceptance of creative evolution as the proper goal of man, for this will eventually transform the spirit and institutions of education, of industry, and of government, opening a broad way to the realization of the highest and finest values in human life, in a form of association where leaders no longer scream and curse and threaten and where men no longer shuffle, cringe and fear but stand erect in dignity and liberty and speak with calm voices of what clear eyes may see.[1]

Thus, when Merriam became unhappily aware that the rules of the accustomed game could be broken and that even a domestic New Deal could not prevent the unwanted intrusion of war, he attempted to reach a final clarity which shows itself more like the 'Heavenly City of the Eighteenth-Century Philosophers' than the 'Behavioural Sciences'. He avowed five beliefs: (1) 'the essential

[1] *Prologue to Politics*, p. 73.

dignity of man'; (2) 'confidence in a constant drive towards the perfectability of man'; (3) the assumption that 'the gains of the commonwealth are mass gains'; (4) the desirability of popular decision 'in the last analysis on basic questions'; and (5) confidence in the possibility of conscious and peaceful social change.[1] His last major book, which he called *Systematic Politics* (1945), carried these later tendencies still further. It was not the scientific system of politics which he had often envisioned; it showed signs, rather, with its oratory of democratic optimism and idealism—a fluent blending of Jeffersonianism with evolution—of a return to *something* like a traditional level of political speculation, even if more like the speculation of the Chautauqua tent than of the university seminar.

Merriam, for all his naïveté—at times a rather engaging naïveté—was the leading apostle of the modern American science of politics, just as Lester Frank Ward had been the apostle of sociology. His pupils rarely allowed themselves the luxury of his flights of rhetoric, but he gave them confidence that social science and progress were compatible and would create a new and revolutionary understanding of political society. In recent years far more 'sophisticated' and logically coherent conceptual structures have been raised, and some actual research, but they stand or fall for their contact with reality on the simple, primitive affirmations such as Merriam made. He is less to be rebuked for his overreaching optimism than to be given our sympathy for the unhappy fact that historical contingency would keep on interfering with the closed system that was his understanding of the progressive nature of American liberalism. If the system could have remained closed in the minds of most Americans, science and progress might for a long while have seemed sufficient guides for political education and conduct. Though the beliefs in science and progress concealed more than they showed, they concealed broadly those things which, until very recently, Americans felt very little need to discuss. Each challenge to the view of the 'closed system', or the growing inadequacy of the view itself, led Merriam to a still more strident affirmation, an affirmation in which 'progress' began to outweigh the quantitative techniques of social science. It did not lead to an attempt to understand the presuppositions of actual American politics and political thought. Merriam had all the equipment for such an enterprise; but he accepted instead of explaining the common fascination with 'science'; his experience remained richer than his formal writings.

Merriam's tragedy was that in reacting away from direct participation in politics he went so far as to transmute an habitual pragmatism

[1] Quoted by himself in 'The Education . . .', p. 20, from his *The New Democracy and the New Despotism* (New York: 1939).

into an abstract and positivistic search for a scientific methodology. He probably did not realize how abstract was the certainty of science; technology was more likely the analogy that had impressed him. Merriam was not able to carry out his own impossible counsel: his 'private' worries at the spread of Fascism and Naziism in the late 'thirties drew him back into political writing of a more traditional kind, as seen in his *Systematic Politics*, a book unhappily loose and shallow except as a tract for the times, but witnessing a modification amounting to a retreat from a pure science of politics. We can regret that we have not the great book that Merriam, the old Progressive, could have given us: the intellectual autobiography of his change of interest and belief through these three stages: politician, social scientist and then would-be political philosopher. If he could in writing his own life have given us an intellectual and political auto-biography of his epoch, as he was well placed to do, he might be more readily forgiven for having challenged a comparison, in the short sketch he did write, with *The Education of Henry Adams*.

It is hard to have had to write harshly about Charles Merriam. To talk to men who were his students is to realize the great disparity between his charm, integrity, sincerity and personal knowledge of American politics, and the sterility of his books and the entrepreneurial haste of his 'public' life as organizer of political science. His students may feel that the foregoing account is partial and uncharitable. Perhaps for this reason we have quoted so largely. But, in the last paragraph, we did use the word 'tragedy'. Merriam's personal qualities of enthusiasm for politics, for the spreading of participatory democracy, for people in general, these were typical of the leading figures of the Progressive Era—an era which, we have said, showed not only the confusion of American liberalism, but also its intense, if unconscious, fund of moral worthiness. Now, to his students Merriam still appeared the 'Progressive' in that style. 'To all these students he gave faith in the capacity of man for a better life through tolerance and reason, coupled with a willingness to fight for progressive ideas,' wrote Leonard D. White in the introduction to *The Future of Government in the United States*, Merriam's *Festschrift*. But Merriam was no American Laski; in fact he retreated from practical politics, and he failed to create the substitute science of politics for which he hoped. He wished, but he did not reason. He wished not in order to provide an understanding of politics so much as an alternative to politics; and it is this wish that has been such a recurrent, though not a necessary, temptation in American political thought. Some of his students were affected less towards 'science' than just towards studying politics in general, and from them come a series of routine, but always needed, studies of American parties, pressure groups, and Federal and State Administration, studies not ambitious—after the first chapter—but useful within their limits and, as a whole, far superior to the few and sketchy British studies of the period. But it was work no different in principle from the older work; it did have more stress on politics and was less narrowly institutional, but this is nothing to do with a science of politics. And others, like Harold Lasswell, became fired by the dream of a science of society, without realizing that it was a retreat from reality, a repudiation of experience for ideology; and, above all, without realizing, as in a sense Merriam came to do, that there was need for a 'reconstruction', or a philosophical appreciation, of the nature of American political thought, not for a Procrustean division between 'fact' and 'value', science and thought. We do not want to prejudge the work of subsequent political scientists, even though they praise Merriam and refer to him as if in his pages there is a grounding for their assumptions. Their work may be better than their assumptions. But, both historically and philosophically, the fundamental assumptions of the American science of politics appear at their simplest, clearest, hollowest and most influential in the writings of the late Charles Edward Merriam.

IX

THE DEMOCRATIC GOSPEL OF RESEARCH

Another important trend, especially after 1900, has been that towards synthesis. The border lines between the social disciplines began to disappear. . . . Also, there has been a marked increase of emphasis upon contemporaneous data. . . . In a static world tradition is perhaps the best interpreter, but in a highly dynamic world, like ours, contemporaneous facts and generalizations from them are necessary to give perspective and to make clear our adjustment needs. Other trends are towards practicality . . ., toward a growing emphasis upon professionalization and the training of experts. . . . Finally there has been a vast corresponding increase in investigation and publication, especially in recent years. All of this indicates that the social disciplines are now reaching that degree of maturity which will permit them to be characterized as sciences, and in their professionalized aspects as applied sciences.

L. L. BERNARD in the *Encyclopaedia of the Social Sciences*

Mit gier'ger Hand nach Schätzen gräbt,
Und froh ist, wenn er Regenwürmer findet.

GOETHE, *Faust*

1. The Ideal of Research

'RARE INDEED', Professor Hans Morgenthau has written, 'is the social scientist who will say, as Bernard Glueck did . . . with regard to the problem of alcoholism: "It is difficult not to be somewhat amused by this general tendency to put all faith in more research as the solution." '[1] Merriam was far from alone in this faith. Indeed, by the end of the 'twenties, political science was under some compulsion to show that it could be as scientific, as research-conscious, as sociology or as a 'unified social science' would be. It did not abandon its old goals of citizenship education (or training); it merely reinterpreted them as the fruits of research.

[1] Morgenthau, *Scientific Man and Power Politics* (Chicago: 1946), pp. 34–5.

156

The Democratic Gospel of Research

The indefatigable Harry Elmer Barnes, in the introduction to *The History and Prospects of the Social Sciences*,[1] a manifesto parallel to Merriam's *New Aspects of Politics*, quoted with approval a noted 'Educator', the President of Northwestern University:

> But the most fruitful researches during the twentieth century will probably be conducted not in the natural sciences but in the social sciences. . . . All our human relations will be improved as rapidly as we make progress in the social sciences, and I am convinced that our universities will make a great contribution here as they did in the discovery of truth in the natural sciences during the nineteenth century.

And the education of the American teacher of politics in the 'thirties became more and more a training in research techniques and less and less an education in history and philosophy. His gains in sociological techniques were all too often at the expense of cutting away the very foundations (inadequate though they were in themselves) of any genuine sociological knowledge. Science organized their teaching as if they preferred to turn out imperfect scientists to imperfect statesmen. Men who had a profound ignorance even of the history of their own national politics, men who knew little but technique, were trained and began to teach. This is a criticism that could not be levelled at Merriam himself, who was always somewhat of the old American Progressive to whom the details of Lincoln's practice of law and of Jefferson's farming were something beloved and symbolic. And the object of their investigations, as we will see, became more and more how to understand the merely contemporary in American politics. Some professed in this to have no end in view; some professed to seek such understanding as a method of control towards a future and more rational order. They became less and less inclined to think through or even to recognize beliefs that they took for granted, beliefs that in fact gave their 'objective' research a moral and a democratic bias. They could regard their investigations as being purely scientific simply because they could take so much as already granted in their tradition, however much 'as scientists' they denied the importance of studying tradition.

Clearly a major condition for the multiplication of purely descriptive research projects is that social and political conditions remain fairly stable—though this often seems contradicted by the stress of the new social scientists on 'change', 'dynamic patterns', 'evolution' and anti-traditionalism. By this two things are meant: firstly, that there are no immediate political problems so great that students of politics cannot justify their absorption in quantitative research; and

---

[1] (New York: 1925), p. xviii; it had more 'Prospects' than 'History', and the history confined itself to those writers who consciously sought after a fully scientific methodology. As a frontispiece, it had a photograph of Lester Frank Ward.

secondly, that the behaviour of the people or institutions studied does *not* rapidly change. But these assumptions might seem peculiarly precarious in our times as a basis for a science of politics, or else narrowly parochial, or even an irrational and compulsive affirmation of a *traditional* theory that no longer adequately explains reality. Difficulties arise within a political doctrine or theory when it does not contain a general enough and a true enough view of man to be reapplicable after circumstances have changed, altering the previous techniques of its application, and destroying the possibility of viewing it as a basis for an objective technique. This is only to restate some implications of the seductive analogy between science as a 'closed system' and American liberalism, at its best, as a 'closed system'. To be technical and quantitative about politics then, as a full political science, fixed 'meta-technical' assumptions must be assumed to exist, whether they be culturally or philosophically derived. It will not be hard to show that the whole faith in the remedial character of research depended upon a peculiar view of democracy and of 'democratic man'.

To understand this view we must look at the character of the research. Charles Merriam made no understatement when he wrote: 'American social scientists engage in a wide range of co-operative research efforts. The pages of the official journal of the American Political Science Association . . . scanned over the last two decades, reveal quite sharply the growing trend toward collaborative effort.'[1] Merriam had taken from Dewey a sharp epistemological distinction between 'fact' and 'value'. 'Value' was something 'subjective', private; 'fact' was something 'objective', public. A test, therefore, of whether one was engaged in genuine research came to be whether or not any reasonably intelligent person could perform the same operations and achieve the same results. The 'subjective' imagination of the individual scholar became suspect to the true social scientist—except possibly as a source of hypotheses to be tested. Solitary work became almost a morbid symptom; it showed a lack of importance, professional fraternity and true scientific method. The great era of the 'projects' and of the Foundations was under way.[2]

[1] 'Political Science in the United States', UNESCO, *Contemporary Political Science* (Paris: 1950), p. 243.
[2] See generally, *passim*, Wilson Gee, *Social Science Research Organization in Ame can Universities* (New York: 1934); Frederic Ogg, *Research in the Humanistic ana Social Sciences* (New York: 1937); Frederick Keppel, *Philanthropy and Learning* (New York: 1936); Harry Elmer Barnes, ed., *History and Prospects of the Social Sciences* (New York: 1925); E. V. Hollis, *Philanthropic Foundations and Higher Education* (New York: 1938); W. H. Cowley, 'Co-operation in American Research', *American Scholar*, I (July 1932); Harold Laski, 'Foundations, Universities and Research', in his *The Dangers of Obedience* (New York: 1930); and the Social Science Research Council, *Bulletins*, a series.

The Democratic Gospel of Research

L. L. Bernard, in his article on the development of the social sciences quoted in our chapter legend, painted the now familiar picture of the '*a priori* laxity' of the old order: 'the work of the classical economists and of the political philosophers gives abundant evidences that generalizations did not always await the accumulation of vast masses of verified data'.[1] 'Significantly enough, fact-gathering operations have become more collective as they become more abundant . . .' Lasswell was to write: 'The idea of a permanent corps of research assistants comparable with the laboratory technicians of the physical sciences was all too new.'[2] There was, however, in this new ideal of scholarship a democratic spirit as well as an expert spirit; and there was, further, an activity of justification, or of promotion, as well as of research.

2. T. V. Smith: The Fraternal Philosopher of Behaviourism

The linking of scientific research to 'the democratic process' occurs most clearly in the writings of Professor T. V. Smith, whom H. W. Schneider in his *History of American Philosophy* ranked as one of the 'Chicago trinity' who had given Pragmatism 'a more systematic and technical elaboration as a theory of government'[3]—the other two of like substance being Merriam and Lasswell. A trilogy of books on political science and power appeared from their pens in 1934 and have recently been republished in one volume.[4] Though Merriam was more like Smith in being the democratic philosopher, as popularly conceived, than was Lasswell, yet Lasswell also took many opportunities of stating his agreement with Smith.[5]

Smith was a politically active pragmatist who taught, as a Professor of Philosophy at Chicago, a doctrine that *identified* scientific method with an interpretation of democracy in terms of equality and majority rule. The theme of his contribution to the trilogy,

---

[1] *Encyclopaedia*, I, 342. To make clear that this data-hoard can be gathered, he notes further, with a somewhat sad mixture of defensiveness and aggression, that: '. . . the spirit in most American universities is decidedly favourable to productive labour instead of to brilliant conversation and elegant leisure' (p. 348). Oh for the Dons of yesteryear!

[2] *Analysis of Political Behaviour* (London: 1948), pp. 5–6.

[3] See p. 92, above.

[4] *A Study of Power*, comprising Harold D. Lasswell, *World Politics and Personal Insecurity*; Charles E. Merriam, *Political Power*; and T. V. Smith, *Power and Conscience, Beyond Conscience* (Glencoe, Ill.: 1950), all originally published as separate but related volumes in 1934. Each author read the other works in MS. though there is no specific joint responsibility.

[5] For example, he concludes the Preface to what is probably his best known work, *Politics: Who Gets What, When, How* (New York: 1936): 'My findings are in many respects parallel to the concluding chapter of *The Promise of American Politics* by my friend, colleague and Representative, Professor and State Senator, T. V. Smith. This is most gratifying to me in every one of my capacities as friend, colleague and constituent' (p. vii).

Power and Conscience, Beyond Conscience, is that the concept of 'conscience' has been ever pernicious to democracy because of its 'recession into the purely private'; its 'dutiful attitude' as contrasted to the claim for 'rights'; and its easy use in the support of '*a priori* absolutist*'* systems. All these aspects of conscience can stake a private claim which denies equality and renders the greatest goal of man, fraternity, impossible: ' . . . the equality dictum may be made to read, "Equalize others in order to rule oneself." So interpreted, the equality dictum represents the self in its fated egocentrism prescribing self-abnegation, in fashion homeopathic.' [1] Only when all men (or things) can be treated equally—as, he says, in the Marxist *ideal* of the classless society[2]—can the idea of 'self' be truly moral, which is to say, truly fraternal. Smith sees 'Behaviourism' alone among all other intellectual methods as guaranteeing this equality. In a typical passage he cites as an example of Behaviourism and 'objective intelligibility', Merriam and Gosnell's studies on the causes of non-voting, and shows how very moral-minded this 'objective' research appeared to him:

> Merriam and Gosnell have investigated objectively the *lack* in the electorate of motion towards the polls, to see why citizens did not *bestir* themselves when and where they *ought*. Though they investigated reasons, the goal of their research was civic motions or lack of motions, and the evidence considered as relevant thereto was other motions of pen or larynx wielded by the perpetrators or withholders of the first motions. We have here, so far forth, objective rendition of complex bodies, a rendition, be it noted, which transforms so-called subjective material (reasons) into objective data (causes) and measures and reports upon them in quantitative fashion.[3]

Thus 'Behaviourism', to Smith, is the method of making morality, socially conceived, objective; and Behaviourism is identified with scientific method; and the fruits will be the 'essence of democracy . . . fraternity'. 'Until this humble scientific method', he says, 'does brick by brick raise the splendid temple of fraternity, no persistence in religious asserveration, no warmth of enthusiasm, will conjure up its walk. Increased knowledge will prove more fruitful than any resort to holy names.' [4]

[1] Smith, *Power and Conscience*, p. 341. The sentiment and style are unusual but the meaning is surely plain—and detestable—enough.

[2] *Ibid.*, pp. 307 ff.

[3] *Ibid.*, pp. 287–8, in Chap. IX, 'Dialectical Behaviourism and Social Order'; the italics are mine, though the emphasis, surely the author's.

[4] Smith, *The Democratic Way of Life* (Chicago: 1939), 3rd ed., p. 35. There are many universities in which this book is still assigned; students enjoy it, for it is written in a very lively manner. Generally, see also his *The Philosophic Way of Life* (Chicago: 1929), subsequently republished in a 2nd ed. as *The Philosophic Way of Life in America* (New York: 1943).

Smith's three articles, 'Conduct', 'Duty', and 'Ethics', in the
Encyclopaedia of the Social Sciences should not be forgotten, both
as evidence of his contemporary prestige and of what the 'Chicago
school' expected of a philosopher. He did them proud. 'Conduct', he
tells us, 'is, in a word, the plotted curve of behaviour.' So, as conduct
is how people behave, he does not have much more to say, as a
philosopher, on that theme, except to chide those religions which
have tried to encourage a conduct based upon faith as well as upon
works. 'Behaviour precedes ideas and in the long run always conditions them.' Any system of thought that does not recognize the
priority of actions to thought is, then, to Smith, a delusion and
probably a fraud as well. 'The concept of duty represents the most
general acknowledgement of the dominance of the social environment upon the individual. The common name for this dominance is
conscience.' [1] But 'conscience', he tells us, is usually believed to be the
will of God. And this identification can easily lead to a rejection of
the practical life itself. 'This experience of obligation, the sense of
duty, seems in the having to be more than a merely difficult calculus
of advantage. Utilitarianism and its contemporary affinities (Behaviourism, Pragmatism, Freudianism) admit that it is more but
deplore the "more".' He leaves no doubt that he is advancing with
his eyes wide open, for he argues that Kant's dictum that duty is not
duty unless done exclusively for its own sake should be 'completely
reversed'. 'The sense of duty is the last silent witness of a past which
the sooner overcome and forgotten, the better . . . the only generalized duty is the duty to be uniformly intelligent.' [2] His article on
'Ethics' pulls together these views; it is a defence of pragmatism as
embodying 'social intelligence' and of a 'scientific ethics' against
'metaphysics': 'Conduct affiliated too intimately with ideals grows
mystical and loses its social significance.' [3] He contrasts 'Utopian' to
'scientific' ethics, noting that it was Marx who first began the shift
from the one to the other, away from the defence of 'the *status quo*'
which has been, he observes, the usual purpose of Christian, Kantian
and 'Utopian' ethics. But the violence of Marxism is not necessary,
he hopes: the pragmatism of Dewey can best give the social sciences
'the honour that is rightly theirs, the honour of vitalizing knowledge
by practice and of informing practice with insight'.[4]

Smith may be broadly correct, after all, to see behind any non-
scientific moral claim 'holy names'. In order to build a democratic
way of life, he tells us, is needed 'not deduction from divine fatherhood, as religion has taught', but 'induction from an enlarged

---

[1] *Encyclopaedia*, V, 293.
[2] *Ibid.*, V, 294–5. Does 'uniformly' mean 'persistently' or 'popularly'?
[3] *Ibid.*, 'Ethics', V, 602.   [4] *Ibid.*, 'Ethics', V, 605–6.

understanding of human nature'. (While one 'induces' one 'enlarges', so he has a case both ways.) He scolds religion for being 'otherworldly' and for basing 'human brotherhood' upon the 'fatherhood of God', instead of seeing that any possible concept of 'God' itself depends upon the fact, he says, of 'human brotherhood'. He does, however, allow 'two functions . . . that in a democracy might be called religious'. Firstly, no human being should 'for long remain detached from some friendly functional group' (this seems to be *trying* to make A. F. Bentley's postulated reality of the group real—or Berdiâev's 'domestication of man' perhaps). Secondly there is 'the enlarging of man's nature so that loyalty to the small group would not militate against loyalty to the human group as such'. And so, he continues, 'from widely scattered religious sources today is going up the most hopeful cry that organized religion has uttered since the Galilean elevated man above the sabbath, the cry that religion and even God must be democratized'.[1]

Smith, of course, was and is a kindly, warm-hearted, expansive man, immensely popular as a lecturer. To the political scientists who admired him he was a repository of an esteemed folksy, cracker-barrel wisdom well blended with a knowledge of modern social science; and to even those who thought him a little vague, a little imprecise, yet certainly he was a good man. He exhibits what Mr. Leslie Fiedler has recently called 'the liberalism of innocence', of those who 'have desired good, . . . have done some; but . . . have also done great evil'.[2] Smith's 'evil' is from the softening of thought that he engenders and from the things he leaves undone by so passionately basing morality solely upon what a majority wants. Perhaps this formulation does Smith an injustice, for he was well aware that a majority claim as such is not necessarily legitimate, which is why he insists on equality and 'the friendly functional group'. This is to be a 'friendly' group; he says nothing about forcing men to be free; it is not the Corporate State. He merely argues that 'metaphysical' beliefs render literal equality impossible and thus render the counting of the majority as if it were the whole or the sum of the parts also impossible. Indeed, on Smith's argument, there seems no reason why a random sample would not yield legitimacy as readily as a majority.

Thus, to T. V. Smith and those who thought that he expressed their philosophy, the essence of science is that its propositions are

[1] *Democratic Way*, pp. 29–35. So, in this transfiguration of all values, the would-be Nietzsche of Democracy only finds 'beyond conscience' the ghost of the Social Gospel in the clothes of a Mr. Billy Graham using the techniques of Group Psychology.

[2] See his *An End to Innocence, Essays on Culture and Politics* (Boston: 1955), p. 24. T. V. Smith's fantastically democratic interpretation of Marx well illustrates Mr. Fiedler's general theme of the softness of American liberalism in the 'thirties in which sincerity and well-wishing swamped discrimination—see Smith's *Beyond Conscience*, pp. 289–311.

public property, demonstrable and understandable to everyone. This is also the essence of democracy. The ultimate value, 'fraternity', is a complete 'openness', a complete dedication to common standards. Revealed religion is, therefore, Smith clearly and boldly states, 'undemocratic'. Democracy, for Smith, is based upon the toleration of all ideas, so long as they remain ideas and do not transfer themselves into patterns of action and thus infringe the common truth and the reformed religion of fraternal equality (though surely to a pragmatist all ideas *must* have some such practical effect—this may be a way, like Hobbes' 'until God wills', of saying 'never'). Social science is, then, the calculation of how this new religion of fraternity can best be implemented. 'Democracy as a governmental form', he tells us, 'is primarily concerned with maintaining the conditions under which citizens may try for some objectification of the ideal in and through action.'[1]

The 'objectification of the ideal' is no longer the business of an aristocratic leadership 'based upon prestige and flowering towards impartiality' (i.e., mere impartiality), for 'leadership based upon special knowledge and flowering towards control of facts for human ends is the democratic ideal'.[2] 'Knowledge is power', Smith frequently quotes, and with 'special knowledge' suddenly being admitted, the last sentence rings ominously, if only in its complete ambiguity on a precarious question. He may often repeat that 'the duty of doubt' and the 'assumption of fallibility' are parts of both science and democracy, but once the 'facts' are known and such glorious tomorrows are possible, there is clearly the basis for an unquestionable scientific control of society. Democratic leadership, then, must be impartial between 'values', according to Smith, but not between 'facts'. But what are 'facts'? Smith never approaches this question. He uses the actual diversities of interest and belief among men as a refutation of religious claims for a 'single truth', but all the time holds out the promise of a future 'splendid temple of fraternity'. 'Piety without unction', he says, 'spells progress.'[3] His occasional lectures on Lincoln acutely grasp the mystical quality of Lincoln's idea of the 'Union'; but he sweepingly embraces this with his own 'religious' fraternalism.[4] He is completely without sense that there are different levels to reality in all discourse.

[1] Smith, *The Democratic Way*, p. 276; see also his *Creative Sceptics: in Defence of the Liberal Temper* (Chicago: 1934), especially p. 265: 'Science is thus related to democracy in ways more deep than mere production and spread of concrete goods. It is spiritually related.' [2] *Ibid.*, p. 206.
[3] *Man's Three-fold Will to Freedom*, being the . . . Dunning Trust Lectures delivered at Queen's University, Kingston, Ontario, 1953 (Toronto: 1953), p. 44.
[4] See *Lincoln, Living Legend* (Chicago: 1940); and *Abraham Lincoln and the Spiritual Life* (Boston: 1951). As every generation, it is said, rewrites its own history, so every American publicist creates his own Lincoln.

Consequences

However, this is no place to comment further on the general adequacy of Smith's ideas (although, in fairness, we should note that recently he has regulated equality from a 'descriptive' to a 'directional' ideal).[1] We are simply exhibiting him, at his face-value in the 1930's, as a philosopher on whom Lasswell and Merriam could explicitly rely for the philosophy of their scientific research. Smith saw partially and shows clearly that for there to be a science of politics or society at all, there must be what A. N. Whitehead called a firm 'base line' and also an ulterior goal. He believed in an atomic commonness between men; that the counting of facts and opinions could objectively decide policy; and that that policy would be part of a process towards a 'temple of fraternity'—a faith in fraternity is, as it were, the final cause.

Like Merriam, he actually wrote best about what he knew from experience—as one would expect of a true pragmatist, which perhaps he ceased to be. His *Legislative Way of Life*[2] is not a great book, but it argued well, with apt examples, the need for holding politicians 'less in disdain' and for recognizing, from his own experience as an Illinois State Senator, that compromise is of the essence of legislation. But this sound fruit of experience, as with Merriam, did not find its way into what he regarded as his important formal writings as a would-be scientific and very democratic philosopher.

3. Quantitative Methods in Politics

The first practical manual for actual statistical techniques in political research was Stuart Rice's *Quantitative Methods in Politics*,[3] a book of considerable influence.[4] But this influence was also that of a suppressed general theory as well as of a professedly limited technique.

[1] See *Man's Three-fold Will* . . . He makes this distinction between 'descriptive' and 'directional' equality in referring to a criticism of egalitarianism made by Professor Butterfield in a previous lecture of the series. But it is hard to see how it meets Butterfield's point, though it does show an awareness of the problem alien to the more influential Smith of the 'thirties (pp. 62 ff.). Smith, like Merriam, throve upon a friendly intellectual environment and, with a sensitive ear for 'trends', now tries to accommodate himself to a somewhat colder climate of ideas.

[2] (Chicago: 1940). 'Democracy means,' he said, 'politically speaking, the process of clearing collective conflicts through a legislature; and it means, socially speaking, the way of living together without condescension' (p. 1). This is certainly *American* democracy and it well points a criticism of some other concepts of democracy—but also, alas, of Smith's own formal academic writings.

[3] (New York: 1928).

[4] A select bibliography in one of the most 'authoritative' sources of contemporary 'political behaviour theory' describes it thus: 'Pioneer statement on the conceptual and methodological problems involved in applying quantitative techniques to political behaviour is contained in Part II: "Conceptual Background." After two decades this volume still stands as indispensable reading for those interested in the empirical aspects of political behaviour research.' ['Research in Political Behaviour', *APSR*, XLVI (Dec. 1952), 1034.]

He wrote that 'there is little doubt that the insistence upon the value of quantitative method has become fashionable among American social scientists', but drew from this: 'the need for caution'. Initially he made no claim to be advancing a complete methodology of political studies or a general theory of politics: 'Quantitative method is one among various methods of discovering truth. . . . It would be foolish to contend concerning any particular situation or problem that a suitable method of measurement . . . will not presently be found, but there may always be some . . . which at a given time have resisted this type of approach. Investigation of these by other means should not for that reason be held lacking in scientific value.'[1] After Bentley, Merriam and Smith, there is a refreshing and wise lack of 'empire building' in the early pages of Rice, a pragmatic insistence on particular aids for solving or understanding particular problems. He recognized that 'no one engages in scientific research unequipped with certain assumptions and presuppositions of a philosophical character'. He made clear that it is no question whether there are such assumptions and that the investigator should be aware of them.

But, rather oddly, Rice then went on to draw a rigid distinction between 'ends' and 'means' and appeared to view all such philosophic presuppositions as equally valid, that is to say, equally prejudiced. Having apparently insisted that every activity of research in the social sciences assumes a prior viewpoint, he then demanded that: 'If social science is really to become a science, it must separate itself from religious and ethical endeavour and from all other efforts to set up values or ends of any sort.' He did not wish, he said, to condemn such values and endeavours: 'The contention is merely that *these things are not science.*' He spoke of the 'scientist in his off-hours as layman' having a sense of 'social, moral or religious obligations',[2] but this is not *science*. Here is a curiously stark division of both experience and judgement. He does not tell us how we can express a 'value' that does not entail evidence or consequences, or how we can express a 'fact' that does not presume a theory as to its relevance and a 'value judgement' as to its significance. If for the purpose of being purely scientific we make this abstraction, tearing apart the actual world of experience, then for the purposes of politics, however defined, we must surely suspend or subsume this separation. There is conceivably a political science that has no reference to 'values' (at least to values in political dispute), or that treats 'values' as opinion and then measures and describes how many and who hold them, but it would have no relevance to politics at all, unless the questions asked were somehow significant. In other words, Rice

[1] Rice, *Quantitative Methods*, pp. 3–5. [2] *Ibid.*, pp. 17–19.

could say, though he does not, that the genesis of the proposition or hypothesis to be tested is of no concern, only its 'truth conditions' are of scientific concern. But he could not then, without appeal to his 'off-hours as layman', judge whether the propositions were *trivial* or not (there might be a science of politics which is, then, as was once said of philology, of those things not worth knowing).

Rice, then, sounds eminently fair at first, but turns out to be unfortunately muddled. Much of his actual work, however, suffered little damage from his own understanding of its significance. Many of the statistical techniques he suggested can still be very useful; and, for instance, his own research into ' "Stereotypes" in the control of political attitudes' could be well used in argument against certain common superstitions of political thought about national character (presumably he had this in mind as 'off-hours layman'). But the main example or project for research that he outlined raises more serious issues.

When he tried to set up a tabular construction to compare the ' "Representativeness" of Electoral Representatives',[1] he was immediately involved in a theory of politics, indeed, one that sees the representation of the direct will of a legislator's constituents as of the essence of democracy. He explicitly contrasted this view to that of J. W. Burgess, whom he quoted as saying: 'The views of a constituency should always be taken into account as contributing to the make-up of the consciousness of the State, but the will of a constituency has no place in the modern system of legislative representation.'[2] Rice stated that his own views on the problem were, of course, '*a priori*' but, nevertheless, they were concerned with '*what is*', not 'like the statement by Burgess . . . a metaphysical problem of representation . . . the question of *ought*'. Surely neither view alone gives a satisfactory understanding of the theory or the practice of representation in the United States; both views contain a grain of truth, but the distinction between them is not one of 'is' and 'ought'. Both views take one set of tendencies in American government (indeed, the point is more general than American government) and try to make of it the whole—in doing this, the obvious distinction is not between 'scientist' and 'metaphysician', but between Jacksonian and Federalist.

However, Rice, preoccupied with 'representativeness', ignores any alternative view of 'Responsible Government' as contrasted to 'Representative Government', or of a 'national consensus' as well as 'particular representativeness'—questions which A. L. Lowell, for

---

[1] Rice, pp. 189–205.
[2] Quoted by Rice, pp. 190–1, from Burgess, *Political Science and Comparative Constitutional Law* (Boston: 1890–1), 2 vols., II, 116.

instance, was careful *not* to prejudge in his studies on public opinion —and he declares that empirically verifiable propositions are alone meaningful. He gives as an example the question raised by Frank Goodnow as to whether a Constitutional Convention is representative of the 'Sovereign people' and whether its enactments are 'binding on the Courts'. 'The questions of Goodnow', says Rice, 'are potentially susceptible of an empirical answer, while the statement of Burgess could be established only by a prior postulation of ends.' [1] But even if the enactments of a Constitutional Convention (a favourite panacea of the Progressive movement) could be shown to influence the decisions of the Courts, so—in that great pragmatic phrase —what? This would not empirically demonstrate the rightness of the actions or the efficacy of such a form of government. Rice seems to assume that this would be demonstrated if the Convention could be shown to be representative of 'the sovereign people'.

What does he mean by 'representative'? He says that the legislator 'is representative' because, firstly, 'voters tend to select men of their own kind to office' and, secondly, 'because he responds to legislative issues on the whole in about the same manner as would his fellow group-members in the constituency'.[2] But, all too obviously, to many, to the degree that this is true, it is the dilemma of Democratic Government, not its automatic condition of justness. He compounds the electorally measurable both with the just and with the democratic. This is no place to argue the respective merits of a broadly 'Representative' and a broadly 'Responsible' view of Constitutional Democracy. It is enough for the argument even to exist on rational grounds for Rice's view of politics to appear, at the best, gravely limited. It is, however, important to our thesis to see that the view of democracy to which Professor Rice subscribed is one that renders plausible the idea of a science of politics.

Rice's view of democracy is one aspect of American liberalism, but it is not the whole. It is that aspect specifically associated with the Jacksonian democracy: the belief in direct democracy through short terms of service, rotation in office and the common or the average candidate rather than the exceptional. It is this same aspect, so easily but not necessarily seen as the essence of American liberalism, that influenced the young social sciences in the Progressive Era and led, with the call for 'Referendum, popular Initiative and Recall', to an over-great absorption in the problem of Representation. From this view of democracy springs the belief that 'the facts' when put

[1] Rice, *loc. cit.*
[2] *Ibid.*, pp. 193–4. 'Group-members' is, clearly, purely *empirical* to Rice, whereas Burgess' 'consciousness of the State' is *metaphysical*—this being A. F. Bentley's theory of group reality again, calling some one else's good goose gander.

before 'the people' would be a cry to Heaven swiftly and precisely answered. The reasons that Rice offers as to why the legislator is representative are clearly far *more* true for the United States than for other Constitutional-Democracies, certainly including Canadian Dominion Government (though not all the Provinces). But even granted that the extreme democratic theory of representation is a sufficient explanation and an unbreakable law in the United States, at best a science of politics raised on such a structure will be, like Charles Beard's early work, purely an American science. The 'constituency' of political science would then be a specific country, not the 'universe of discourse' or 'nature'. But this consideration does not seem to have made the Behavioural School any the more sceptical of general law in politics; rather, it seems to have strengthened their psychological certitude that Science, Democracy and what Jefferson called 'Americanism' are a trinity destined to march in the foremost files of time: the success of the American 'experiment' confirms the observation of a natural Progress.[1]

Professor William Anderson, writing about American political science a decade after Rice, can himself illustrate splendidly the psychological coherence of this theory or belief:

An empirical and practical spirit came to pervade most of the studies. . . . As a result of the new approach and the greatly increased activity in the study of politics, what has been called the 'science of politics', using science in the sense of a natural science, seemed to be in the making. . . . American political science stands today somewhat away from the contemplation of the State and sovereignty, and towards the study of actual political processes. . . . The new emphasis not only serves to humanize political science, but also to change the focus and to expand greatly the opportunities for fruitful political research. This approach is, also, more in conformity with the spirit of a democratic people that still believes in progress and the importance and dignity of the individual human being.[2]

However, we should note that Anderson then, in his last paragraph, suddenly injects what seems to be a sensible note of caution, as Rice did in his opening pages:

This is not to say that the study has reached a fully rounded maturity. It may well be that the present secular and empirical approach needs to be corrected by a redefinition of the place of values and ethical factors in relation to politics. Perhaps, too, American students of politics have permitted their studies to become so fully conditioned by the ideas and circumstances of their own country that theirs has become a science of North American rather than of world-wide application.[3]

[1] See T. V. Smith's praise of Rice in his *Beyond Conscience*, pp. 288–9.
[2] William Anderson's supplementary chapter to Anna Haddow's *Political Science in American Colleges and Universities, 1636–1900* (New York: 1939), pp. 264–6.
[3] *Ibid.*, p. 266.

But, like Rice, Anderson leaves this unexplained. He does not explore what is meant by a 'redefinition' and he certainly does not retract the hopes he has sketched before—indeed, his last sentence, with the hope of 'world-wide' application, seems to intensify it. His later writings and reviews show no sign of any 'redefinition' of the main claim. Probably what he had in mind was the denial by many of the more extreme Behaviourists that 'values and ethical factors' had any autonomous causal effect at all in politics, or were, as Bentley regarded them, just rationalizations of interest. Probably Anderson was feeling after the step that Lasswell and others later took: to grant that such factors have or appear to have an effect in politics, but then to study them scientifically as 'opinions', who and how many hold them and to what types of personality structure, psychologically conceived, do certain 'values' adhere.[1]

4. The Great Case Book

When, in 1931, the 'Committee on Scientific Method' of the Social Science Research Council issued its long-planned *Methods in Social Science, A Case Book*, Stuart Rice was the editor and Harold Lasswell was the 'coinvestigator'. The volume emerged from discussions originated by Charles Merriam when he was President of the Social Science Research Council as a step towards 'the integration of the Social Sciences'. The volume was clearly intended to be both a Landmark and a Beacon Light. It was the largest co-operative project yet attempted; it included all the social disciplines, and the contributions were presented in a scientifically constructive order.[2]

The first 'Case Analysis' (i.e., an essay with numbered paragraphs) was by Professor McQuilkin DeGrange: 'The Method of Auguste Comte: Subordination of Imagination to Observation in the Social Sciences.' 'Order, precision, clarity of thought, architectonic vision, philosophical power, synthetic unity—such were some of the characteristic qualities that Comte brought to the task of consciously creating a new Science. . . . The full fruit of his labours was prevented

---

[1] Cf. Oliver Garceau, 'Research in the Political Process', *APSR*, XLV (March 1951): 'Yet normative theory . . . has an indispensable role in empirical research. Values are data of political process. They very properly set priorities for research. The heritage of political philosophy will prove to be a source of hypotheses for research, and our political values will guide the use of research findings' (p. 84).

[2] *Methods in Social Science* (Chicago: 1931). The essays were called 'Case Analyses' and were divided into nine sections: '1. The Delimitation of the Field of Enquiry. 2. The Definition of Objects of Investigation. 3. The Establishment of Units and Scales. 4. Attempts to Discover Spatial Distributions and Temporal Sequences. 5. Interpretations of Change as a Developmental Stage. 6. Interpretation of Temporal Sequences with Consideration of Special Types of "Causation". 8. Attempts to Determine Relationships among Measured but Experimentally Uncontrolled Factors. 9. Attempts to Determine Quantitative Relations Among Measured and Experimentally Controlled Factors.'

by death. Only the guidance of this method remains.'[1] It was a generous estimate of Comte and well bore out its title.

Political science was well represented, although W. Y. Elliott's essay in the first section, 'The Possibility of a Science of Politics: with special attention to the methods suggested by William B. Munro and George E. G. Catlin', was something of a gad-fly in the ointment. Catlin, then of Cornell, was given the unique privilege of an immediate three-page reply, no doubt to repair the damage wrought by Elliott's famed mixture of philosophical sensitivity and polemical violence. Frank Knight had also shown some scepticism about the premises of the volume in the Economics article: he argued that physics was more 'metaphysical' in its foundations than social *scientists* realized. But perhaps Rice and Lasswell had a certain professional pride in answering a maverick political scientist. Elliott had maintained that there was indeed a sensible practical distinction between the interests of the 'political scientist' and the 'political philosopher', but that the 'rough laws' and classificatory activity of the former had little to do with the methods of natural science and that politics, to achieve a wholeness, must somewhere deal 'with values in an ideal scale'.[2]

Catlin replied that it was a false objection to say that there could be no science if questions of value were involved: 'There is, it would seem, on the contrary, no objection to *supposing* that wealth is good. . . . The business of the scientist is to study those methods which a man must adopt to attain this or that end *if* he happen to choose it.'[3] He concluded that: 'In political science, "rough laws" are possible: the writer would, however, prefer to call these laws "incompletely understood, deduced and demonstrated" rather than "rough". There are no fringes of caprice in a law *qua* law.'[4] He says '*qua* law' just as many still say 'a political scientist *qua* scientist is objective, but *qua* citizen comes up with "insights", "values" or "hypotheses".' This is no answer at all to Elliott's doubt as to whether such laws are possible in principle—except 'roughly' for small segments of political life; or to Knight's doubt that they are possible or desirable in practice. (The systematic nature of the Case Book might seem sadly shattered when these threads are left untied even in the first few articles.)

---

[1] *Methods in Social Science* (Chicago: 1931), p. 58.

[2] *Ibid.*, pp. 70 ff. and p. 92. Elliott recognized that Catlin and Munro represented 'the prevailing currents' more than he himself.

[3] *Ibid.*, p. 90. He does not reply to the short answer that Frank Knight had already given to this form of argument: '. . . such a specialization is impractical'. The social scientist, as a man, cannot leave 'the application to "others", but must insist on having something to say about policies and ends' (pp. 68–9).

[4] *Ibid.*, p. 94.

In Section VII, 'Interpretations of Relationship among Unmeasured Factors', Lasswell offers an analysis of 'The Comparative Method of James Bryce'. He makes a good criticism of Lord Bryce's failure ever really to characterize the 'Democracy' of his *Modern Democracies*. But he is also disturbed by the whole 'impressionistic' and unsystematic character of Bryce's observations. He does pay tribute to Bryce's 'talent for striking up an acquaintance with a "random sample" ', a talent which 'should not obscure his ability to discover the best observers in a given society, and his exertions to keep on mutually valuable terms with them'. (This is a revealingly pragmatic account of Bryce's gregarious friendliness.) 'There is no evidence, however,' continued Lasswell, 'that Bryce ever systematically classified various types of well-informed people, and exerted himself to discover the variations among them in opinion about a specific issue.' (The 'coinvestigator' presumably possesses something more than an address book.) He suggests strongly that a 'fixed list of questions' is often a convenient 'guide in the collection of material' it may be 'mailed out formally', used in a 'face-to-face interview', or 'kept in the background' and consulted from time to time.[1] However, Lasswell's main criticism of Bryce is levelled, not at his method of work, but at his 'pessimism about politics as a science'. 'The dogmatic, and even romantic, assertion that the "feelings and acts" of men are incapable of measurement does not appear to rest upon careful scrutiny of modern economists, to say nothing of the work of professional psychologists.' [2]

Lasswell here seems not unlike T. V. Smith in viewing the 'claim' as more important than the specific content of any research. The claim is, indeed, vastly important; we can scarcely imagine how different government and society would be could it be true. But somehow throughout the Case Book there is a disproportion between the often painstaking detail of the cases reported and the general claim.[3] Nothing approaching a scientific law emerges from any of the Case Studies, although there are plenty of shrewd precepts for aiding greater objectivity in research and for gaining comparability of results. On the one hand, there is the type of the opening

---

[1] *Ibid.*, p. 471. His footnote on that page is of interest by way of comparison:
'The Viscountess Bryce, in a gracious reply to an inquiry, has written: "I do not think that he ever made a formal list of specific points to work from in respect of comparisons. . . . In planning his books he had always in mind from the beginnings a clear outline of their purpose and their form and the scale on which they were to be constructed, which he gradually filled in with the details, the illustrations and the comparisons which occurred to him as he built up the picture." '
'Picture' is what is called a 'give-away word'. Lasswell would never have used it himself.   [2] *Ibid.*, p. 479.
[3] *Ibid.*, No. 50, Catlin's 'Harold F. Gosnell's Experiments in the Stimulation of Voting', pp. 697–707, illustrates this.

171

essay on Comte, heralding a new science, but promising research to exemplify its claims in, as W. Y. Elliott remarked, a footnote; and on the other hand, a host of investigator's precepts, like those of Kimball Young, the sociologist, in his 'analysis' of Frederick Thrasher's study of gangs, wisely warning investigators against the wearing of glasses and the use of cultivated English in slum areas.[1] There is little or no middle ground. Some recognition of a suppressed major premise which can at least emotionally sweep together the detail and the generalities seems implied by the inclusion of an analysis called: 'The Concept of Progress and Its Influence on History as Developed by J. B. Bury', by Sidney B. Fay, an historian. But the analysis is mere précis and praise of Bury. It lost a needed opportunity to explore the presuppositions of the idea and of Bury's own ambiguous attitude towards it. All Fay adds is that the influence of Darwin has strengthened the idea even more than Bury had supposed, and that recent scientific advances bore it out still further.[2]

Probably because the book was so obviously American in its authorship and style of thought, *The American Journal of Sociology* invited Karl Mannheim to review it. His review is of great interest. He treads cautiously at first, evidently well aware that he is reviewing a work deeply imbued with a national sentiment and with what Santayana had once called (*à propos* Dewey) 'a new and difficult kind of sincerity'. He pays proper respect to the practical spirit of the book and the care for detail showed in many of the Case Studies; this he contrasts favourably to the intense abstractness of most German sociology. But, he continues, 'we must admit a very marked and painful disproportion between the vastness of the scientific machinery employed and the value of the ultimate results'. Subjects and titles, he says, evoke the highest expectation, 'yet, after having reached their conclusions, one is tempted to ask, disappointedly: "Is this all?"' [3] Mannheim makes the now familiar complaint that American students of society have branded all philosophy as 'metaphysical escapes' and have shown 'a curious lack of ambition to excel in the quality of theoretical insights into phenomenal structures'. They are anxious 'not to violate a very one-sided ideal of exactness. One almost ventures to say,' he ventures, 'such works aim in the first place at being exact, and only in the second place at conveying a knowledge of things.' Mannheim then argues that it is better first to have a sense for an important subject matter and only then to worry

[1] *Methods in Social Science*, p. 521

[2] *Ibid.*, pp. 287–97.

[3] From the *American Journal of Sociology*, XXXVIII (Sept. 1932), 273–82, reprinted in Karl Mannheim, *Essays on Sociology and Social Psychology* (New York; 1953), p. 187.

about exactness. He diagnoses this tendency to triviality from an over-concentration on method due to yielding 'too much to the fascination of natural science'.[1] The comments of Mannheim are just. The only pity is that within the scope of a short review he could not apply the techniques of his own 'scientific' sociology of knowledge to this American social science; the attempt would have been interesting.

To return to political science alone: Professor Elliott's contribution had quoted a sentence from William B. Munro's Presidential Address to the American Political Science Association (1928) which admirably sums up the assumptions of the scientific school: 'But the science and the art of government still rest upon what may be called the atomic theory of politics—upon the postulate that all able bodied citizens are of equal weight, volume and value; endowed with inalienable rights; vested with the attribution of an indivisible sovereignty.' [2] (Munro did not deny that much of government was an 'art', but he looked forward to more and more of it becoming a 'science'.) Munro, thus, with complete self-awareness, assumed a Lockean atomic individuality and the reality of natural rights as the basis for a science of politics. It was one of the original peculiarities of the Natural Rights philosophy, as it arose in Western thought largely to replace speculation which assumed Natural Law, that it was used to form a fixed 'base line' for the construction of a science of politics.[3] 'Multiply not thy entities'—we may not choose to regard this as science simply because the assumptions of the 'base line' are so large and are so shifting; but for the American school, as for Hobbes, the belief of the creators that it was science seems open to little doubt. This belief was itself a political belief, held with a psychological certitude that did service for the lack of any logical distinction between science and philosophy.

An 'artificial' scientific order, as Lester Frank Ward used the word, in order to maintain a relationship with justice at all, and still be calculable, must assume a fixed and clear Natural Right. It is not the assumption of Natural Right as such that then causes the difficulties, but the assumption of the clarity and precision of its content. The creators of a political science confessedly based upon Natural Right have not realized how a large part of politics arises from the tension between the affirmation of a natural right and its varying content in varying circumstances to various people. And the difficulty of a scientific certitude is even greater if Natural Law were to

[1] Mannheim, *ibid.*, p. 189.
[2] 'Physics and Politics: an Old Analogy Revised', *APSR*, XXII (Feb. 1928), 3; quoted by W. Y. Elliott in *Methods in Social Science*, p. 73.
[3] See Chapter VIII, 'The New Political Science', Leo Strauss, *The Political Philosophy of Thomas Hobbes* (Oxford: 1936).

be taken as a basis—indeed, it would be almost a self-contradictory conception, for by Law being external to will, there is no possibility of the individual being treated as both the 'atomic' unit of calculation and as the calculator.

In this chapter we have sought to show that the spread of co-operative research in the name of a science of politics has been based upon a simple and a dubious view of democracy. The equality of man meant the same thing as the significant identity of units to be measured. Of course, for many things this is true; but for many other things, at the heart of the notion of the political, it is not. The actual political beliefs of the men and the books we have noted are at least an exemplification that a limited political theory is possible, in that they seem to bear out Aristotle's concept of democracy: the belief that because men are equal in some respects, they are equal in all. (Is this not 'the tendency' of democracy when unchecked by notions of Law?) An obvious idealism moved these men, but ideals, no more than facts, are all on the same level of reality. 'We are all here on earth to help each other,' Mr. W. H. Auden has said, 'but what the others are here for, God only knows.' Morals as well as facts have no order apart from philosophy. It has been one of the generic weaknesses of the American liberal temper to accept sincerity as rectitude. The founders of the science of politics, then, accepted 'natural rights' and treated them as if democratic procedure, when conceived as the rule of the majority, could never conflict with them (an assumption, again, that is cultural, not philosophical). They treated them as social *demands* upon government, not as limitations. In doing so they lost sight of the distinction between liberty and egalitarian-democracy that, notably, De Tocqueville had already drawn. Mere liberty, they rightly regarded as anarchy. But full democracy, they could never conceive as a possible tyranny. The note that Smith sounded, Merriam and Lasswell accepted, and Mannheim observed, that all 'metaphysics' was necessarily at war with democratic liberty—this was their fundamental error.

Liberty and tolerance are important not because metaphysical distinctions do not matter, but because they matter profoundly. They continue to exist because the metaphysical is not the physical. The belief in *a* road is not the same as an authenticated signpost to any particular road. A truer apperception of reality is to be gained, in the philosophy of politics as in general philosophy, by experiencing and understanding the variety of different ways in which men actually talk about good and evil, virtue and political justice, not by discarding experience and ordinary speech in favour of a new and technical pseudo-scientific vocabulary. The importance of staying close to the mundane ground of ordinary speculation which the political scientists seek to avoid is at least shown in the dialectic method of Plato or his master. True, the 'dialectic method is not a game that two can play', but the thinker when thinking is thinking only his own thoughts—he need not confuse truth with what a large group of men, researching together, can all agree upon.

But strangely, at first sight, though the social scientists were achieving some agreement amongst themselves, they were falling out of agreement with the actual politics of their time. By the end of the 'twenties the old pragmatic, reformist spirit among political scientists was largely dead. The pragmatic spirit had reaped the fruit of its own sowing; when in the era of Harding and of Coolidge the political scientist was no longer wanted by society as critic and leader, as he had been in the 1900's, he did not venture to intrude himself, he retired into a professionalized 'quest for certainty' to become, what Dewey himself never was, a fit target for A. N. Whitehead's gibe that it is more important for a proposition to be interesting than to be true. They often spoke the truth, an exact truth, but about trivial things. Pragmatism, when its gods of an affable public opinion deserted it, changed into positivism, without many noticing the difference.[1] The political became less interesting to political scientists than the sociological.[2] When the New Deal supplanted the era of Harding, Coolidge and Hoover—truly the era (as Harding said) of 'normalcy'—political scientists certainly entered government service in large numbers; but most of them returned to politics as 'experts'. There was not apparent any revival or creation of a function of independent criticism, nor yet any historical or philosophical clarification of the ambiguous content of the uniformity of belief in American liberalism. A book like Max Lerner's *Ideas Are Weapons* (1939), though often spoken of as a sign of a renewed vitality of political thought, yet all too obviously depended, like the social science research movement, upon the assumption that the 'ends' of American life were 'given', 'fixed' or clearly apparent in the real will of the people or the 'common man', and that their full social realization only depended upon improved 'means', techniques, tools, weapons, instrumentalities.

[1] Later, Robert Lynd did, of course, in his well-named *Knowledge for What?* (Princeton: 1939).
[2] This is well exemplified in the closing chapter of Raymond G. Gettell's *History of American Political Thought* (New York and London: 1928), Chap. XIX, 'New Influences on Political Thought', pp. 611–15 especially.

X

THE CONCEPTUAL BEHAVIOUR OF HAROLD LASSWELL

The friends of democracy who have turned to science have been acutely dissatisfied with the ambiguity of inherited political, social, and philosophical literature. To speak of the movement toward science as a revolt against philosophy is to fall into error. It was not impatience with democratic morals that led to the de-emphasizing of general definitions; it was discontent with the chronic incompleteness of formulation in the traditional literature. The turning to the specific is more properly to be understood as a stampede to complete philosophy, to reconsider every generality for the purpose of relating it to observable reality.

HAROLD LASSWELL, *The Analysis of Political Behaviour*

. . . He did the very best he could
With things not very subject to control,
And turned, without perceiving his condition,
Like Coleridge, into a metaphysician.

BYRON, *Don Juan*

1. The Promise of Methodology

TWO distinguished sociologists, of by no means the most uncritically 'scientific' persuasion, have recently referred to the 'special position' that Harold Lasswell occupies in American social science. 'There is hardly anyone', they said, 'who equals him as a living symbol for continuity and interdisciplinary integration in social research.'[1] Lasswell is the most well known of contemporary American political scientists. Though not all political scientists would agree even with his general position, yet he is the acknowledged master of the specifically scientific school and has probably influenced more work in other people than any political scientist alive today. His own writings have achieved an eminence, in their size

[1] Richard Christie and Marie Jahoda, editors, in the symposium, *Studies in the Scope and Method of 'The Authoritarian Personality'* (Glencoe, Ill.: 1954), p. 22; see also p. 18.

176

and complexity, somewhere between a Skyscraper and a Maze.[1] He
has devoted his great abilities, year in and year out, through many
books and by many different concepts, to 'pure causal analysis', not
sacrificing science for any preoccupation with 'applied or reforma-
tive theory'.[2]

Although he was the pupil of Charles Merriam who has tried
hardest to fulfil his master's hopes for scientific method in political
studies, yet he has avoided the excessive homiletic quality of
Merriam's advocacy and has patiently set out to construct various
'conceptual frameworks' by which society might be understood and
then, possibly, controlled more scientifically. He did not confuse
science with 'fact gathering' or with a purely inductive logic; he
grasped both the logical and the practical primacy of theory to
observation in natural science. Although in recent years he has tried
to identify scientific method with the democratic spirit, he has never
wholly shared the somewhat naïve democratic fervour of Merriam
or Smith. His thirty years of abundant work have been to provide
'a model for the orientation of research', or a 'set of provisional
postulates for political behaviour research' or 'theoretical formula-
tions of power politics'.[3] In the introduction to *Power and Society*,
written jointly with Abraham Kaplan, he puts his basic position
clearly:

Theorizing, about politics, is not to be confused with metaphysical
speculation in terms of abstractions hopelessly removed from empirical
observation and control. Such speculation characterized the German
Staatslehre tradition so influential at the turn of the century. The present
work is much closer to the *straightforward* empirical viewpoint of Machiavelli's *Discourses* or Michel's *Political Parties*. But this standpoint is not
to be confused, on the other hand, with "brute empiricism"—the gathering
of 'facts' without a corresponding elaboration of hypotheses—a position
to which the descriptive politics of De Tocqueville [*sic*] and Bryce sometimes appears to come dangerously close. 'It is facts that are needed,'
Bryce exclaims, 'Facts, Facts, Facts.' Of themselves, of course, 'facts'
are mere collections of details; they are significant only as data for
hypotheses.[4]

[1] Two of his most influential books—*Psychopathology and Politics* (1930) and
Politics: Who Gets What, When, How (1936)—have received the unique honour among
American writers today of being bound up with a new work, *Democratic Character*,
by the Free Press (Glencoe, Ill.) as *The Political Writings of Harold Lasswell* (1951).
[2] As David Easton has claimed—see his *The Political System* (New York: 1953),
pp. 119–23; and also his 'Harold Lasswell: Policy Scientist', *The Journal of Politics*,
XII (Aug. 1950), 450–77.
[3] These phrases are taken from three successive Lasswell items in the 'Selected
Critical Bibliography on the Methods and Techniques of Political Behaviour Research'
at the end of a collaborative article, 'Research in Political Behaviour', *APSR*, XLVI
(Dec. 1952), 1036.
[4] *Power and Society* (London: 1952), p. x, my italics.

Leaving aside the two curious judgements on Machiavelli and De Tocqueville, we can say that he makes clear that there is, in some sense, a constructive role for political theory: he sees that *mere* research is apt to be a mere waste of time. Lasswell cannot be accused of neglecting theory for practice; his constant claim is to be trying to bridge the two (though by 'practice' he has clearly meant, until quite recently, research and not politics). 'The task of the hour', he stated in *Psychopathology and Politics*, 'is a development of a realistic analysis of the political in relation to the social process.' This would depend upon 'the invention of abstract conceptions and upon the prosecution of empirical research'.[1]

These 'conceptual frameworks' seem meant to correspond more to the analytic procedures of modern Economic theory than to anything previously thought applicable to the study of politics. This he himself has recently made clear, in explaining why research projects like Jacob Adorno's *The Authoritarian Personality* have not taken place within political science—a passage worth quoting at length because it contains his understanding of a part of our general problem:

Although academic political science in the United States has gone further as a specialized discipline than in Europe, the growth of the subject as a behaviour science has been retarded by several factors. The neighbouring discipline of economics, for example, developed much farther. . . . The members of an Economics department could study the market without conducting a rear-guard action with colleagues who specialized on 'economic philosophy' or 'economic law'. In departments of Political Science the specialists on 'political philosophy' (often called 'political theory') were historians of past writings on the 'State'. Possessing a voluminous and dignified tradition they were so weighed down with the burden of genteel erudition that they had little intellectual energy with which to evolve original theory for the guidance of either science or policy. Academic economists were fortunate to have a less voluminous and a less dignified inheritance. And they were comparatively unencumbered with legalism. Hence they dealt with questions of policy in a less formalistic framework. More of their energy went into the construction of theoretical models for empirical research. In contrast with economics the systematic evaluation of political theory was left in a curiously stationary condition. Hence empirical work in political science received a minimum of constructive aid from scholars responsible for political theory. This led to a great schism between the great corpus of general tradition and empirical studies. The latter were too likely to be both parochial and noncumulative.[2]

---

[1] *Psychopathology* . . ., pp. 45–6. He continued: 'It is precisely this missing body of theory and practice that Graham Wallas undertook to supply in England and Charles Merriam has been foremost in encouraging in the United States' (p. 46).

[2] From his contribution to *Studies in the Scope and Method* . . ., eds. Christie and Jahoda, pp. 195–6.

Even within this paragraph there is a curious and revealing shift of tone and style between the sarcasm of 'voluminous and dignified tradition' and 'genteel erudition', and the final reference to the 'great corpus of general tradition'. In part, this is no more than the benevolence of an elder Statesman, prepared to indulge all factions in a common profession of which he is now a leader. But it also shows a real shift in his thinking, a shift that has taken place, however, without his repudiating any of his previous positions. Whereas his early writings view 'philosophy' and 'value theory' as the allies of obscuranticism and the enemies of science, his more recent writings have spoken of 'Policy Science'. Social Science is now a means to an end, a dividing of the world into two parts, questions of 'what' (speculative and relative, though usually democratic) and questions of 'how' (scientific).[1]

This ambiguity between a *shifting of ground* and *development* is also seen in his attitude to 'prediction' in social science, a concept that has often been taken as the most important criterion for a genuinely scientific theory. In 1934, he said that in the task of 'abolishing uncertainty' the '*crucial* test of adequate analysis is nothing less than the *future* verification of the insight into the nature of the master configuration against which details are construed'.[2] But by 1951 he is writing: 'It is insufficiently acknowledged that the role of scientific work in human relations is *freedom* rather than prediction.'[3] The interpretation of Lasswell is difficult because, like Merriam, he has a reluctance or an inability ever to repudiate openly earlier 'false scents' and unhelpful concepts; this adds a quality of confusion and complexity to his later writings, apart from his formidable technical vocabulary, so that it takes all his high intelligence and dexterity to sustain a feeling of unity in them.

The content of his many 'conceptual frameworks' has varied. Marxism at one time influenced him much; he was critical of such a 'reading of private preferences into universal history', but found the *methodology* of Marxism immeasurably superior to any other yet known.[4] However, his first genuinely unique conceptual framework

---

[1] See *The Policy Sciences, Recent Developments in Scope and Method*, edited by Lasswell and Daniel Lerner (Stanford: 1951)—unless otherwise indicated all quotations below from *The Policy Sciences* are from Lasswell's own contribution: 'It is not necessary for the scientist to sacrifice objectivity in the execution of a project. The place for non-objectivity is in deciding what ultimate goals are to be implemented. Once this choice is made, the scholar proceeds with the maximum objectivity and uses all available methods' (p. 11).

[2] *World Politics and Personal Insecurity* (Chicago: 1934), p. 17, my italics.

[3] *Political Writings*, p. 524. His definition of 'freedom' is unusual, but we will return to this later.

[4] *World Politics . . ., passim*, see especially pp. 135–6 for qualification and pp. 22–4 for affirmation; see above, p. 141, fn.

he drew from Freud, not Marx, the argument of his *Psychopathology and Politics*. His second conceptual framework, or series of frameworks, centre around 'power' and 'the political élite': *Politics, Who Gets What, When, How* is the clearest systematic treatment of this. His wartime *Democracy Through Public Opinion* is less a new framework than a retreat from his temptation with the idea of an élite of social scientists into the democratic orthodoxy of Merriam, Smith and Rice, although he tends to supplant the method of Electoral Representation by the method of Public Opinion Polls and Surveys as a source of democratic policy and legitimacy. This touches on his third significant set of concepts, summed up in *The Language of Politics, studies in quantitative semantics* of 1949 (it largely drew on his wartime work as head of the War Communications Research Project at the Library of Congress).

None of these categories is self-contained or without relation to the earlier ones. *Power and Society, a Framework for Political Enquiry*, jointly written with Abraham Kaplan in 1952, combines his earlier 'power' analysis with the study of the 'language and symbols' of politics by offering, somewhat after the manner of Sir George Cornwall Lewis, an attempt to give a refined clarity to the terms used in what he calls '*hypotheses-schema*'. Similarly, his *Power and Personality* of 1948 tried to draw the Freudian categories of his *Psychopathology and Politics* up into the 'group structured' realm of his writings on power. Lastly, his leadership and share in *The Policy Sciences, Recent Developments in Scope and Method* reinterprets his previous work, but without any repudiation, from pure science into applied science. And underlying all these works there is an insistence on a strictly 'behavioural approach' to politics and society: *The Analysis of Political Behaviour* (1947) systematically urges the abolition of prejudice and bias in research and policy by means of largely quantitative objective procedures.

Now, the above paragraphs are a simplification that pay little tribute to the complexity and variety of his frameworks and, more latterly, to his 'insights'; nor to the fact that, leaving possible contradictions aside, all his concepts are not entirely absent from any of his books, even, in germ, in the earliest.

Professor Lasswell is, then, not a settler, he is a pathfinder and a border scout. He has either led in person nearly every migration into the 'field' in contemporary American political science or else the project-leader has borne his authenticated charts, and also his passports to tribes and disciplines along the route. He has blazed the trail for small armies of settlers, but, as the wagons stop moving and the ploughs are dragged out, he always gallops off to yet more virgin soil, leaving the Social Science Research Council to organize a

Territorial Government. He leaves us dazed by the many accounts of the many border-lands he has explored for a while, but his general direction is always the same, the West of Science. His originality, width of knowledge, energy and his refusal to become 'hidebound' in his thinking are admirable, but his movements do become a little bewildering for those who want not merely to do 'research', but to do research with the latest concepts and the newest tools. They are apt to appear outmoded before they have had time even to unpack.

His assertions about actual political trends may sometimes seem no more than trite. But such criticism does not seem to affect Professor Lasswell very much: he takes the position that the science of politics is, after all, but a young science, and must perfect its methodology before it can make significant findings.

For his fundamental assertion is that there is a crisis in politics which is, at heart, a crisis in the methodology of political theory. It is not primarily a failure in political prudence, a derangement between ethics and politics, nor yet a shift in geo-political factors; but it is a crisis in the way we look at politics at all, in what we have hitherto counted as relevant knowledge and proper techniques. It is in this light that we must examine Lasswell's main concepts, now on his own grounds, analytically, no longer primarily historically or politically. His attempt to solve the problem of 'value' in politics by understanding political behaviour in terms of personality structure makes his conceptual framework of *Psychopathology and Politics* his most strongly based and systematic challenge to the historical and philosophical attitude to political studies. So we will deal with this last and at greater length.

2. Power and Élites

'When we speak of the science of politics,' wrote Lasswell, 'we mean the science of power.'[1] This was the theme of his volume in the trilogy, *A Study of Power*, which, together with volumes by Merriam and Smith, first came out, as we have noted, in 1934, and was republished in 1950. Merriam's political theory was so ambiguous and vague largely because of his failure to distinguish between 'power' and 'authority'—or, as some writers would prefer to put it, his confusion of *political* power (i.e., constituted power) with power in general. This lack of distinction distorts the nature of politics and avoids the problem of the nature of legitimate authority.[2] This argument also touches Lasswell, but there is no need to repeat it: his absorption with power as a 'conceptual framework' raises additional problems that illuminate his own underlying political thought.

The first paragraph of Lasswell's *World Politics and Personal*

[1] *Language of Politics*, p. 8. [2] See above, pp. 150–1.

Insecurity asserts: 'Political analysis is the study of changes in the shape and composition of the value pattern of society. Representative values are safety, income and deference.' And the 'distribution of any value' resembles a pyramid: 'The few who get the most of any value are the *élite*: the rest, the rank and file. The *élite* preserves its ascendancy by manipulating symbols, controlling supplies, and applying violence. Less formally expressed, politics is the study of *who gets what, when, and how.*' [1] Amid a typical footnote (a long and diverse list of books bearing on a theme in the text, not an attempt to make good a particular point) he then refers to Mosca's *Elementi di Scienza Politica*, Michel's *Corso di Sociologia Politica* and Carl Schmitt's *Der Begriff des Politischen.* He argued that there was a World Revolutionary situation unique to our age which was creating such an expectation of violence and insecurity, and was causing such a disarrangement of individual and group personality, that a new solution for a new and total problem must be found.

His solution seemed to oscillate between restating the problem in the language of Marx and then of Freud. A revised Marxism became one 'developmental possibility', something not strictly a science, but something that *if* we could agree to accept its postulates, would then allow a scientifically determined and demonstrable course of action. He heads the last chapter, 'In Quest of a Myth: the Problem of World Unity':

> The pre-requisite of a stable order in the world is a universal body of symbols and practices sustaining an élite which propagates itself by peaceful methods and wields a monopoly of coercion which it is rarely necessary to apply to the uttermost. This means that the consensus on which order is based is necessarily non-rational; the world myth must be taken for granted by most of the population. The capacity of the generality of mankind to disembarrass themselves of the dominant legends of their early years is negligible, and if we pose the problem of unifying the world we must seek for the processes by which a non-rational consensus can be most expeditiously achieved.[2]

This breathtaking extension of Sorel's manipulative 'myth of the General Strike' is the oddest mixture of unrealistic assumptions couched in realistic language. He reminds himself that in stressing the importance of a myth held by an élite the 'world material level' must not be forgotten: 'We allude here to the possibility that ideological uniformity depends upon material uniformity, and that the principal problem of spreading a world myth may be how to standardize the world material environment.'[3] This sudden inversion of cause and effect raises some doubt as to whether the concept of

[1] *World Politics*, p. 3. [2] *Ibid.*, p. 237. [3] *Ibid.*, p. 238.

'myth' is necessary to his analysis at all, except in deference to a new fashion. But, be that as it may, this manipulation of the external world is to be solution to the 'World Revolution of our times', a way to the 'externalization of anxiety'. But on the other hand, the 'internalization of anxiety' is also a possible solution, under the symbol of Freud. How, is not precisely clear, but it is to be through Lasswell's own 'configurative analysis of the pyramids of income, safety and deference'. Somehow, it appears, the analysis itself will create this internalization.

However, in either case, whether the method of manipulation be the neo-Marxian concept of a world myth, or an extension of the Freudian concept of analysis, there will be an élite of manipulators. The composition of this élite then moves readily from those to be studied into those who are studying. He speaks several times in different words of the 'possible though no doubt unforeseeable outcome of academic activity' that might 'rearrange the value pyramids for the benefit of the specialist':

> It is indisputable that the world could be unified if enough people were impressed by this (or by any other) élite. The hope of the professors of social science, if not of the world, lies in the competitive strength of an élite based on vocabulary, footnotes, questionnaires, and conditioned responses, against an élite based on vocabulary, poison gas, property, and family prestige. [1]

This modest chain of reasoning reaches the same end as that of Lester Frank Ward's scientific sociology: the rule of the sociocrat or the specialist, the proud temptation that all students of the social sciences seem to meet at some stage in their thought, master or are mastered by it. This élitism is the thread of all his work in the 1930's. In *Politics: Who Gets What, When and How*, he defines the study of politics as 'the study of influence and the influential'. 'The élite', he defines, 'are more influential than the many, the mass.' The ascendancy of an élite 'depends in part upon a successful manipulation of its environment. Methods of management involve symbols, goods, practices.' [2] Then, whether to hold out hope for social scientists or for us all, he makes at the end of the book an interesting and probably a true general judgement: 'Western civilization is activistic: it fosters

---

[1] *Ibid.*, p. 20.
[2] *Politics: Who Gets What*, pp. 443–4. Lasswell was not alone in his scientific élitism: see James Burnham's *The Machiavellians* (New York: 1943), and also Thurman Arnold's *The Folklore of Capitalism* (New Haven: 1937) and his *Symbols of Government* (New Haven: 1935). He wrote the latter book in the hope that 'a competent, practical, opportunist government class may rise to power' (p. 271). See also Chap. 3, 'Scientific Management and Public Administration', and Chap 6, 'Who Should Rule' of Dwight Waldo's *The Administrative State* (New York: 1948) for an excellent discussion of élitism in the study of Public Administration.

the manipulation of man and nature, it favours the externalization rather than the internalization of human impulses.'[1] But this points to a dilemma as well as to an opportunity, and to how dangerous and ambiguous is the 'power-élites' analysis with its stress on manipulation and activity while it refuses to ask the in part moral questions, 'for what purposes?' and 'within what limits?'—questions also a part of Western civilization. Lasswell does not come near to seriously considering these questions in his writings on power and élites.

The goal of 'one world' is not an answer, but an evasion of an answer—especially when 'ideological uniformity' and 'material standardization' are the conditions he thinks necessary for 'one world'. He can only assure us, what we hope because of such evasions is false, that *given* such a goal, social science can find the techniques.

What led to this strange if temporary flowering of Sorel and Mosca's dialectic reaction to Marxism in the intellectual companion of the great democrats, Merriam and T. V. Smith? In part, the 'tough-minded' factualism and 'Boss rule' consciousness of the old muck-rakers could prepare this ground. But this is clearly not a sufficient explanation. Lasswell's *World Politics and Personal Insecurity* is itself a kind of dialectic reaction against Wilson's liberal inter-nationalism, as well as a way of rejecting the content but accepting the broad method of Marxism. Earlier the Progressives had attacked the older Liberal-Republican educators as 'mere moralists' who would not face up to 'reality', facts brutal and sordid; but they had had a deep moralism of their own. Lasswell must have been trying to exorcise this underlying morality, especially what Mr. George Kennan has called the 'Wilsonian sentimentalism'. In doing so, he has to attack, for a while, the very notion of popular will and consent upon which the progressive reformers and social scientists had rested, substituting the harsh 'realistic' notion of élites and power. (His attitude is of a piece with the grim and cynical 'realistic' novels of the 'twenties and the stiff-jawed flirtations with Marxism by the intellectuals in the 'thirties.)

But whether the American climate in the long run starved the substance out of such concepts, or whether Lasswell was merely trying out a set of class-conscious European clothes which he after-wards had completely altered, certainly he has come to divorce the notion of an élite from that of a class entrenched in power, which it was to Mosca and Pareto. By 1952 he is actually protesting at the notion being regarded as undemocratic. Social mobility, he argues, means a rapidly changing élite, 'the élite of democracy (the ruling

[1] *Politics: Who Gets What*, p. 454.

class) is society wide'.[1] Now this is a very tame rabbit indeed, compared to the exciting human bestiary of Sorel and Pareto. The word 'élite' continues to resound through textbooks and classrooms of American political science and sociology but it merely allows students to indulge a belief in 'toughmindedness' while at the same time remaining good (but *realistic*) democrats—'you are all the élite'.

Now certainly Lasswell did a needed service in drawing attention —once again—to the type of person who is found in government and politics; but this problem can be stated in a less pretentious and misleading way. The conceptual rigidity of the initial claim that élites are universal, and the subsequent dilution of the concept rather than its frank rejection, has only delayed and obscured genuine thought on the role and stability of political leadership in a society of high social mobility. Nothing is more difficult than to persuade an American audience, academic or otherwise, that, for example, Soviet controls do not depend alone upon power as force, the Terror and the fear of the Purge, but also, unhappily, upon widespread consent. This is the failure of a liberal imagination to comprehend an illiberal world (as many American writers are now pointing out), but it is also due to the widespread teaching of a false theory of politics.[2] 'When we speak of the science of politics,' says Lasswell in 1949, 'we mean the science of power.' This is just not true, even for an understanding of his own writings, unless 'power', like 'élite', is so devalued and extended in meaning that it no longer bears its ordinary connotation. 'Power', wrote Lord Chesterfield to his godson, 'may fall to the share of a Nero or a Caligula, but *authority* can only be the attendant of the confidence that mankind have in your sense and virtue'.

3. The Language of Politics

'The central theme of this book is that political power can be better understood in the degree that language is better understood, and

---

[1] *Power and Personality*, pp. 202 ff.

[2] This is well pointed out in a review of W. W. Rostow's *The Dynamics of Soviet Society* (New York: 1953) by S. Hendel in *Soviet Studies*, VI (July 1954), 56–9. He criticizes the 'stark simplicity' of the view contained in the book that 'the history of Bolshevism and of the U.S.S.R. . . . may be understood, essentially, as a struggle for internal and external power—with all other considerations either subordinated or abandoned to the naked power drive'. Professor R. A. J. Schlesinger, in the next issue of the same journal (Oct. 1954), reviews Barrington Moore's *Terror and Progress: U.S.S.R.* (Cambridge, Mass.: 1953) in an article called 'Models and Facts'. He makes the same complaint about this 'intellectual framework which is shared by a majority of American students of the subject . . . that of "power pure and simple" ' (p. 135). Professor Schlesinger's own prejudices would only re-enforce the point. We should note, in fairness, that some brilliant American scholars of Soviet affairs, untouched by the scientific movement, have given in their own works a strong refutation of the power view. See, for example, Professor Merle Fainsod's *How Russia Is Ruled* (Cambridge, Mass.: 1953).

that the language of politics can be usefully studied by quantitative methods.'[1] It would hardly be possible even to envisage disagreement with the first assertion, if it was not so understood as to infer the second. Lasswell by 1949 had evidently read C. K. Ogden and I. A. Richards' *The Meaning of Meaning*, amid his restless search for concepts, and from it had added another layer of conceptual vocabulary to his already greatly reformed political discourse. But this was no road to Vincennes or sudden opening of Euclid for Lasswell; he had already shown a great interest in the manipulative use of 'symbols', slogans and 'key-words' in propaganda. (He saw early that it was no use investigating 'the facts' unless one can also learn how 'the facts' are communicated throughout society, and how their communication could be bettered.) But it enabled him to advance a general claim for the importance of 'Content Analysis' for political science. He claimed that by treating concepts as 'language' and not as 'meaning', that is, as 'signs, symbols or symbol-signs', the incidence of certain key political symbols could be studied quantitatively. In theory, if statistical methods grew refined enough, the degree of intensity could be measured by which nameable political 'values' are held by certain individuals or groups. This is the task of Content Analysis. The results of such studies might contribute 'to the problem of interpreting significant political trends'.

Obviously, in the study of propaganda—indeed, 'mass-communication media' in general—much interesting and often unexpected information can be gleaned by a quantitative listing according to *agreed* categories of *agreed* words or their *agreed* equivalents for some limited aspects of policy. We stress the amount of judgement needed even for the most elementary operation, but this is not to say that, for instance, we could not learn something about Nazi ideology if we had listed the number of times, to use Lasswellian phraseology, Fuehrer-symbols were used compared to Racial-symbols in a representative selection of Party speeches or newspapers. But the contributors to the volume were not able to advance any example of foretelling a future trend of policy in any situation at all. Lasswell adduces examples of similar methods in literary studies, without noting, however, that they are mostly concerned with the establishing and dating of a text, not with making a prediction. (Statistical techniques have been used in studies of imagery, for instance in Miss Carolyn Spurgeon's work on Shakespeare and Keats, but the inevitable inflexibility of categories has made them far from satisfactory.) Political terms, in proportion to their importance, are not likely to be interpreted quantitatively without large

[1] Lasswell, Nathan Leites and associates, *Language of Politics: studies in quantitative semantics* (New York: 1949), p. v.

(and finally decisive) classificatory assumptions. If we take our Fuehrer-Race question, for example, and ask help from the students of quantitative semantics in discovering which was the most important element in Nazi ideology, it is doubtful whether any quantitative answer could be given that does not raise more questions than it answers. How would, for instance, concepts like Hitler as *Volksvater* or '*Ein Volk, Ein Reich, Ein Fuehrer*', be classified? Can the latter synthesis of the dialectician be properly broken down into three countable components without distorting the style of ideology of which it forms a part?

Now, this example may be too complex for Content Analysis to deal with. The triviality or the tautologous character of the work produced in the volume in question is extreme. Its proponents, of course, are either concerned with useful commercial tasks much more humble and humdrum than Lasswell's vast claims justify, or else as social scientists they regard, as Lasswell often says, 'the perfection of the tool' as a slow prior step to the development of a significant science. As the opening sentence of the book shows, there is a great confusion between Lasswell's attempt to come to terms with what he regards as *modern* 'logical positivism' and his hopes still to create a quantitatively expressed general science of society, more after the pattern of the older Comtean positivism. However, despite this obvious confusion and the fact that several of his other conceptual frameworks are intellectually far stronger, Content Analysis has led to more actual research than any other of his frameworks. This, alas, is clearly due to the relative simplicity of conducting such research, not to the importance of the possible results.

The Hoover Institute Studies in Symbols bore out the above assertion.[1] In the Hoover studies, Professor Ithiel de Sola Pool was concerned to find out how many times 'symbols designating democracy' have been used in the national press of various countries, especially the Soviet Union. A. L. Lowell, in his pioneer studies in public opinion and politics, had insisted that the opinions reported must be genuinely reflective opinions in order to be anything more than profoundly ambiguous scratches upon paper. This did not deter Pool, who saw some unexplained value in establishing statistically that the Soviet press uses the word 'democracy' frequently—though not

[1] See especially the first two monographs in this series, Harold D. Lasswell *et al.*, *The Comparative Study of Symbols: An Introduction*; and Ithiel de Sola Pool *et al.*, '*Prestige Papers': a survey of their editorials* (Stanford University Press: 1950). These were part of a Carnegie financed project of the Hoover Institute, the 'RADIR' project (Revolution and the Development of International Relations). Series A are general; Series B are on élites; Series C, from which we draw our examples, are on symbols. The project subsequently moved to the Massachusetts Institute of Technology as part of M.I.T.'s programme to assure a well-rounded education to its students.

Consequences

as frequently as the American press, as he demonstrates. Of course, Pool knew what democracy *meant* already—the studies are, after all, concerned with symbols and language, not with meaning, for he allows himself the *obiter dicta*: 'If we classify the main elements in the modern Western conception of democracy [which he doesn't] we come up with three main constellations of ideas, namely: representative-government, freedom, and an orientation to the people' [1] —categories of crystal clarity.

He concluded his study on the 'symbols of democracy' by asking: 'What conclusions of broad social relevance has this effort provided?' And he answered: 'Broadly speaking, we have noticed an increasing concern with the notion of democracy. . . . Today the judgements expressed about democracy are strongly favourable, irrespective of the practice in a given country.' [2] To ask if any political inferences could follow from this would be an unfair question: the proposition is meant to stand as a monument to scientifically verified truth in the behavioural sciences.

It may be a plausible philosophical position to say that all we can mean by 'democracy' is what people do in fact mean by 'democracy', how they used the word in their ordinary discourse. But, even in this sense, we learn nothing significant by counting how many times they use it. Lasswell, torn between his desire to avoid 'meaningless' propositions in politics, as understood by modern positivism, and his desire to formulate general laws, in the manner of nineteenth-century positivism, poses questions that are in practice, if not in theory, meaningless, impossible to verify:

Our problem may therefore be posed as follows: Under what conditions do words affect power responses? If we let the 'power response' in which we are interested be referred to by the letter R, the problem is to find what words in the environment of the responders will affect R in one way rather than another, given certain predispositions on the part of the audience (other environmental factors being held constant). When will a revolutionary appeal be rejected or endorsed? A reformist appeal? An instigation to radical action? To moderate action? [3]

[1] Pool, *Symbols of Democracy*, Hoover Studies, Series C, p. 2.

[2] Pool notes that the procedure followed in this study was outlined by Harold D. Lasswell and that he drew up the list of symbols to be counted. The actual counting and tabulation was done by a staff of seven women (presumably stenographers) under Professor Daniel Lerner, utilizing, he tells us, 18,900 newspaper editorials.

[3] *Language of Politics*, p. 18. Cf. the Rev. Laurence Sterne on this general problem: 'Now there are such an infinitude of notes, tunes, cants, chants, airs, looks and accents with which the word *fiddlestick* may be pronounced in all such cases as this, every one of 'em impressing a sense and meaning as different from the other as *dirt* from *cleanliness*—that causists (for it is an affair of conscience upon that score) reckon up no less than fourteen thousand in which you may do either right or wrong.

'Mrs. Wadman hit upon the *fiddlestick* which summoned up all my Uncle Toby's modest blood into his cheeks. . . .' (From *The Life and Opinions of Tristram Shandy, Gentleman.*)

This is opening up new vistas for research with a vengeance, all equally hypothetical, like a parody of economic theory (one can suggest schemes for page after published page when their nature is such that no one could attempt them). And the style and background of such a statement is of the literature of pseudo-science, something dangerously open to sheer charlatanism. His best ideas are far better than this, but he himself seems incapable of distinguishing between the good and the bad in his work: he argues each 'conceptual framework' with the same earnest and laboured intensity.

Professor George Catlin, who often crops up as an authority in Lasswell's footnotes, has repaid the compliment and in so doing curiously exposed the ambivalence of the scientific school between the old and the new positivism. 'At Chicago and Yale', Catlin wrote, 'Professor H. D. Lasswell has used an admirable technique, adapted from the economists. It is a species of political logical positivism and involves a study of semantics.'[1] One sympathizes with Catlin; the difficulty with adopting 'logical positivism' as a symbol of modernism is that it is, after all (in so far as it now has a precise reference at all), *logical*, and not concerned with substantive meaning. Perhaps a *'political* logical positivism', such as Lasswell and he seem to want, will not suffer from the sterility of *logical* positivism as a guide to action. Professor Catlin evidently hopes for such a guide, for he remarks: '. . . what we require is not "no ideology", but a better ideology and one very carefully considered—at least as much as Marxism, the product of a century of brain work. We need a political logical positivism, a new political scholasticism, for a new world.'[2] This sort of nonsense is the great temptation of our age: that to 'defend' *political* freedom—which such crude reasonings show is a brittle achievement not to be taken for granted—we become ideologists ourselves, dupes of a frightened passion for a total certainty.

How well Lasswell's 'quantitative semantics' qualifies as 'political logical positivism' is hard to say, because his own ground shifts between the old and the new, between the positivistic and the sceptical. At first, we have seen, he asserts as a 'central theme' what are in fact two themes: the first, that a study of the language of politics is needed (presumably, at its best, akin to some of the work of the 'New Criticism' in literature); and the second, 'that the language of politics can be usefully studied by quantitative methods'.

---

[1] George Catlin, 'The Utility of Political Science', in Berger, Able and Page, *Freedom and Control in Modern Society* (New York: 1954), p. 266.

[2] *Ibid.*, p. 282. One wishes that Professor Catlin had expounded the nature of this 'new political scholasticism' more fully in his big book, *The Story of the Political Philosophers* (London: 1939). The whole enterprise of the book shows a fascinating ambivalence between, in his own words, the 'rational Grand Tradition of Culture' and 'the beginnings of a Science of Politics' (p. x).

But by the third chapter Lasswell has merged these two propositions together and can assert: 'The point of view of this book is that the study of politics can be advanced by the quantitative method of political discourse.'[1] And this, to judge by the other contributions, is the fairer statement of the viewpoint of the book. They are all concerned with the theory or practice of Content Analysis; there are no analytical essays on 'Seven Types of Ambiguity in the Phrase "New Deal"', for instance; there is no 'Well Wrought Urn', only the compilation of ashes. Between the opening chapter, 'The Language of Power', and the third chapter, 'Why Be Quantitative?', there is, more promisingly, a chapter on 'Style in the Language of Politics'. He draws some obvious contrasts between the style of the proclamation of the Imperial Durbar in Delhi in 1911 and some writings of the Mahatma Gandhi and of Nehru. He well shows that style is more than the sum of the meanings of the separate words in a writing, and is a part of meaning and effect; but he then does *not* make any attempt to relate this to the quantitative procedures of Content Analysis, which, being based on disparate words or phrases, ignores the question of style. 'In the long run . . . the study of style may make its largest contribution in relation to the problem of interpreting significant political trends,' he asserts,[2] but does not square this with his similar earlier claim about the content analysis of key symbols.[3] Clearly, an analysis of a political writer's style can be a useful clue to his calibre and integrity—as various essays by such writers as George Orwell, Leslie Fiedler, Lionel Trilling, F. O. Matthiessen and Edmund Wilson have tellingly shown. (It is a pity that Lasswell has never written on such figures as political critics and commentators, nor any of them on Lasswell as a writer.)

In the chapter on 'Why Be Quantitative?' he argues that 'quantitative method' as well as reducing 'the margin of uncertainty in the basic data', will also aid 'the special objectives of humane politics'. 'Whatever improves our understanding of attitude is a potential instrument of humane politics. Up to the present, physical science has not provided us with means of penetrating the skull of a human being and directly reading off his experience. Hence we are compelled', he continues, 'to rely on indirect means of piercing the wall that separates him from us. Words provide us with clues . . .'— hence, quantitative semantics can aid a 'humane politics': 'a commonwealth in which the dignity of man is accepted in theory and fact'. But, in the midst of this *tour de force* of quasi-totalitarian reasoning, he remembers himself, and adds in a rare explanatory *footnote*:

There is, of course, no implication that non-quantitative methods should

[1] *Language of Politics*, p. 40.   [2] *Ibid.*, p. 38.   [3] *Ibid.*, pp. 14–15.

be dropped. On the contrary, there is need of more systematic theory and of more luminous 'hunches' if the full potentialities of precision are to be realized in practice. As the history of quantification shows (in economics, for instance), there is a never-ending, fruitful interplay between theory, hunch, impression and precision.[1]

There is that difficulty with the meaning of Lasswell's writings which Falstaff found in the size of Mistress Quickly. 'Luminous hunches' are then admissible, even desirable; but what of a systematic analysis of the *meaning* of political concepts—or are political concepts only meaningful as *hypotheses* for quantitative verification? At times he seems to suggest the latter; but then can 'the dignity of man' be verified, or is it more than a luminous hunch? But these questions are beyond the pale of the *Language of Politics*. In the *Policy Sciences* and other later writings he is more aware of them and attempts an answer.

4. The Policy Sciences

In *The Policy Sciences, Recent Developments in Scope and Method* (1951), Lasswell set out to show that the most scientific of the several social sciences were not purely methodological and conceptual, as was being increasingly murmured, but were intensely practical. However, it did not lay the ghost—as the subtitle indicates; it was more concerned to give a new explanation for its appearance. But there is no need to press this point; we should accept Lasswell's contention as best explaining his work: that a methodological reformation must precede any approach to the 'world revolutionary process of our epoch'.

Lasswell, paradoxically, always showed some signs of striving to break from the self-imposed bonds of his own sharp distinction between 'political science' and 'political doctrine'. Undoubtedly, he was affected somewhat like Merriam by the threatening international events of the late 'thirties. He began to affirm the direct practicality of the 'science of politics' and also its commitment to a particular view of man. In 1942 he wrote:

With the more inclusive science of politics many special sciences are possible. A special science is concerned with the fulfilment and preservation of specific forms of state and society. The science of democracy—one of those special sciences—bears much the same relation to general political science that medicine has to biology.[2]

[1] *Ibid.*, p. 51.
[2] *Analysis of Political Behaviour*, p. 7 (these are collected papers, so the dates differ). His use of 'with' is unhappily vague. To say 'within' would imply a subordination of the 'science of democracy' which he evidently wishes to avoid. To say 'along with' would make them of co-ordinate status, which logically is untenable. He is probably using 'with' in the very broad and vague sense of 'in the circumstances of'.

The first two sentences seem to imply that there are or could be an Authoritarian and also a Totalitarian applied science of politics— perhaps even a science of Parliamentary Government as distinct from Congressional Government. But then to use the analogy of 'medicine . . . to biology' seems to narrow the field to one, unless Authoritarianism and Totalitarianism become Faith Healing and allied quackeries. This analogy may, however, just be a very loose *façon de parler*, or an anticipation of what only later he sets out to prove. '*One* of those special sciences' should clearly be taken at its face value until he explicitly changes his viewpoint. Thus the 'Policy Sciences' (his plural refers to disciplines and not to different forms of society) appear not as pure knowledge, but as applied knowledge; and 'the science of democracy' at first appears to be a thing relative, contingent to an already existing democratic society (which seems to jar with his and Merriam's early view that science must change this society utterly).

Professor David Easton, also anxious to create the theoretical basis for a science of politics, has pinned his main hope on Lasswell, but has implored him to make up his mind on this very issue. Lasswell, he says, 'vacillates between a relativistic Weberian approach and a scientific attempt to validate values'.[1]

In *The Policy Sciences*, then, Lasswell appears at first to adopt a relativistic viewpoint: 'It is probable that the policy-science orientation in the United States will be directed towards providing the knowledge needed to improve the practice of democracy.' But, the very next sentence continues: 'In a word, the special emphasis [of the book] is upon the policy sciences of democracy, in which the ultimate goal is the realization of human dignity in theory and fact.'[2] 'Human dignity', whatever it means, as the essence of democracy, is surely put forward as an absolute value. He had already said that since 'the dominant American tradition affirms the dignity of man, not the superiority of one set of men's influence . . . emphasis will be upon the development of knowledge pertinent to the fuller realization of human dignity.' So the earlier sense of a peculiar American manifest destiny which had mingled with the scientific movements and the sociologists of progress, is now continued by Lasswell— together with, apparently, a continued implicit belief in 'natural rights', although what exactly he means by 'dignity of man' is far from clear.

This is a matter of no small importance. To elucidate the meaning of 'dignity of man' seems a proper end for a critical activity, not an

[1] Easton, 'Harold Lasswell: Policy Scientist', *op. cit.*, p. 34.
[2] *Policy Sciences*, p. 15. C. J. Friedrich observes, in a masterly review, that on this shaky proposition Lasswell 'builds his entire approach'. 'Policy—A Science?', *Public Policy*, IV (1953), 269–81.

unexplained beginning. Professor Lasswell does not then go on to prove himself a Kantian of note. Instead, there is a curious attempt to point to a precise creative moment of history that seemingly forever defines American values:

> When the scientist is recommended to take note of value objectives, he quickly discovers conflicts within his own culture and personality. . . . In a word, there are legacies from a world of caste which prevailed before the French and American revolutions gave impetus to the idea of social mobility on the basis of individual merit.[1]

This is a new *laissez-faire* dressed as sociology; it is a gross historical over-simplification; and it is a quasi-Marxist assumption that conflicts of value only exist in a 'caste' society (for by 'caste' he surely means no more than 'class', except to give an exotic inter-disciplinary lilt to his sentence). It betrays an apparent lack of any feeling for the differences between the Anglo-American and the French revolutionary tradition. The idea of 'social mobility on the basis of individual merit' could be, it is true, both that of Napoleon and of Jefferson, but the setting of each is so different that the same stone is not the same jewel. This rationalistic and revolutionary interpretation of the American War of Independence seems an essential prior belief for the plausibility of a science of politics. That American politics has in fact been more of an unbroken tradition than the social scientists were willing to recognize, and has contained more consciousness of moral limitations also, is probably the main reason why they themselves have in fact hedged or avoided the explicit illiberalism of French St. Simonian and Comtean thought.

The title of Lasswell's contribution to the *Essays in Honour of Charles Merriam* was actually 'The Developing Science of Democracy' (he says 'of', not merely 'for'). In the *Policy Sciences* his possible qualification that 'the policy science of democracy' is only one type of social science for one society wears fairly thin by the concluding chapter. From beneath his scientific garments the aura of the divinely annointed democrat shines forth to give even the most statistically minded of the contributors the flushed face of virtue, if not the blush of innocence. By the end of the book, democracy and science are indistinguishably interwoven, a cloak of authority that is pictured as being able to ensure a unified democratic world. And, again, the whole argument can scarcely be understood but for the strong undercurrent of a belief in a necessary progress: 'The forecast remains,' he says; 'the world is moving toward homogeneous social structure, regardless of whether political unipolarity

---

[1] *Policy Sciences*, p. 10.

is early or late.' Lasswell certainly notes that there are great difficulties along the road to this goal, but, given more scientific method, it can be reached: 'Our review of world trends toward bipolarity and toward scientific and democratic homogeneity has shown how often they can interfere with one another. A new level of techno-scientific culture must be shared widely before its full benefits can be attained.'[1]

This is a large point of substance to emerge from what is in largest part a treatise on scope and method. Even if it is granted that *given* the goals, the means can be arrived at scientifically, his claim remains an example of how much disagreement there is likely to be about the content of those 'goals' (even granting also that 'goals' can be sensibly formulated in such a manner at all).[2] There should now be little doubt that to draw up a new method and a new scope of political analysis and research is, in fact, to presuppose desired conclusions, though not necessarily precise, meaningful or widely acceptable conclusions. When research takes place under specific instructions towards a precise and limited end, there seems little to cavil at if it is called 'scientific' *in a popular sense*, and if the researchers, as, for instance, many U.S. State Legislative (Research) Councils, claim that their work is 'purely factual' and 'applied science'. But, as the above quotations illustrate, Lasswell's aims are not so modest: he is not interested in making research a tool of an existing politics, but rather in the creation of a new scientific world society and a *bi*-polar (a concession to reality) politics. He does make clear that his conclusion is a 'forecast' and not a 'law', but a 'forecast' nevertheless is not a 'prophecy'. We might agree, on general grounds of history and experience, that his forecast seems likely—alarmingly likely for those who have a taste for diversity, not integration. But before we can make a reasoned judgement on whether Lasswell's 'techno-scientific culture' is the vision of the Millennium or of *1984*, we must examine what he means by 'the dignity of man'. This can only be inferred from his writings; he does not directly tell us. But it is perfectly clear that he attaches 'value' to the phrase: it vibrates in his style as something more than an hypothesis that x per cent of Americans or American social scientists believe that man is dignified. To look at his concept of 'the dignity of man' is also, then, to look at his concept of 'value', which is also to understand his mode of inference between policy and science, or science and policy.

Quite simply he says: 'By a value we mean an object of human

[1] *Policy Sciences*, p. 116.
[2] Max Weber has written that 'the inversion of "cause and effect" propositions into "means-ends" propositions is possible whenever the effect in question can be stated precisely'. ['The Meaning of Ethical Neutrality', *The Methodology of the Social Sciences*, translated by E. Shils and H. A. Finch (Glencoe, Ill.: 1949).] Can such a large goal as Lasswell's be termed 'precise'?

desire.' 'Three values', he says, 'may be named whose proper relationship determines whether we are justified in calling any group democratic. The values are power, respect and knowledge. Where the dignity of man is taken into account . . . such values are widely shared in a free society.' ¹ It would be less confusing if he called these values, 'preferences'; he could then retain 'the dignity of man' alone as a 'value'—it is clearly prior to the 'values' he names. Thus he can speak of 'morals', but these morals are purely socially derived.

Such a belief, or nexus of 'values', is the 'starting point' or 'goal value' for his 'hypothetical constructs'. 'How do we go about', he asks, 'inventing and evaluating hypothetical constructs about our epoch? Our reply: select according to goal values.' ² Here his concept of 'value' and of 'hypothetical constructs' seems akin to that of Economic Theory, but he never pauses to note the different nature of the subject matter; nor the limiting assumptions that the economists themselves generally recognize; nor yet, connected with this last point, the greater modesty and caution in the conclusions of most modern economists.³

This selection 'according to goal values' is a reinterpretation, at least, of his earlier pure scientism (and his scientific élite now seem limited in their initiative to inventing techniques of finding out what really are 'the goal values' of a majority or of a consensus of society). He can now specifically assert that the science of politics reaches its highest form in progressive American thought:

> By taking human dignity as our central focus, we are in step with the ideal values of the American tradition, and with the progressive ideologies of our epoch. Liberalism and socialism are united in affirming the free man's commonwealth as a goal of human society. That man's dignity is not to be realized in this world is the principal forecast of whoever takes a dim view of human perfectability.⁴

This assertion of a 'central focus' if it is central to anything must be central between the 'starting point' or 'base line' and the 'dignity' which is *to be* realized. In other words, this 'dignity', unlike the *essential* worth of man' that many publicists take from the Christian tradition, is a *potential* to be realized and not an *essence*, something that can neither be created nor destroyed. Perhaps this is to press his words too closely, but it is to show that his base line becomes

---

¹ *Analysis of Political Behaviour*, p. 36. The list of 'values' is sometimes more extended. In Appendix A of *The World Revolution of Our Times: a Framework for Basic Policy Research* (Stanford: 1951) he lists the criteria of these 'basic goal values': Power, Respect, Rectitude, Affection, Well-Being, Wealth, Skill, and Enlightenment.
² *World Revolution*, p. 5.
³ See, for instance, Gunnar Myrdal, *The Political Element in the Development of Economic Theory* (London: 1953).
⁴ *World Revolution*, p. 8.

something other than the Natural Rights tradition, the self-evident propositions of 1776, as we have previously interpreted it. It is, on closer inspection, an immanence that will result in a complete reconstruction of all values: T. V. Smith's 'beyond conscience', the 'techno-scientific culture', the withering away of those who, like the framers of the Federal Constitution, specifically take 'a dim view of human perfectability'. Theoretically speaking, his identification of values with preferences and of all morality with the method of science will only be naturalistically true in the future 'homogeneous social structure'. In the long meantime he can still consistently hold, as he certainly does, to his distrust of evaluative philosophy.[1]

Despite his talk of 'ideal values' he strives to retain his 'naturalism of discourse' by distinguishing 'goal thinking' from 'trend thinking' and 'scientific thinking', the latter two being 'naturalistic'.[2] Therefore, in his *World Revolution of Our Times,* he treats the 'ideal values' of American democracy as themselves, in an anthropological sense, 'myths'. In the 'Criteria of Basic Goal Values', which he offers in Appendix A, he qualifies every assertion—often sensible and interesting judgements about what people commonly think of as desirable attitudes—by saying: 'according to the prevailing myth'. The order of values within the myth is, of course, 'to be ascertained by empirical investigation'. One is tempted to say that the only way this concept could gain naturalistic meaning is when the other meaning of 'prevailing' is realized: success would create its own order.

'A legitimate aim of education', he tells us, 'is to seek to promote the major values of a democratic society and to reduce the number of moral mavericks who do not share the democratic preferences.' This sentence could be innocuous or empty, but when he seems to deny any distinction between value and preference (indeed here he uses the words as synonyms!) and has such grandiose goals for 'the science of democracy', then one sees the uncomprehended inner-logic of a tyranny of public opinion (democratic values 'empirically derived'), administered and justified by a class who would seem to be the dialectic synthesis of the bureaucrats and *les idéologues,* the Lasswellian social scientist. Presumably among these 'moral mavericks', by his own logic, are all those who take 'a dim view of human perfectability'. The Founding Fathers and most practising Christians would be discouraged from joining Lasswell's dignified herd.

However, though there is this inner-logic of political doctrine in his work, we have still not understood an inner-logic of theory. It is a theory that he himself may not have adequately comprehended,

[1] See the section called 'Transcendence' in *World Revolution,* pp. 2–3. 'Theological conceptions typically invoke "God" as the key symbol. . . .', etc.
[2] *Analysis of Political Behaviour,* pp. 92–3.

but which, nevertheless, underlies the claim of the whole scientific school and is a far stronger claim than any of his fully articulated 'conceptual frameworks'. After all, if there is still not a suppressed consistency, how can a man sensibly believe that moral problems are resolvable merely by empirical investigation? As often as he tries to merge values with preferences, the concepts fly apart, incorrigibly—as when he speaks of the 'ideal values' of American life or says: 'Science can ascertain the means appropriate to the completion of the moral impulse—means at once consistent with the general definitions of morality and compatible with the fulfilment of moral purpose.' [1] To consider whether he can ever hope to resolve these paradoxes is to consider the meaning of his continued interest in psychology, specifically in psychoanalysis, a life-long interest and advocacy that here finds its deeper relevance both for his own work and for the interpretation put upon factual research by the whole scientific school.

5. The Therapeutic Image

From the time of Walter Lippmann's *Preface to Politics* (1913), many American political scientists had been greatly fascinated by the new schools of psychology. In what Ward had called 'the psychic factors' they hoped to find the *real* level of reality that would best explain both behaviour and ideas. It would seem that where there is a society in which individualism is claimed by publicists to be both non-doctrinal and universally shared, and in which social scientists profess to avoid moral commitments at all, then this individualism is inevitably reduced to 'personality structure' as 'the ultimate explanation': in understanding human nature, philosophy is reduced to psychology; just as in understanding society as a whole, politics is reduced to sociology. For most political scientists psychoanalysis was to be, as William James in his old age had told Freud, the 'Psychology of the future'. But it was a use of psychoanalytical theory that leapt far beyond the patient clinical practice of Freud, or even his late-period speculative essay on *Civilization and Its Discontents*. 'Political prejudices, preferences and creeds', wrote Lasswell in 1930, 'are often formulated in highly rational form, but they are grown in highly irrational ways. When they are seen against the developmental history of the person, they take on meanings which are quite different from the phrases in which they are put.' [2] However, by 1950, he is warning that in the 'experience of American political scientists' psychology will achieve the best results when taken 'not as a synonym for the entire field of politics, but rather as a set of tools for disclosing new facts or suggesting new interpretations'. He noted that: 'If

[1] *Ibid.*, p. 1.   [2] *Psychopathology and Politics*, p. 153.

this is a more modest conception than has been promulgated in the past, it is not tantamount to a declaration that the contributions of psychology to American political science or policy are trivial.'[1] Just what these contributions are, he does not say; but, again, it is a methodological claim that he makes—a claim that conceals a deeper theory or analogy.

We have already noted at some length the importance of the belief in Progress in reconciling, psychologically at least, pure scientific research with moral conduct. If we ask, 'What is the mechanism of progress?', the answer appears either as 'natural selection', for Spencer and Sumner; or as a cumulative and directed 'co-operative intelligence', for Dewey and his followers. But there is another type of reconciliation at least logically independent of 'Progress'. This compares or even identifies the purely descriptive and 'objective', factual study of politics with the psychiatric situation, as *therapeutic*. The psychiatrist deals with the irrational by what is recognized as reasonable procedure: expressed at its simplest, by the mere uncovering of hidden information. He does not try to exhort or force a pattern of rationality upon the patient (in the manner that Lasswell pictures the authoritarianism of political philosophers); he merely tries to make a diagnosis by uncovering a deeper mental reality, and the making of this diagnosis is, in the patient's new awareness, a return to rationality. The diagnosis, when made by analyst *and* patient, *is* the cure. Therefore, or similarly, the objective discovery of how the political process really works is in itself a rationalizing process, given that the groups and individuals studied either participate in the process of study or are made aware of the findings (hence the vast and recent interest in 'communications research' and 'propaganda'). So, just as the psychiatrist is not an indoctrinating agent, the activity of the political scientist is held to be neither ideological nor purely pedagogic, but therapeutic: the study of practical politics is ultimately the practice of a higher politics. *Any* objective investigation into the 'political process' is a contribution, great or small, to a 'rationalizing' process.

Now, Lasswell does *not* ever explicitly say this so precisely. But two obvious general points convince us of the propriety of such an interpretation. Firstly, there is clearly at work, amid the contradictions of the many 'conceptual frameworks' which he himself explicitly advances, some underlying, half-understood, principle of consistency. Secondly, he explicitly hopes to gain the kind of under-

[1] UNESCO, *Contemporary Political Science*, p. 527. This is as near as he ever comes to a *personal* retraction or modification. He notes correctly that the Political Science department at Chicago was the centre in the inter-war years 'of the movement to explore the significance of psychology for politics. Charles E. Merriam was the significant figure' (p. 536).

standing and results in politics that the psychoanalyst can gain in his individual clinical practice.

The chapter called 'The Politics of Prevention' in his *Psychopathology and Politics* saved that book from being merely a series of disparate case studies of neurotic and even psychotic politicians, such as to leave one otherwise with the general impression that the quest for power and public office is always a form of disease. He argued that the traditional 'political methods of coercion, exhortation and discussion' assume that politics can only solve problems when they have happened. 'The ideal of a politics of prevention is to obviate conflict by the definite reduction of the tension level of society by effective methods, of which discussion will be but one.' He continues: 'The preventive politics of the future will be intimately allied to general medicine, psychopathology, physiological psychology, and related disciplines. Its practitioners will gradually win respect in society among puzzled people who feel their responsibilities and who respect objective findings.' [1] And he adds: 'politics is the process by which the irrational basis of society is brought out into the open'.

This hope for the 'obviation of conflict' in social life is, to the extent to which Lasswell presses it, of the stuff of Utopias, not of moderate reform.[2] And its fulfilment depends not upon direct political action in a Marxist manner, but upon a technique of research and education of social scientists, something akin, at least superficially, to the patient, detailed and modest-sounding work of Freud. 'The achievement of the ideal of preventive politics', he clearly tells us, 'depends less upon changes in social organization than on improving the methods and the education of social administrators and social scientists.'[3]

The claim, then, is no small claim, and it has an engaging simplicity and reasonableness. Without this concept of 'therapeutic action' it is hard to imagine why normally intelligent and moral men are so deeply enthusiastic in limiting their life work to purely descriptive, purely factual studies.[4] And this claim is another way

---

[1] *Psychopathology and Politics*, p. 202.

[2] Lasswell wrote the article on 'Conflict' in the *Encyclopaedia of the Social Sciences* (New York: 1930), V, 194–6. It brings out clearly how large a role 'the obviation of conflict' plays in his thought. It begins: 'Social conflict results from the conscious pursuit of exclusive values.' He notes that the 'philosophy of compromise . . . seems to concede in advance that there is no truly inclusive set of social aims'. He hopes: 'It may be that the manipulation of collective opinion for the sake of raising the prestige of science will contribute towards this sense of unity of man with man', which will obviate conflict—and presumably liberty too.

[3] *Psychopathology*, p. 202.

[4] G. E. G. Catlin also appears to assume the 'therapeutic image' in his *A Study of the Principles of Politics, being an Essay Toward Political Rationalization* (New York: 1930); see especially the last two pages, 458–9 (despite his earlier warning against sweeping uses of psychology, p. 30).

of fulfilling the deep hope that we have seen throughout the scientific movement, of superseding politics as a mode of social activity. He can speak of 'the political personality' who fails to adopt 'images of authority' as part of the self and thus 'construes the social process as a vast arena of conflict'.[1]

So, as he tells us that the main role of a 'preventive politics' is to relieve tension by removing conflict, his 'preventive politics' presupposes that ordinary politics is an irrational sickness that needs to be cured. This claim parallels the epistemological claim of the modern 'Linguistic' school of philosophers: that philosophy is a therapy to restore language to practical and normal usage from the incursions of carelessness, metaphysics and moral philosophy. The therapeutic intent of Lasswell's work is a plausible and pleasant thing; we can eschew doctrinal politics and the uncertainties of mere discussion and yet, at the same time, act vigorously by the prosecution of research towards making a brave new world free from conflict. 'The whole aim of the scientific study of society', Lasswell says, is only, in its immediate task, 'to make the obvious inescapable'.[2]

Before examining more closely the therapeutic view of research, we should pause for a moment to show its relevance to Lasswell's concept of 'freedom'—a concept, after all, not unimportant to any writer on politics. We have already noted his reassuring remark that 'the role of scientific work in human relations is *freedom* rather than prediction'. Now we can cite his definition of freedom in full:

> By freedom is meant the bringing into the focus of awareness of some feature of the personality which has hitherto operated as a determining factor upon the choices made by an individual, but which has been operating unconsciously. Once elevated to the full focus of waking consciousness, the factor which has been operating 'automatically and compulsively' is no longer in this privileged [*sic*] position. The individual is now free to take the factor into consideration in the making of future choices.[3]

Leaving aside the fact that this is where the problem of *political* freedom begins, not ends (indeed to some, of moral freedom also), this would be, if taken literally, a description of a breakdown of *all* inhibitions, a kind of uncontrolled explosion of psychic energy, unless some rationalizing and therapeutic factor was assumed—as

[1] 'Effect of Personality on Political Participation', in the Christie and Jahoda, *Studies in . . . Scope and Method*, p. 209. See also *The Democratic Character*, the third vol. in Lasswell's *Political Writings*, p. 498: 'The psychiatrist feels at home in the study of ardent seekers after power in the arena of politics because the physician recognizes the extreme egocentricity and sly ruthlessness of some of the paranoid patients with whom he has come in contact in the clinic.'

[2] *Psychopathology and Politics*, p. 250. ('Freedom consists in the recognition of necessity'? No, of course, he doesn't *really* mean this.)

[3] *Political Writings* (the *Democratic Character*), p. 524.

obviously it is. For he then immediately speaks of such freedom leading to 'the more perfect realization of democratic values'.[1]

This therapeutic presupposition of Lasswell's is of such general importance to the idea of a science of politics—indeed of positivism in its widest sense—that we now need to examine some statements of the 'therapeutic' viewpoint more explicit and intensive than can be found in Lasswell. Undoubtedly, research can have therapeutic effects in many small groups: numerous studies attest this.[2] Perhaps such an effect can be obtained in any small group discussion *where all are well known to each other* (as Aristotle remarks of the maximum size of the just *Polis*). There is, indeed, an unhappy tendency for the European student of politics to give the genteel groan of agreement to any attack on such studies, however ignorant and prejudiced. It is, however, no accident that there are no such examples of thera-peutic research to be found in relation to any significant political problem: the difference in scale is decisive. But still, their cumulative utility could be far greater for *social studies* and they do furnish a clue, analogy or method for Lasswell's vision of a total planned analysis of society, or the 'general theory of society' of which some of his followers and other parallel minds now speak.

But there are two grave objections to this whole analogy drawn from psychoanalysis. The first is perhaps only a practical one: that for it to be a true analogy, research in political science would have to involve the 'subject' or 'subjects' far more than at the moment seems possible. Lasswell looks at psychoanalysis almost exclusively from the analyst's point of view, despite his reputation as a dis-tinguished lay analyst. But this could be answered on traditional democratic lines; Lasswell could find many passages in his later works urging greater public participation in politics—we have already noted his ambivalence between direct-democracy and élitism. But the second objection is an objection in principle.

[1] Compare this to Freud himself as shown in a letter to James J. Putnam, his early American disciple, reproving his over-great hopes:
'The unworthiness of human beings, even of analysts, has always made a deep impression on me, but why should analysed people be altogether better than others? Analysis makes for *unity*, but not necessarily for *goodness*. I do not agree with Socrates and Putnam that all our faults arise from confusion and ignorance. I think that too heavy a burden is laid on analysis when one asks of it that it should be able to realize every precious ideal' [quoted by Ernest Jones, *The Life and Work of Sigmund Freud* (New York: 1955), II, 182].
The point is not that Lasswell differs from Freud—which for us is unimportant: but that Freud's view is far more sensible!
[2] For example, Jacob L. Moreno, *Who Shall Survive? A new approach to the problem of human interrelations* (New York: 1934) and *Sociometric Control Studies in grouping and regrouping with reference to authoritative and democratic methods of grouping* (New York: 1947); Elton Mayo, *The Human Problems of an Industrial Civilization* (New York: 1933) and *The Social Problems of an Industrial Civilization* (Boston: 1945; London: 1949); and Alexander H. Leighton, *The Governing of Men* (New York: 1946).

We have already touched upon the objection in its most general form. 'How, in scientific terms, can a problem be selected as significant for investigation?' Lasswell has replied that we should accept democratic values (though he is ambivalent as to whether these are wholly or partly an ideal or a social construction). Now, in a rule-of-thumb sense, this is not difficult advice to follow; but it is notoriously very difficult to decide what is *un*democratic behaviour—who are Lasswell's 'moral mavericks'? *So the precise problem is to find out how the 'political therapeutist' defines significant deviation, or, in terms of the analogy, disease.* This is crucial. Unless there is a clear and acceptable standard of 'normal' behaviour in psychoanalysis itself, we are no better off than before in the attempt to find, as a product of factual research, a naturalistic ethics for politics.

To Freud himself all life was potential disease, and what is recognized as disease by society and the doctor is a breakdown in the psychic mechanisms of social adjustment. Freud had stressed that 'it is not scientifically feasible to draw a line of demarcation between what is psychologically normal and what is abnormal . . . the distinction, in spite of its practical importance, possesses only a conventional value'. He spoke of the 'neurotic ego [being] . . . not any longer able to fulfil the task set to it by the external world (including human society)'.[1] And, of course, in practice psychiatrists take their view of what constitutes disease and thus normality from their understanding of the conventions of the society in which they live (although a 'preventative medicine' would raise a more difficult problem). But to extend this practice from the individual patient to the group and then to the concept of politics in general, this is to pass more and more away from an easy commonsensical judgement. For it is precisely how political authority may legitimately determine those limits of deviation beyond which the normal and acceptable becomes disease that are the subjects of the fiercest political dispute and the greatest disagreement about what constitutes evidence. 'The nature of the normal' has, in a vital sense, been the major problem of all great *political* thinkers, their dominant and necessary theme. In this prior question the task of history and philosophy in elucidating the rationality of tradition seems pre-eminent; and yet these are the very ways of knowing what the science of politics seeks to replace.

Lasswell himself gives no thought to this problem and, surprisingly, although in the United States both field research in the social sciences based on psychological premises and on the actual practice of psychoanalysis far outstrips any in Europe, this fundamental

---

[1] Sigmund Freud, *Outline of Psycho-Analysis* (London: 1928), see pp. 7, 20, 26, 46 and 64 for definitions of the *normal*. See also Ernest Jones, 'The Concept of a Normal Mind', *International Journal of Psycho-Analysis* (XXIII), 1942.

problem has been most seriously considered by some British writers.[1] British psychiatrists, after the Nazi victory in Germany and the occupation of Austria, had a close-at-hand responsibility thrust upon them—symbolized by the presence of the refugee Freud. From these events arose an obvious dilemma: 'would or should analysis of a Nazi in Germany leave him a Nazi still? Might not even an analysis of a dissident Bavarian liberal, say, make him, on the "conventional" view of normality, a good Nazi?'

Roger Money-Kyrle is sure that there is an answer in terms of psychiatric theory.[2] He advances the view that 'philosophic-liberalism' or 'humanism' is closer to the *ego* reality structure than the *super-ego* fantasy mechanisms of the Totalitarian State. 'We can now be certain', he asserts, 'that the characteristic of a non-humanist opponent is an elaborate defence against unconscious and ultimately irrational anxieties within himself.' [3] His confidence in this was re-enforced by the very practical task of creating de-Nazification tests for the Allied Control Commission in Germany. There he was faced by the problem that although he felt that he could make a scientific judgement from an interview and questionnaire about whether the subject was an incorrigible Nazi or not, yet still, by the terms of this technique, he wondered if he had any moral right to make such a judgement which would involve political penalties for the subject. But he is able to conclude that psychoanalytical theory does show the non-humanist as irrational, and analysis does produce desired results, all without any moral intent by the analyst. He says that to assert that desirable ends can be furthered when their nature is unknown may sound paradoxical; but analysts do this constantly and the more they stick to the task of helping the patient to discover the unconscious impulses that influence his conscious thoughts and acts, and the less they intrude their own wishes, the more likely they will be to cure the patient 'with some changes of character that are welcome to themselves as well':

That such changes turn out to be in the humanist direction must also be welcome to the analyst. But this is not something he deliberately tries to

[1] See: H. V. Dicks, 'Personality Traits and National Socialist Ideology', *Human Relations*, III (London: 1950); Ernest Jones, 'Evolution and Revolution', *International Journal of Psycho-Analysis*, XXII (1942); Roger Money-Kyrle, *Psycho-Analysis and Politics* (London: 1951); J. T. MacCurdy, 'Psychology and Politics', being three posthumous articles edited from his unfinished manuscript, *British Journal of Psychology*, XL and XLI (1950).

[2] MacCurdy expressed well the conventional view of most British and American psychiatrists: 'In making his diagnosis the psychiatrist, like the layman, uses as a standard of comparison the hypothetical normality of the average member of the community. . . . This limit (of encouraged differences) is not set by the psychiatrist, not by a court, but is the consensus of opinion characteristic of an age or community' (*ibid.*, XL, 99).

[3] *Psycho-Analysis and Politics*, p. 139.

bring about. He does not try to force any particular character on anybody, both because he knows he would probably fail and ruin his analytic work, and because such a totalitarian use of moral force is incompatible with his own psychology.[1]

Now this is precisely the natural bridge between morality and research that Lasswell seeks. But the difficulty we have raised still remains. Money-Kyrle has only shifted it to the notoriously vexed point as to whether the 'ego reality structure', which he sees as being close to 'philosophic-liberalism', is itself a culturally determined factor or not. If it is, he would still have no 'right' to jeopardize the life, liberty or property of any Nazi, although we would then expect this as *his* 'normal' behaviour, as an English liberal. He seeks to meet this difficulty, however, and makes clear that to him: 'Normality in the psychoanalytic sense is not an average but an optimum. . . . Optimum normality might be described as optimum freedom from unconscious fantasy.'[2] Later, he argues that if competing political groups had more psychoanalytical insight they would be able to discuss their rivalries: ' . . . in an atmosphere of greater realism, and with much more mutual sympathy and less tension. . . . Since such group relations would be the result of replacing false by true pictures of, or beliefs about, our own and other groups, they could be described as rational, or, what is the same thing, the clinically normal.'[3]

So the question of rationality can be reduced, according to Money-Kyrle, not to a relativism of group ethos, but to the corrigible truth or falsehood of certain (presumably significant) beliefs of a culture. This is the *clinically* normal. We are acting unreasonably when we hold verifiably false beliefs that involve us in unpleasant consequences. When at the end of his book we learn that psychoanalysis is aimed at the exposure of error and delusion, just as 'what is called political analysis is likely to be socially therapeutic, and so worth pursuing on its own account', we learn that we have learned very little more than we knew already. And the dilemma which underlies the simplest formulation of this 'therapeutic image' remains, for we are not told how the 'clinically normal' of political analysis is derived. What Money-Kyrle has really succeeded in doing is to show that there is no incompatibility between psychoanalysis and 'liberal-humanism', but he has not shown that there is a necessary relationship between them, nor that either or both exhaust the class of all possible types of political legitimacy. For his remark about political

---

[1] *Psycho-Analysis and Politics*, pp. 148–9.
[2] 'A Psycho-Analytic Contribution to Ethics', *British Journal of Medical Psychiatry*, XX (1944), 38.
[3] *Psycho-Analysis and Politics*, p. 105.

analysis being *likely* to be socially therapeutic, he offers no adequate ground. It is difficult to see how he can, while he believes that all rational political doctrines must be empirically verifiable as true or false to have meaning or utility. They must be a 'true or false' picture—of what? He wishes by psychoanalysis to emancipate politics from a purely historical understanding—'traditional determinism', as he says—but he is never specific about how, or by what criteria, we do single out a particular 'mistake' as being more significant than a host of mistakes of a trivial or clinically indifferent nature. When such judgements are made they are obviously a synthetic judgement upon an understanding of the whole situation; they will be composed of history and philosophy as well as of general experience and specific 'scientific' knowledge—the same kind of judgement that is needed to say whether some programme, policy or piece of research has proved 'socially therapeutic' or not. (In other words, the qualities called for in the psychiatrist when analysing neuroses with a political fixation are much the same as those of the true politician or statesman.)

Money-Kyrle's work, like Lasswell's, becomes involved in a curious ambivalence between logical positivism (Money-Kyrle explicitly makes clear his debt to Moritz Schlick, his former teacher in philosophy), and tendencies inconsistent with this, which arise from the fact that the very notion of 'disease' is not recognizable in these terms, and from the fact that some not directly verifiable sense of 'the normal' must be gained which is not merely the sociologically normal. The type of understanding most often needed, and in fact most often used, is, surely, that very sense and knowledge of a *tradition* of politics that is a foolishness more than a concern to most modern social scientists, psychiatrists and philosophers.[1] Thus the 'therapeutic image' even at its very strongest and most explicit, as in Money-Kyrle, is far from creating a 'preventive politics' that would exclude the uncertainty, the resignation to conflict and the arbitrariness that Lasswell attributes to traditional concepts of politics. The substitution of psychological knowledge for historical analysis as an understanding of politics only begs more questions than it can answer.

All of Lasswell's many 'conceptual frameworks' fit into the therapeutic image. His stress on 'power' and on 'élites' were in part genuine theories of the sociology of politics. Even if they did not discover those evasive 'recurring uniformities of human behaviour',

---

[1] When a 'therapeutic' philosopher does gallantly venture into something more than criticism of 'the vocabulary of politics'—the late Mr. T. D. Weldon's *Vocabulary of Politics* (Penguin Books: 1953)—it is odd to see that he concludes by conjuring with the name of Burke in the name of empiricism.

yet certainly they pointed to aspects of politics often neglected in what he calls 'the democratic myth'; in many respects they were an overstated rebuttal of the simple moralism of progressivist individualism. But his hope to reduce politics to psychology is doomed to sterility. For different types of personality will all too obviously play different political roles in different types of institutional structure. If in Madison's great Tenth Paper of the *Federalist*, we add 'personality-type' to the concept 'faction', we see that the business of politics, while it is compatible with liberty, is not to destroy faction (or differing personality types), but to limit their harmful effects. The work of clinical psychologists both for individuals and for small groups may reduce the general level of tensions in a society, possibly far more than some of us can yet imagine, but this they can do— indeed, as by education—only *indirectly*; they cannot of themselves become or supplant political government, nor resolve all conflicts. For all conflicts are not those of personality any more than they are all of economic interest.

To take a last and an important example. Professor Paul Kecskemeti has asserted that: 'the problem of totalitarianism has become one of psychopathology: an approach which has played a considerable role in American social psychology since Harold D. Lasswell's *Psychopathology and Politics* (1930).'[1] But all this means is that a type of personality has been postulated that is called 'totalitarian', based on surveys and interviews in the United States, a non-totalitarian country. But the nature of totalitarianism cannot be understood merely in terms of psychopathology without viewing the great importance of *ideology* in totalitarian régimes as mere rationalization; without ignoring the modern social and economic conditions peculiar to the emergence of totalitarianism.[2]

Lasswell, despite his concept of 'the world revolution of our times', does not in fact recognize that modern totalitarianism is something unique, something more than old authoritarianism new writ large. Kecskemeti notes that Lasswell 'reached conclusions substantially parallel to those which have emerged in more recent American research'. The work he refers to, as isolating key factors 'underlying totalitarian personality formation',[3] is Adorno's *Authori-*

[1] Writing in his introduction to Karl Mannheim's posthumous *Essays on Sociology and Social Psychology* (London: 1953), pp. 4–5.

[2] As some still do. See a recent example, Frederick L. Schuman's review of the UNESCO, *The Third Reich*, in *APSR* (Dec. 1955), 1173–4. But Hannah Arendt's *The Origins of Totalitarianism* (New York: 1950), curiously titled in the English edition, 'The Burden of Our Times', should at least be an effective rebuttal of this view, as is C. J. Friedrich's 'The Unique Character of Totalitarianism' in *Totalitarianism* (Cambridge, Mass.: 1954) and also Friedrich and Brzezinski, *Totalitarian Dictatorship and Autocracy* (Cambridge, Mass.: 1956).

[3] *Essays on Sociology and Social Psychology*, p. 5.

tarian Personality again. Jacob Adorno certainly does not use the word 'totalitarian' in connection with his study, but, as Edward Shils well observed, the word 'authoritarian' even is only introduced in the title and two or three times *in passing* in the text. It is used as a synonym for the extreme 'right' of their 'right-left' personality scale of political attitudes. The curious nastiness of the word 'authoritarian' to the egalitarian liberal tells the reader more about the political thought of the authors than their concept tells him about political régimes; and, a smaller point, the high weighting given to anti-Semitism in their attitude-scale explains their failure to note the fading reality of the 'left-right' continuum of political attitudes: the authoritarian of the left is oddly neglected.[1] Adorno and his co-workers completely ignored questions of institutional structure and of the relation of personality to régime. The Constitutional State would surely be the poorer, not the richer, for the exclusion of all Adorno's 'authoritarian personalities', those who are, presumably, Lasswell's anti-democratic 'moral mavericks'.[2]

Lasswell, in conclusion, like Merriam, is to be understood primarily for the conviction which he had helped to spread that the study of politics is important (as it is, though probably not as much as he thinks) and can be scientific after the manner of the natural sciences. The many instructors in political science who complain constantly that their discipline is not as systematic or as scientific as even economics and sociology, take heart at the work of Lasswell. They feel that some day what they think of (often falsely) as their pedestrian work teaching State and Local, or Comparative Government, and their often suppressed avocation to do really scientific research, will be given a place by Lasswell in a new conceptual framework which will herald a genuine science of politics.

But, we have sought to show, Lasswell dwells mainly in a bleak

---

[1] See Edward Shils' interesting critique, 'Authoritarianism: "Right" and "Left"', in the Christie and Jahoda symposium, *Studies in the Scope and Methods of 'The Authoritarian Personality'*, *op. cit.* The editors commented that *The Authoritarian Personality* 'follows much upon the lines of Lasswell's early work', i.e., his *Psychopathology and Politics*.

[2] Shils, *ibid.*, puts this point well, a telling criticism from a distinguished American sociologist of the whole psychopathology approach:

'[It is hard to support] the . . . views that a large number of authoritarian personalities as such could produce an effective authoritarian movement. Movements and institutions, even if they are authoritarian, require both more and less than authoritarian personality structures. On the other hand, a liberal democratic society itself could probably not function satisfactorily with only "democratic liberal personalities" to fill all roles.

'The tasks of a liberal democratic society are many and many different types of personality structures are compatible with and necessary for its well being. Even authoritarian personalities are especially useful in some roles in democratic societies and in many other roles where they are not indispensable, they are at least harmless' (pp. 48-9).

and barren world of abstract and arbitrary concepts and of bare and unrelated facts. It is a somewhat cold brave new world in which as part of the revolutionary ideology an *Ancien Régime* is pictured where political and moral philosophy necessarily claimed a direct empirical political authority and where all authority, whether in politics or in education, was necessarily 'authoritarian' and anti-democratic. Lasswell himself, it is a presumption to say, is no dull mind; he is widely read and has a really exceptional intelligence; but his impatience, his eclecticism, his refusal to think through his assumptions, and his unresolved jumble of different types of concept and levels of meaning are fatal to the clear scholarship and the political sense of the many he attracts by his skilful manipulation of, to him, the twin symbols of 'Science' and 'Democracy'.[1]

Ultimately, despite the slow congestion of his technicalities and, often, just the plain obscurity of his utterance, there is a recklessness in his thought; there is a willingness to repudiate or to neglect the best in the political tradition of America and the West for his vision of a world-wide techno-scientific culture, his standardized material environment free from conflict, free from 'moral mavericks', free—we may add—from character and humility. His 'dignity of man' is not a witness to an affirmation of a vital element in the morality and politics of the Western world, but a witness to its degradation. 'I think, then, that the species of oppression by which democratic nations are menaced is unlike anything that ever before existed in the world. . . . I seek in vain for an expression that will accurately convey the whole of the idea I have formed of it; the old words *despotism* and *tyranny* are inappropriate: the thing itself is new, and since I cannot name, I must attempt to define it.'[2] Lasswell's theories do not define what De Tocqueville had in mind; they are dangerously near to being an example of it.

If one is not really alarmed at the direct totalitarian implication in Lasswell's manner of thought, it is because one does not take it seriously, because one believes it to be impossible to apply. But its negative consequences for American political education are at least worrying. This is not Lasswell's originality and influence alone: it

[1] There is a review of the *Policy Sciences* by Professor Hans Morgenthau in the *APSR*, XLVI (March 1952), pp. 230–4, in which he justly comments: 'There is an element of tragedy in the spectacle of two superbly endowed minds failing so thoroughly in spite of great ability and great effort. Yet that tragedy is not so much the tragedy of two men as the tragedy of political science and of philosophy in America. For as Mr. Lasswell is the product of a school of political science which was, if not hostile, in any case indifferent, to the necessary contribution of political philosophy to political science, so Mr. Kaplan is the product of a school of philosophy which sees in the history of philosophy primarily a history of errors.'

[2] De Tocqueville, *Democracy in America*, ed. Phillips Bradley (New York: 1948), II, 318.

should be patent that his thought is a symptom, albeit an unnecessarily aggravated one, of a deeper derangement in the wider thought of American liberalism, a derangement that has made plausible the confusion of science with technology and thus the generalization of this confusion, away from the proper boundaries and the logical coherence of science, to subsume all politics.

PART FOUR
Inconclusions

XI

SCIENCE AND POLITICS

It [English Idealism] was not a revolt against science, it was a revolt against the philosophy which claimed that science was the only type of knowledge that existed or ever could exist. It was not a revolt against the intellect, it was a revolt against the theory which limited the intellect to the kind of thinking characteristic of natural science.

R. G. COLLINGWOOD

1. 'Concerning the Alleged Scientific Method'

THE MAIN TASK that I have set myself is now done. I have traced the history and examined closely some of the fruits of the American science of politics. These last two chapters may be an act of supererogation, this chapter especially. But there are some conventional topics which, although one suspects them to be more empty of consequences than is commonly supposed, yet can be avoided only at the risk of appearing discourteous to the concerns of others and of being suspect of an evasion. And I now use the first person to touch upon the topic of 'scientific method' as a sign of hesitancy more than of conviction.

Although I have found it a more natural usage to speak more often of 'scientific method' than of 'scientism', yet nothing I have written so far has meant to preclude the possibility that the logic of 'the science of politics' could be based upon a misunderstanding of 'scientific method' or 'science' rather than upon a misapplication. It can confidently be said, even before entering into this obscure and often passionate realm, that 'the scientific spirit' can in no manner be blamed for bad political theory. What I regard as Professor Lasswell's repudiation of the great and good Western tradition of constitutional politics does not flow from the spirit of modern science, but from his own culturally conditioned (but not determined)[1]

---

[1] Or else many of my American friends could not have been so helpful to me in this venture.

derstanding and envy of *technology*. We all know that the pure scientist himself often has to fight hard against the practical, financial and psychological allurements of applied research. I have not suppressed Merriam and Lasswell's writings on the philosophy of science; they simply do not exist. But I think that I have already shown, perhaps more than fully, the great concern of Lasswell to reduce politics to a series of statistical techniques. But, be this as it may, there still remains the question of what grounds there are for the belief that there is a method or methods of natural science which can be extended to the so-called social sciences.

In the writings of social scientists many different understandings of science emerge, both of its method and of its scope, though all who identify themselves with 'scientific method' appear to claim that 'recurring uniformities' can be found in human social behaviour. Some have taken a simple 'facts and induction' view of science; others, more recently, have thought that they think in terms of what some modern philosophers and logicians have called 'the hypothetico-deductive method' (notably Professor Karl Popper). It might seem that Lasswell's 'conceptual frameworks' are an adoption of this 'hypothetico-deductive' method. But we have already seen that there is the utmost confusion in Lasswell between his 'propositions' and his 'goal-values', a confusion possibly endemic. His apparent use of hypothesis is sometimes a circularity of argument—he shows by Content Analysis that all people believe in democracy because democracy is what all people believe in; sometimes it is trivial—as in most of his studies in propaganda; but, more often, though he professes to take opinions as data, his propositions or hypotheses are an expression of a hope to alter people's opinions and behaviour in more 'scientific' directions, according to his 'ideal value' of the 'techno-scientific culture'.

Some natural scientists, of course, share Lasswell's persuasive and Utopian attitude to science and society. The so-called 'scientific-humanists' are often not shy of arguing on grounds of logic that scientific method alone is meaningful, and then, far from being sceptical about the possibility of a genuine social science, share the impatience of so many social scientists that politics has lagged 'so far behind' physics, and offer broad and seductive hints of a humanitarian science of society. For instance, there is a widely used book, *Readings in the Philosophy of Science*,[1] designed to fit undergraduate and graduate courses in Science, Philosophy and 'General Education'. It reprints articles from learned journals and books by a distinguished list of modern philosophers and scientists, including

---

[1] (New York: 1953), eds. Herbert Feigl and Mary Brodbeck.

Carnap, Einstein, Russell and Reichenbach. Most of the articles are of a technical nature, but Professor Feigl in his introductory chapter sets out to answer certain 'stock charges' which, he says, are often levelled at 'science' as such. One of these charges he formulates thus: '*Science cannot determine values. Since scientific knowledge can (at best) find out only what is the case, it can, by its very nature, never tell us what ought to be.*' Without the Thomist formality of citing the grounds for this assertion, he proceeds to his *sed contra*:

> This final challenge comes from theology and metaphysics. . . . The answer to this in a scientific age would seem to be that a *mature* mankind should be able to determine its own value standards on the basis of its needs, wants and the *facts* of the social condition of man. But it is true that science cannot dictate value standards. . . . This means we have to act on the highest probabilities available. . . . But such estimates of probabilities will be made most reliable by *the* scientific method. Common life experience and wisdom, when freed from its adherence to pre-scientific thought patterns, is not fundamentally different from scientific knowledge. . . . There is an important common element in *mature* thinking (as we find it in science) and *mature* social action (as we find it in democracy): *progress* arises out of the peaceful *competition* of ideas as they are put to inter-subjective test. *Cooperative planning* on the basis of the best and fullest knowledge available is the *only* path left to an *awakened* humanity that has embarked on the adventure of science and civilization.[1]

One may doubt whether this is any longer typical of responsible scientific opinion; but it is to this kind of writing that the social scientist and his unfortunate students turn.

However, even among those genuine scientists who have interested themselves in social problems, there are some who can only disappoint the social scientist. Professor Norbert Wiener, the mathematician, writes that he has declined pressing invitations by some sociologists to try to expand the social implications of his 'Cybernetics' into a general theory of social causation: 'I cannot share their hopefulness that sufficient progress can be registered in this direction to have an appreciable therapeutic effect in the present diseases of society.' For, he argues, the modern theory of 'small samples' in economic and sociological statistics 'once it goes beyond the determination of its own specifically defined parameters and becomes a method for positive statistical inference in new cases, does not inspire me with any confidence, unless it is applied by a statistician *to whom the main elements of the dynamics of the situation are either explicitly or implicity felt*.'[2] Now such a view puts the typical advocate of a

---

[1] *Ibid.*, pp. 17–18. Let *my* emphasis serve for criticism.
[2] *Cybernetics: on control and communication in the animal and in the machine* (Cambridge, Mass.: 1948), p. 191.

science of politics in a dilemma: for to appeal to the implicit feelings of experience of the observer is perhaps to open up all the doors of 'subjectivity' that he wishes by 'scientific method' to close, or is, at the best, to admit of 'scientific method' as a thing much more flexible than his case demands. Wiener himself does not seem to think it important to make clear whether the social sciences are inherently 'unscientific' or not, but he does seriously question the common notion that social science is scientific in so far as it can measure—'the complete description', as A. F. Bentley put it, 'will mean the complete science':

. . . in the social sciences we have to deal with short statistical runs, nor can we be sure that a considerable part of what we observe is not an artifact of our own creation. An investigation of the Stock Market is likely to upset the Stock Market. We are too much in tune with the objects of our investigation to be good probes. . . . Our investigations in the social sciences . . . will never be good to more than a very few decimal places, and, in short, can never furnish us with a quantity of verifiable, significant information which begins to compare with that we have learned to expect in the natural sciences. We cannot afford to neglect them; neither should we build exaggerated expectations of their possibilities. There is much which we must leave, whether we like it or not, to the un-'scientific' narrative of the professional historian.[1]

The contrast between the ideological *attitude* of Feigl and the scientific *attitude* of Wiener is sharp. And the difference cannot be bridged by any semantic agreement about the use of the word 'science', indeed, it would be quite pedantic to avoid the use of the word in many general contexts. There need be no misunderstanding of what we do *not* mean when we say, for example, that Noah Webster's lexicography was 'more scientific' than Dr. Johnson's, or that J. E. Neale's *The Elizabethan House of Commons* is 'admirably scientific'. But, all the same, the word in many contexts is obviously both a slogan and an understanding. For this reason, while it is important to make an obvious distinction between a 'hard' and a 'soft' usage of the word (virtually between the modern Anglo-American and the German sense),[2] yet there are so many shades of opinion between the two extremes, so much complexity and confusion to the issue, that such a distinction will only be treated by many social scientists as a well-meaning attempt at mere mediation.

[1] Wiener, *loc. cit.*

[2] Cf. Professor W. A. Robson: 'Political science . . . is a science in the sense that any organized or teachable body of knowledge is a science. It is not a science in the sense that physics or chemistry is a science; for these and other natural sciences are able to formulate general laws which associated in a precise manner particular causes and specific effects.' [*The University Teaching of Social Science: Political Science* (UNESCO, Paris: 1953), p. 51.]

There is somewhere a remark attributed to Poincaré that while physicists have a subject matter, students of society are almost entirely preoccupied with considering their methods. There is, indeed, no simple antithesis of rival viewpoints, of 'strong' and 'weak' of 'precise' or 'imprecise' science, although there is a vast literature of controversy. Differences of degree in the claim for the general applicability of 'scientific method' become differences of kind according to the varying personal judgement and prior social beliefs of the various authors and authorities.

But perhaps three broad viewpoints can be usefully distinguished. Firstly, some writers would maintain that there is no essential difference between the *methods* (or the method) of the natural sciences and of the social sciences, but that the degrees of probability of the derived laws are significantly different. Secondly, some would centre attention upon the *degree of generality of substantive theories*—more than upon the methods by which they are derived, and either claim that the social sciences can achieve laws almost as precise as physical laws or else, while holding this view in principle, regret that the purely practical difficulties against formulating social laws are immense, possibly decisive. And, thirdly, some would centre attention upon the truth conditions of natural science and claim that the scientist's concept of experimental or observational *verification* is the only mode of truth in any science, but then within this position the possibility of a genuine social science is still in question. All three viewpoints can be applied in varying combinations, in whole or part, to an understanding of the social sciences, each as either *inference* or *analogy*; and, further, these three notions of scientific method, of general theory and of verification can be argued as showing the absolute incompatibility between scientific and social truths—and this last form of argument could be maintained, in the most radical form of scepticism, without necessarily asserting that there are any social truths at all. I think it is not amiss to stress an apperception of chaos more than of simplicity lurking behind the subject of 'logic and scientific method'.

Morris Cohen, the American philosopher, in his much read *Reason and Nature*, gave a short summary of why social phenomena are more complex and variable than the subject matter of natural science, even when viewed purely behaviouristically. He pointed to: '(1) . . . their less repeatable character, (2) their less direct observability, and (3) the greater difficulty of isolating one factor at a time.' [1] Cohen argued that the most scientific kind of formulation that the social sciences can hope for, after rejecting the notion of 'laws of history', is 'type analysis': 'concepts like humanity, Christianity, the Renaissance,

[1] Cohen, *Reason and Nature* (New York: 1931), p. 351.

etc., that enable us to organize history and the cultural sciences . . .—convenient symbols to sum up a group of facts.' He then repeated his main thesis that 'the fundamental unity of common sense, social science and natural science is apparent', but that 'it will not do to dismiss the differences in certainty, accuracy, universality and coherency . . . as "mere matters of degree" ', for 'mere' matters of degree, he states, are important. On this argument it would not seem to matter what we call 'science', although he concludes with reference to 'type analysis', somewhat weakly: 'Though it is proper to distinguish this level of thought from the plane attained in the natural sciences we should not deny it the adjective *scientific* unless we are ready to eliminate such names as Galen, Leeuwenhoek, Pasteur, and Darwin from the rosters of science.' Cohen is certainly the pragmatist and not the logical positivist. It is interesting to see that although, as he presented it, there seemed no point of substance at all involved in whether we call history and ethics 'sciences' or not, yet in fact the cultural shaping of pragmatism shows through in the obvious prestige he attaches to the word. Cohen's book is an almost perfectly fitting methodology for the many political scientists whose actual work is pragmatic but who long for the supposed security and certainty of the natural scientist.

The obvious sharp difference between the precision of both the methods and the laws of the natural and the social sciences only deepens the question, What is it that the advocates of a science of politics mean by 'scientific'? To ask this question now, after considering the diverse views of Feigl, Wiener and Cohen, is to raise at least the suspicion that the whole concern with methodology is a falsely posed question. For a general method of research can hardly be at stake. There is no contradiction involved in saying that all disciplines have, in some sense, a common method; but that equally they all have their own peculiar methods arising out of the peculiar nature of their subject matter.

James B. Conant titled a chapter of his admirably lucid *Science and Common Sense*, 'Concerning the Alleged Scientific Method'. He chided 'a distinguished American biologist' for claiming the superiority of 'men and women effectively trained in science and in *the scientific method*' in problems of politics, industry and everyday life. Conant asserted: 'I believe that almost all modern historians of the natural sciences would agree . . . there is no such thing as *the* scientific method' [1]—a belief more questionable than the proposition it contains. (And there are no signs that Mr. Conant's subsequent public service was shaped by his own pre-conceived ideas as a scientist—as the social scientists like Lasswell would want and

[1] Conant, *Science and Common Sense* (New Haven: 1951), pp. 42 and 45.

expect of him in his unique opportunity, although, certainly, both his scientific career and his Ambassadorial career may be inspired by a deep, if imprecise, concern for truth and duty.)

Methodology is, surely, most often a retrospective way of describing what we did to discover truths in particular situations. Certain tricks of the trade can be learnt which will probably help us in discovering fresh truths, but we learn them from someone who knows how to use them, and one of the things we learn is that such a person is constantly adapting or inventing fresh methods to discover or verify the truths about fresh problems. Writers on methodology have been willing at times to recognize this as a description of the *genesis* of scientific theory: that each new theory merely modifies an old, builds on a traditional corpus of knowledge and technique, never presents a completely new theory and is only directly concerned with what constitutes verification when there is a clear contradiction between two deductive theories. But there is a reluctance to apply the same notion to ideas in the social realm: 'social engineering' is admitted, by analogy to technology, but only when it has purged itself of the moral philosophy and the philosophy of history, which are the traditional content of social theories and the inferences from the judging as well as the making and the witnessing capabilities of man.

There are some signs of realization among 'scientific' social scientists that science is itself largely a traditional body of knowledge, and also that the modifications by which one theory gradually gives way to a new one are often the product more precisely of the imagination and intuition that come to a good craftsman, than of the manipulation of a fixed canon of 'methods'. The frequent statements on this score made by Albert Einstein in his last years may have much to do with this. The advocates of a science of society in the 1920's and 1930's wrote a great deal of nonsense under the influence of the outdated belief of late Victorian science (as found in Karl Pearson's *Grammar of Science*, for instance) that objectivity in social theory was directly analogous to the supposedly purely methodological, inductive-deductive path of scientific discovery. But Lasswell is now quite happy to pay tribute to the role of 'insight' (it has recently become quite a fashionable word among social scientists), as long as these insights lead to verifiable results. He now praises, as we have seen, people who were anathema to him in his youth, as sources of 'insights' and, as he sees Bryce's work, of 'hypotheses'—to be verified. There are signs that it is coming to be realized that there are no general rules of method that can guarantee the discovery of new and valid knowledge. The important issue at stake, then, is not of method, *but of the mode of verification.* What is to be counted as true, however derived? What in general, in science and in human affairs, is meant by a 'true theory'?

I think it is clear that what the modern proponents of a 'science of politics' have sought for, above all, from philosophy has been an exclusion of empirically non-testable statements.[1] This is the common thread of concern, of far more import than either the framing or the actual assertion of general laws of society—in so far as any of these concerns are even logically prior to the beliefs in a science of politics. The writings on methodology that have come from social scientists have, in fact, been far more polemics in favour of 'science' than even 'how to' books; they usually mean by science simply a system of propositions testable by the direct observation of 'facts'. Feigl's *Readings in the Philosophy of Science* illustrate this. They tell us little about how scientists actually work and actually come to agreement; instead, they exemplify explicitly a particular modern theory of philosophy and, implicitly, a peculiarly modern theory of politics. These polemics are unnecessary in natural science because recurrent uniformities over long or infinite periods are everyday working assumptions; but in the social sciences no one has yet offered any example of a significant general law that is not hedged higher than its fruits by assumptions of *ceteris paribus*. This view of the priority of testability over generalization in the minds of social scientists seems the only respectable explanation for Content Analysis: it is deemed more important to reach statistically testable conclusions than socially significant generalizations; for the latter call for an act of agreement, a broad and less tangible historical or sociological judgement, indeed a personal or moral agreement, as the Americans well say, *to go along with* the conclusions. In this light, those who still expect to find general laws in social science are only too apt to find themselves in the unfortunate position of Professor Catlin, warmly demanding 'a political logical positivism' as a new 'ideology' in response to the challenge of Marxism.[2] They adopt the very philosophy that allows the least possibility for meaningful social generalization and explanation, and then, human, all too human still, try to make wishes into spells.

2. Concerning the Imprecise Concept of Politics

Clearly, to believe in a broad similarity in the criteria of truth between the natural and the social sciences is either to limit arbitrarily the range of meaningful discourse in politics, or else, as Cohen

---

[1] 'Scientific thinking', wrote Lasswell, 'is naturalistic in the sense that all propositions are looked upon as being confirmed or confirmable by data' (*Analysis of Political Behaviour*, p. 92). This is one of the rare, and thus so short, definitions of science that he gives.

[2] See above, p. 189.

tends (with his Jamesian sense of the diversity of man's purposes) possibly to under-estimate the clarity of what constitutes truth in the natural sciences. R. G. Collingwood was surely right to see the essence of positivism as an extension of the philosophy of the natural sciences into all philosophy. There is only a small doubt that such a philosophy can provide us with an adequate epistemology for scientific truths; but there seems every reason for doubt that it can help us in framing social theories and evaluating social truths.

For though politics is normally the application of experience to the creative conciliation of differing interests, yet in times when the preservation of the political is challenged, we cannot help but talk in evaluation terms, of good and evil. It is now often argued that the notion of ethical decision arises from conflicts of purpose between individuals or groups. The political scientist as 'scientist' wishes to remove all these conflicts in order to avoid the indeterminacy of ethical decisions. I think that it is not likely that conflict will disappear, but I think, to go a step further from the notion of conflict, that there are metaphysical grounds for ethical decision, simply because conflict also involves the physically paradoxical notion of *sacrifice*. The notion of ethics would be meaningless if it were just the description of the behaviour of the victor or the survivor, as in any theory of inevitable Progress or of a pseudo-scientific determinism. We commonly observe that situations can occur in everyday life in which sacrifice, even of life itself (*contra* Hobbes), is preferred to guilt (even though *we* did not knock the brat into the water) or to the notion of dishonour (that notion of 'honour' which Hobbes, probably correctly, felt to be at the root of the—inherent—instability of law). It is a proper usage of words when we say of a murderer, 'he is less than a man' or 'he is inhuman'. For there are some things within the physical capability of a man that he cannot do and still be regarded as human. It is so also with the notion of the political. Even when a political régime is duly constituted, agreed to as having authority in the conventional sense of a society, it cannot aim to survive (or to maintain its traditional territories) *at any cost* without ceasing to be a political régime, and becoming what Aristotle would have classified as a corrupt form of régime, probably today, a totalitarian régime. There are, then, limits to what even a duly constituted political régime may do. It is doubtful whether they can be meaningfully listed or precisely indicated in advance of crisis, protest and personal conduct; but that they exist at all is a premise of civilization. There seem to be a large number of ways of conducting a limited politics, but it is seemingly only in the practice of the totalitarian régimes and in the dreams of the social scientist that it is believed, as David Rousset expressed his understanding of the concentration camp, 'that everything is possible'.[1] This is to talk of an extreme condition, but the breakdown of politics may throw a little light upon some of its premises that are irrelevant to natural science and not explicable by its techniques and mode of thought. Only in these kind of terms can we understand why, even when a correct social generalization is made about behaviour, we can still, on occasion, honour the one defaulter among the ninety-nine conforming statistics. We must respect Antigone, even though it is Creon whom we really understand. Let me make clear that I raise the notion of 'ideal conduct' to delineate and to subordinate the sphere of the political, *not* to say that politics *is* the grasping for or the unfolding of the ideal.

Lasswell himself, we have seen, cannot help but talk at times in terms of moral evaluation. The notion of 'therapy' underlying his work is both an evasion and a tacit acknowledgement of the insufficiency of 'scientific' techniques to comprehend ethical positions. His error is not that he is really a scientist in politics, but that he is misusing the word 'science' to evade the study of the true origin and nature of his 'value goals'. If he did not lack initially any historical understanding, then the content of his ideal would probably be different—indeed his burning moral zeal might also, by taking on reflection and perspective, gain a more rational structure. The question that Lasswell will not consider is what he means by the premise or assumption of 'the dignity of man', indeed, what is meant by introducing such notions at all. I do not think that he is entirely wrong to use such notions even though they make nonsense of the other main elements of his political theory. Some such assumption is needed for any conceivable political theory, just as some initial assumption like 'the uniformity of nature', or the modern logicians' view of the principle of verification itself 'as a rule of thought', is needed if there is to be a theory of scientific theories at all.

Just as in Lasswell's 'dignity of man', a metaphysical viewpoint also underlies the purportedly logical rule of 'methodological individualism'—a phrase of Karl Popper's. It is no accident or convenience that this rule appears in political support of a type of liberalism, or that, in the concluding chapters of Popper's *Open Society and Its Enemies*, it appears much like the 'essentialist' view which the earlier chapters had so warmly castigated. This 'rule' is a rather ingenuous attempt to build a bridge from the logical principle of verification, as applied to the logic of the natural sciences, and to a particular, fortunately habitual and rather amiable, political doctrine. It would be a true summary of the reasons why we do not

[1] Quoted by Hannah Arendt, *Origins of Totalitarianism* (New York: 1951), p. 413.

count 'group reality' and 'group mind' concepts as basic explanations in political science, even if it did not apply to some of the purely statistical concepts in nuclear physics or to explanations of, for instance, insect behaviour in zoology. But does the rule remain just logical when we consider the behaviour of people who believe, for example, that only the class or the race is real, and proceed to rationalize society on that basis, and exterminate other classes and races? Of course, such a belief is the belief of individuals; even if they are willing to sacrifice their lives for the greater collectivity, it still remains their own decision and action. But the question of whether their sacrifice is reasonable or not, is not one of logic; and, further, the attitude of the methodologists (at least the ones I am thinking of) is rarely 'logical', even if worthy and expected, in face of the annihilation of whole groups of men. I think that the 'rule' also explains their own outraged behaviour, which we could not fully value if it were merely a reflex of, in Mannheim's sense, an ideology. The limitation of politics, while remaining truly political, from any such 'final solution' of conflict as the extermination of conflicting groups depends, as such moments of crisis illuminate, upon some sense of individuality that is not merely methodological. It depends upon a transcendent essence of personality that is not created by ourselves and thus cannot be utterly lost by anything that is done to us or even by anything that we do ourselves.

The 'scientific-humanists' are dangerously close to making that identification of human worth with right reason and then civic virtue that was the typically pagan element in the politics of Classical Antiquity. Our modern notion of liberty would be inconceivable but for the shattering of this identification by the Christian revolution of the first centuries A.D., a turning of men's thoughts to understand why even (or especially) the poor, the ignorant, the unreasonable and the unsocial have a transcendent worth (dignity?) that should be loved and can at least be respected. I do not wish to argue that Christianity is the only ground on which this reduction is possible— I do not know, nor know how to know, if this is the case. But I do argue that grounds of some such an order exist. In normal times these are known to us intuitively, but they become empirically evident in the breakdown of the political relationship—or in the totalitarian attempt to surpass it. For liberty, which exists to some degree in all *political* régimes, is not an end in itself—no more than the liberation or expansion of 'personality', but is the opportunity and the ability to attach value to concepts that are not of themselves directly political, social or, indeed, concerned with the mere business of staying alive. If liberty were an end in itself, then there would be no meaning to any values that are not socially determined and thus politically manipulable if their pattern is understood. Now, this is, in fact, precisely the claim of the science of politics: that *all* values are reflections of social structure, in other words, 'ideology'. But it is no accident that this social determination of all truth is also the premise of totalitarian ideology. For totalitarian ideology differs from the ideology of the *status quo* as described by the 'sociology of knowledge' precisely in that because it believes that all knowledge (except that of the new ideologist) is so tightly determined by social structure, that therefore, for there to be a new and rational order, all of the existing structure must be shattered, broken, discarded, violently overturned; partial reform is not possible, only total reform. We have seen this chain of reasoning in the more excited claims of the social scientists, though the vehement rejection of 'mere' politics by Merriam and Lasswell, unlike that of Marx, is palpably of the abstract word and not of the concrete deed.

In other words, the concept of politics can only be defined in the knowledge that it is a limited activity and that the limitations are, on the one hand, obviously physical, but also, on the other, metaphysical. It is the fate and perpetual ambiguity of politics to be the most important activity between two realms, two realms of knowledge that deal with different subject matters: the physical grounds of phenomena and the metaphysical grounds of belief. Now, this is not to say anything at all original, or at all precise about politics; there is a difference between knowing of a thing and knowing what it is. It is merely to say that politics is normally a practical, empirical, secular activity, which calls for little more than experience, common sense and honesty in its practitioners; politicians are not and should not be scientists or metaphysicians—though neither are they, in the modern sense artists, as is often said, though better perhaps, in the manner that Eric Gill saw the sculptor, craftsmen. But when the traditional concept of politics is challenged, in theory by the idea of a science of politics (which is really an attempt to reduce politics to ideology), and in practice by a politics of ideology, then it must be shown and, I think, can be shown, that there are real limits to politics.

This is little more than the sketch of a hint at a theory of politics, but if the area of concern has any meaning at all, it is sufficient for the present purpose of illustrating that the activities of politics and of political studies have little of the nature of scientific research. 'Scientism' is not scientific method in politics; it is an idealistic attempt to overcome the limitations and uncertainties of politics through an analogy that confuses the genesis, the verification and the application of the theories of the natural sciences.

It will not be amiss to state an example of a theory of politics that is meaningful, but not in the sense that the laws of science are meaningful. Let us take the celebrated final sentence of Alexis De Tocqueville's *Democracy in America*: 'The nations of our time cannot prevent the conditions of men from becoming equal, but it depends upon themselves whether the principle of equality is to lead them to servitude or freedom, to knowledge or barbarism, to prosperity or wretchedness.' [1] Let us grant the utmost rigidity of a scientific law to the opening assertion in this sentence (although the spirit of his work would suggest that 'cannot' is better read 'can hardly', a trend or a tendency, not a law.) Even so, he then presents us with a dilemma. It is what we will make of this broad *condition* of equality that is the important thing, something which cannot be elucidated by any fresh 'law'. But the assertion remains meaningful. It is, incidentally, clearly a more accurate forecast than Marx's notion of an increasing inequity. The question becomes not merely 'What do we mean by equality?', but—to echo Burke on *Conciliation with America*— 'What in the name of God can we do with it?' (or within it). De Tocqueville, like most modern historians, thinks in terms of *conditions*, not of causal laws of history.[2] Conditions limit our freedom of choice and can be delineated, as in the present example, in a manner not measurably precise, but certainly politically important. But the conditions still leave alternatives as wide as 'servitude or freedom', though both in an institutional setting likely to be, as De Tocqueville shows, unprecedented.

Lasswell, we have seen, also foretells a growing equality, indeed in a 'techno-scientific culture'. But he starts by postulating his 'goal-values', disclaiming that they are derived rationally or from deep historical study, and then proceeds to search for 'invariant inter-relationships' that can be manipulated to that end. Trends or tendencies, such as De Tocqueville deals in, are not causal laws (in this we can agree with Lasswell), but equally they are not derived from such arbitrary, simple and highly questionable 'goal-values'. De Tocqueville offers us, then, a tendency of history and an *understanding* of politics, not a law, based on a wide study of political sentiments and institutions: he finally offers a more concise picture of the dilemma that confronts us in the modern period. He describes the relationship between the non-Feudal original institutions of American society and the idea of democracy—it is conceivable that he exaggerates the force of this idea, but to refute him calls for a similar kind of attempt at a complete understanding of American history: there are no 'crucial observations' or particular experiments that can do this. He offers an empirical understanding of the relations of ideas

---

[1] (New York: 1948), ed. Phillips Bradley, II, 334.
[2] Cf. De Tocqueville's own fullest account of historical and political theory, as it is found on pp. 67–8 of J. P. Mayer's edition of his *Recollections* (London: 1948).

to institutions that is unsurpassed in modern political literature. And, in so doing, he uses a distinction of great importance for political theory, though one that *because* of its manipulative importance is now blurred in common thought: he distinguishes between *democracy* (as equality) and *liberty* (as the condition of right). He does this because he has a prior notion, not ungrounded but neither scientifically derived nor derived from majority opinion, of a proper condition of liberty and right. He writes in order the better to understand 'mighty evils which may be avoided or alleviated'; his analysis of the conditions of political theory and historical trend only show more vividly than before the need for a philosophical dimension of politics.

I dwell upon De Tocqueville as an example of a political theory more meaningful and important than anything that has or is likely to emerge from the 'scientific school', because I think that it is still the most obvious task of American political theorists to come to terms with the theory of democratic institutions given by De Tocqueville. He is praised in prefaces and quoted in chapter legends, but his theory of democracy and of liberty is not systematically applied or even widely understood. He is a greater political-sociologist than Marx and yet it has been Marx who has been the more studied even in the United States, probably in large measure because his theory *claims* to be strictly scientific. ('The freest people on earth' have a strangely morbid taste for determinism.) De Tocqueville dwells in the less precise and the more elusive human world of understanding and judgement. But almost every phrase he wrote in any of his works has a systematic bearing on the nature of democracy in America; little that Marx wrote has any relevance to American experience at all.

In conclusion, let me try to summarize simply the early argument of this chapter. There are three concepts that the adjective 'scientific' can qualify when it is used by the social scientist: firstly, a method as in the natural sciences; secondly, verification as in the natural sciences; and, thirdly, a theory with a degree of generalization as in the natural sciences—all or some of these things can be meant. As for the first, Conant is surely right that there is not nearly enough evidence or agreement to justify speaking of '*the* scientific method'. As for the second, I think it reasonable to maintain that there is a common logic of verification among what are conventionally called the natural sciences, but if this is applied systematically to the social sciences, it would drastically limit the range of propositions that we do in fact regard as important. As for the third, there is no true analogy to political theories, for these, while pre-eminent though not omnipotent in society, are not autonomous like scientific theories, but are limited in their generality by the very fluctuations of the conflicting interests that call them into being; and further, they are inextricably interwoven with a moral viewpoint, sometimes even when that viewpoint has little empirical realization.

The force of the idea of a science of politics, then, is not to be understood in terms of a perversion of scientific reasoning, which has an integrity of its own, but as a caricature of American liberal democracy, a growth upon it, when it loses touch, by scorning history and philosophy, with its roots: the protestantism of conscience against mere power.

XII

AMERICAN POLITICAL SCIENCE AND AMERICAN POLITICAL THOUGHT

Should history ever become a true science, it must expect to establish its laws, not from the complicated story of rival European nationalities, but from the methodological evolution of a great democracy. North America was the most favourable field on the globe for the spread of a society so large, uniform and isolated as to answer the purposes of science.

HENRY ADAMS

1. The Virtues of the Ordinary

IT WOULD be unjust, after having spent so many pages in criticism of American political scientists, not to enlarge very briefly upon our clear initial qualification that political science in the United States is and has been wider than those who seek for a science of politics. Indeed, there are some signs that the advocacy of a science of politics has now lost its earlier momentum and its dominance even may soon be in question.

The solid tradition of institutional analysis that stems from Wilson, Lowell, Goodnow and parts of Beard's work in the 1900's (and was much aided by the example of Bryce), has continued all the while and has far more to show for itself than the highly abstract theories and the mainly trivial research of the scientific school. Unencumbered by any more methodology than 'realism', 'pragmatism' and 'common-sense', there have been a series of special studies of particular aspects of American politics of a scholarly standard only surpassed by the very best of contemporary American historians. It would be both impudent and imprudent to essay a list, but a few obvious examples that come to mind are V. O. Key's *Politics, Parties and Pressure Groups* (1942) and his monumental *Southern Politics*; E. P. Herring's *Group Representation Before Congress* (1929); A. N. Holcombe's *The Political Parties of Today* (1924); P. H. Odegard's *Pressure Politics*, *the Story of the Anti-Saloon League* (1928); E. S. Corwin's *The President, Office and Powers* (1940) and his *The Constitution and What it Means Today* (1921, now—in 1954—in its eleventh edition); W. E. Binkley's *President and Congress* (1947) and his *American Political Parties, their natural history* (1943); J. P. Harris's *Election Administration in the United States* (1934); and G. H. Haynes' *The Senate of the United States* (1938) . . . the list could be continued.

But a weakness appears when one looks beyond these tall and well-rooted trees, even when they are in stands or groves, to try to see the shape of the whole wood. It is all too rare to find in them any sense of their relationship to American politics as a whole. For a general understanding of American politics the average American student is still forced into the attenuated mediocrity of far too many of the far too many textbooks; and the better student, in despair of these books, and the stranger, in ignorance of them, still turns to his De Tocqueville, his Bryce, possibly his Wilson; to Laski and Brogan among the moderns, or to the essays of a few native historians like Carl Becker, Crane Brinton and Henry Steele Commager. For all the textbooks with introductory chapters about 'the American way of life', there has yet to come from an American political scientist a general understanding of American politics that can equal the work of certain foreigners, except perhaps the now badly dated *Congressional Government* of Woodrow Wilson and recently the huge enterprise of Max Lerner's *America as a Civilization*. This lack is not primarily due to the enervating effect on speculation of the quest for a scientific method in politics, but it arises from the same conditions that made this quest appear so promising: the lack of perspective of pragmatists upon the apparent unity of their own presuppositions.

The work of most of the 'institutional school' has been saved from walking Merriam's high-road of generality by a certain pragmatic distrust of theory at all, and the best work—like V. O. Key's *Southern Politics*—has been saved from mere fact-gathering, shapelessness or triviality by a shrewd and habitual sense for the play of character and circumstance in party and factional politics (and by dry humour in accurate self-criticism, which was characteristic of the old Progressive tradition). But the work of generalization, the making explicit of a general understanding, has all too often been left to those whom we may call with no exaggeration, the hucksters. All this is the cause, not the result, of the unfortunate compartmentalizing of 'Political Theory' from 'American Government' and even from 'Comparative Government'. (American education generally, not merely political science, is dominated by the paradox of the *student* being forced to 'spread it thin' over far too many subjects, and subjects being broken up into far too many courses, while the *instructors* usually are driven to specialize within a subject more and more narrowly.)

The pragmatist as specialist usually has little of the hostility to the teaching of political theory at all that is shown by the would-be scientist; he often has a kind of old-American respect for such powerful book learning. He does not believe that the expository, classificatory 'history of political thought' as taught in the manner of Dunning and then of Sabine has too much to do with politics or political studies (a view which has much more than a grain of truth), but he would not wish to see it removed from the curriculum, as would many of the real social scientists. But he wants it to remain 'theoretical' and 'purely educational'; he suspects any generalizations about practice it may make—like the rule of the Cyclops, 'each to his own'. The best special studies of a hard core of common-sensical American political scientists, when taken as a whole, and related to the central problems of politics as a whole, vividly illustrate both the weaknesses and the strengths of the pragmatic attitude as a social-philosophy. There is more accurate information to be found about contemporary American government and politics than for any other nation, and yet there is remarkably less knowledge about the causes and conditions which could reveal the coherence, the significance and the underlying tendencies of this information.

One specific development of the last ten years should at least be mentioned, because it lies somewhere between the interests and methods of the pragmatic institutional school and those of the 'scientific' school: voting behaviour research. From this field have come some well-grounded, if hardly surprising, generalizations about the factors of social and economic status that incline a person to vote for one party rather than the other. I am not thinking of the attempts to predict election results—which have little to do with political science[1]—but of the attempts to understand why people vote as they do.[2] Now many of these studies are extremely fascinating and come as near to being 'scientific', in a popular sense, as anything in the social sciences. But however statistically refined they grow, they still depend, as Norbert Wiener said of the theory of 'small samples' in social research generally, upon 'a statistician to whom the main

[1] And should have still less, as Professor Lindsay Rogers argued in his pleasant and well-authenticated philippic, *The Pollsters* (New York: 1949).

[2] The leading studies are: Paul F. Lazarsfeld, Bernard Berelson and Hazel Gaudet, *The People's Choice* (2nd ed., New York: 1948); Angus Campbell and Robert L. Kahn, *The People Elect a President* (Ann Arbor, Mich.: 1952); Berelson, Lazarsfeld and William McPhee, *Voting* (Chicago: 1954); and Campbell, Gerald Gurin and Warren Miller, *The Voter Decides* (Evanston, Ill.: 1954). The last volume is a product of the Survey Research Centre of the University of Michigan, now the leading institute in this field. See also Samuel J. Eldersveld, 'Theory and Method in Voting Behaviour Research', *Journal of Politics*, XIII (Feb. 1951).

elements of the dynamics of the situation are either explicitly or implicitly felt'. The correlations will grow more accurate only as the questions that are put to the material reflect a deeper understanding of the long-run prejudices and peculiarities of American society.

Some of the students of voting behaviour do feel that their work is part of a general science of society, but some are scarcely interested in such questions, seeming to be just happily fascinated by the statistical theory and the practical difficulties of such research. The probabilities which they can establish illustrate the differences from anything like the laws of natural science in the social sciences, not the similarities: here too, *ceteris paribus* reigns, as witness how much form of social and income stratification was upset in the running during 1952 when the Korean War became a party issue. However worthy and fascinating such studies, the vote is, after all, but a small part of 'the political process'. There is a very real danger that the importance of voting can be exaggerated at the expense of the more important problems of party responsibility, influence and internal structure.[1] Obviously, some of the experts in this field, despite their sophistication in statistics and modern sociology, are still tempted by the old Progressive and Populist illusions that the more people participate in voting and the more they vote according to their 'objective' social and economic 'interest', the more smoothly politics will function. And there is also a danger, not so much that voting research can be elevated into a science of society—although there is plenty of talk of 'the decision-making' process as being the core of politics and the heart of voting, but that it will attract students of politics for the wrong reasons, for its precision and measurable objectives. This is not an argument against such studies—far from it; but it is an argument against the influx of people who, unlike the first generation of the advocates of a science of politics, are content to ignore the major problems of politics so long as they can appear to be scientific. 'Larger problems of the social milieu and, ultimately, of philosophy, enter into any defensible judgement of scientifically significant problems,' as Professor Barrington Moore, Jr., came to realize: 'Ill at ease in such questions, many technicians search for pseudo-security in a form of pseudo-precision.'[2]

The time may be near, as a growing body of criticism like Barrington Moore's illustrates, when American political scientists will be

[1] A co-operative project that pointed in a more fruitful direction was surely the American Political Science Association, Committee on Political Parties, *Toward a More Responsible Two Party System* (New York: 1950). The book has many defects, but it was centred on the main problem of modern Constitutional government.
[2] 'The New Scholasticism and the Study of Politics', *World Politics*, VI (Oct. 1953), 124; also my 'The Science of Politics in the United States', *Canadian Journal of Economic and Political Science*, XX (Aug. 1954), p. 315.

able to offer some general understanding of American politics. This will not be because a Foundation will subsidize another team of scholars to write another report on the state of contemporary political science, but because there is a growing need for self-understanding due to the profoundly changed context of American life.

From this need there may even come the possibility of some political scientists being able to recapture a sense of writing, if not for the whole 'educated' public, at least for the whole universe of discourse. The first political scientists of the Progressive Era had this sense, until Arthur Fisher Bentley foreshadowed a type of writing, by a second generation of 'realists', for which the audience was purely the profession (and a few indulgent inter-disciplinary specialists) and in which all too often a jargon reigned that only the profession could readily understand. Bentley, in his *Process of Government*, at least thought that he knew well what he was attacking—a moral didacticism masked as learning; but—it is hard to avoid the conclusion—his leading present-day disciple, Professor David Truman, in *The Governmental Process*, has lost all touch with even what he is attacking. And too many books by political scientists are now addressed neither to problems nor to public—as once Beard's and Dewey's were—but only to prestige and preferment in a needlessly bureaucratized profession. Pragmatism did try to give self-understanding to American society, but its vision was too narrow and its logic was too circular. It was powerless to protect itself against becoming immersed in the latent scientism of the culture; it was willing to criticize almost everything except the pride in technology and the absolute faith in progress which became called 'scientific method'.

Now, after the Second World War, there is little plausibility left in the hope that a professional science can provide the intellectual equivalent of the old envied isolation of American life, although the sympathies of old passionate allegiances and the momentum of the whole institution of research and teaching have now, ironically, become factors of inertia, a frustration to the active and intelligent. The world now presents the very antithesis of the idea of a closed system; matters of skill and matters of judgement are all too obviously unavoidable.[1]

A more precise factor is apparent in the above connection. An infusion of *émigré* and refugee scholars has certainly helped to widen perspectives from the rather narrow field that was an unfortunate consequence of the nativism and realism of Charles Beard.

[1] I think that it is no coincidence that the first sustained criticism of scientism with especial reference to American political science came from a Professor of International Relations, Professor Hans Morgenthau's *Scientific Man and Power Politics* (Chicago: 1946). But this is not to say that the 'scientific school' are not trying to create 'developmental constructs' for international politics: Lasswell is much interested in this.

Some of them, in varying degrees, like Francis Lieber of old, in accepting the American way of life, have tried to distinguish the light of universal example from the paths of a unique dispensation.[1] The dissatisfaction with the science of politics as political theory has created a large journal literature of debate, and although it has hardly got past the critical stage, clearly there are some writers and more teachers of political theory who are not ignorant of American institutions and who may pave the way for a restoration of American political thought.

Professor Morgenthau speaks of the need for: '. . . the restoration of the intellectual and moral commitment to the truth about matters political for its own sake. That restoration becomes the more urgent in the measure in which the general social and the particular academic environment tends to discourage it.'[2] Even in the UNESCO *Contemporary Political Science* Professor Thomas I. Cook criticized the 'scientism' of American political science and spoke of the need of a 'conscious search for unifying roots', a proposition that clearly applied not merely to the study of politics but to American political thought in general.

There have been of late several powerful critics of scientism within American political science: there are those 'commonsense liberals' like Professors P. H. Odegard, Charles McKinley and Arthur Holcombe who believe that the 'scientists' have deserted politics; there was the critique from the pitiless heights of Professor Eric Voegelin's high Calvinism; from the warmer pagan sympathies of Professor Leo Strauss's Platonism; from the gentle Anglican-Thomism of Professor John Hallowell and from . . . the list could again be added to. But none of these systems are likely to sweep all before them as the vaguer but emotionally stronger and more culturally popular American science of politics swept most before it. A restoration of political thought is more likely to come through what is needed to tackle the problem and subject matter of a clearer national self-understanding. This is the common task of both 'institutionalists' and 'theorists': to rediscover American history.

2. Paradoxes and Perspectives

The idea of a science of politics is, then, an idea that became at once profoundly American, and yet profoundly at odds with almost

---

[1] I think particularly of Hannah Arendt (though she is firmly 'outside' the profession), C. J. Friedrich, the late Waldemar Gurian, the late Franz Neumann, Sigmund Neumann, Hans Morgenthau, and Leo Strauss—the list is only partial. I do not cite these names as an invidious comparison with native scholars for it is still one of the great glories of American life that America attracts, receives and assimilates such people.

[2] 'Reflections on the State of Political Science', *Review of Politics*, XVII (Oct. 1955), p. 459.

all that is best in American political experience and expression. For while it throve upon a belief in a natural unity and unanimity in American thought, yet it has cut itself away from the actual reasonings and experience that underlay the great political literature of the early Republic. This literature carried within itself the danger that it could be treated wholly as doctrine, as a set of natural principles to guide all subsequent political action, not as a monument to a high ability in an existing practice of politics.

The skill with which Americans have in fact conducted their domestic politics is constantly hidden, and often hindered, by the willingness of American scholars and publicists to think more of the promise of American life than of the actual historical pattern. The glittering and decorative generalities are extracted from the early State Papers and treated as principles, timeless and unique; but they are ignored *as examples* of a practical and concrete political activity, to be emulated in style, but not repeated in content. Instead of drawing from their history a confidence in their ability to subsume recurring political problems, the American social scientist now draws on an ideology that seeks to overcome all need for 'subjective' judgement, ability and the knowledge of a tradition by turning politics into a technique of administration. In a manner, he but recreates the dream of Tom Paine to replace the rule of Government by the rule of Society; a dream that could even be indulged by stolidly anti-Jacobin Americans to give some popular clarity to the confused issues of the War of Independence, a temporary great stroke of politics, but, in the long run, an indulgence which has created untold confusion when Americans have tried to think about the purpose of their politics. All to often Americans have deceived themselves, as Condorcet did, that the great Federal Constitution was a triumph of pure reason, a masterpiece of technique, instead of the fruit of a long tradition of compacts and Colonial government.

The basic difficulty in American political thinking, and in the interpretation of it, lies in a very obvious and often noted fact: that the forces of traditionalism in America are the forces of liberalism. The American Colonies were, in broad effect, if not in absolute detail, already the astonishing spectacle of an England from which all the great conservative institutions had suddenly migrated. The 'Revolution' was, indeed, viewed as a war to maintain independence, or, more precisely, a multitude of independences. 'I think with you,' wrote John Adams to Jefferson in 1818, 'that it is difficult to say at what moment the Revolution began. In my opinion, it began as early as the first plantation of the country.'[1] From this continuity of liberalism in America, there flow two apparently paradoxical conse-

[1] *Works* (Boston: 1850–6), X, 312.

quences: a traditional anti-traditionalism, and an almost compulsive uniformity in individualism. If we take either as political principles or slogans, how meaningful they appear while there are 'rocks of power' for the waves of the 'dissidence of Whiggery' to beat against; while Locke can be read to Bolingbroke, to a Jacobite or to a High Tory by way of reproof, how much more meaningful and clear he seems. But when even John Adams and Thomas Jefferson can quote Locke to each other as their mutual creed, then the Lockean settlement becomes a rather imprecise work of descriptive sociology, not a critique of practical political wisdom; like De Tocqueville's apperception of a growing equality, it still leaves room for either an elevation or a degradation of what Henry Adams was to call the democratic dogmas. The passion of a belief in an original and continuing unity has come far to outweigh any clarity as to the nature of that unity and of the alternatives within it.

The paradoxes, of course, are only paradoxes from a rootedly European point of view, by which I mean both the views of Europeans and of those Americans who still try to define their own nature solely in terms of contrast and opposition to rejected Europe. To the ordinary American these 'paradoxes' are almost ideal solutions. But perhaps there is an intermediate perspective, of mind, if not of location, in which the resulting confusion in American political thought can be rescued from falling, almost in desperation, into the deep but no longer secure habits of ordinary American thought, the traditional anti-traditionalism and the uniformity of individualism which make the idea of a politics of mere technique so plausible. But first we must restate and develop our understanding of that plausibility.

The assumption of 'an atomic unity' between individuals as a basis for a science of politics was noticed explicitly in W. B. Munro and implicitly in all the other figures of the movement[1] (even in A. F. Bentley, for Bentley's 'groups' are no more than individuals writ large, individuals organically associated according to their 'interests', interests that *are* the personality of the individuals, and thus of the groups). That 'pleasant uniformity of decent competence', as De Crèvecœur had hailed the character of 'this new man, this American', slipped gradually into an assumption that individuals were or should be so much alike that all their behaviour in political and thus group activities could be reduced to measurable and recurrent uniformities. 'The reality of atomistic social freedom', Louis Hartz has written, 'is the master assumption of American political thought.'[2] But this reality has had an ambiguous effect. On the one

---

[1] See above, p. 173.
[2] *The Liberal Tradition in America* (New York: 1955), p. 62.

hand, it has been the 'free labourer' of Lincoln's words, with the pleasing absence of the servile mentality of the European working classes; and, on the other hand, it is the uniformity of opinion and the deadening of speculation about rational choice. Even the 'self-reliant individual', whom Frederick Jackson Turner sought to comprehend by his theory of the frontier, becomes—in Turner's own analysis—explained away as a *type* determined by environment, not as a free individual at all.

There is nothing more poignant in this dilemma than Jefferson's own prescription of precise books in politics for the University of Virginia, and his firm control of the doctrines of the Professor in one Chair alone, that of Law and Politics. What if 'Federalist poison' should subvert young men from their 'hard-won' individualism? Now the gross exaggeration in Jefferson's view of the Federalists is at least as significant as his remedy. The clarity of doctrine in his own Americanism could be unquestioned, so long as he could mistakenly treat, at least in politics, a John Adams as a would-be Monarchist and Tory. But when John Quincy Adams returns to the House of Representatives in humble Republican style after being defeated for another term as President, and begins the positive campaign against slavery, one aspect of unclarity, at least, is exposed; both sides then conjure with the sacred texts of Jeffersonianism, even to the death.

Political science, as a discipline, first arose in the United States to fulfil the practical task of maintaining a belief in the unity of American sentiments. This 'reality' was the subject matter of civics training. Certainly some of its academic founders tried to import intellectual categories drawn from German history, but these proved, perhaps not unhappily, sterile and inapplicable. However, instead of then turning back to a critical understanding of their own national history, the political scientists of the succeeding Progressive Era attacked history and philosophy in general, as conservative and obscurantist drags or brakes upon a further unfolding of the promise of the original American principles. They advocated a pragmatic science of reform, but it was, as a *pragmatic* science, at the mercy of the social ethos that it sought to make more rational. When, with the defeat of Wilson, that ethos changed from reformism back into an older purely economic form of liberal (but conformist) 'progressivism', political scientists were left with three alternatives, none of them entirely exclusive of the others. They could outflank mere politics by the alleged method of natural science, now understood more according to the logic of positivism than of pragmatism; they could retreat into non-contentious, purely factual studies; or they could continue to teach citizenship. All three alternatives were

strengthened by the fact that, with the passage of years, the g¡
State Papers of the Revolutionary epoch tended to be viewed less as
explanations of particular actions in particular circumstances, than as
timeless principles, needing neither rethinking nor clarification. It
would not be fanciful to call the would-be science of politics of the
1920's and 1930's the industrial equivalent of the early citizen literature. For when the actual *content* of those writings could no longer
serve as the actual explanations of the ever-growing success of 'the
American experiment', what was more natural than an appeal to
technology? The understanding of the American political tradition
becomes more and more rationalistic instead of reasonable.

For it has been technology and not science that has been the real
master-concept for most American political scientists. One of the
consequences of the belief in the unity and clarity of American
thought, which comes into play here, is a great closeness of academic
speculation to popular thought. Just as there has been a popular hope
to reduce all apparently great problems in American politics to legal
terms, so there has been an academic hope to reduce the study of
politics to mere technique. Both notions not only deny that there are
'real' political differences—which is largely true—but they assume
also the existence of a set of principles that are objectively applicable
to every aspect of practice. But, of course, both hopes are literally
impossible. If issues like segregation are surrendered by Congress to
the Supreme Court, the Court can only deal with them by writing
decisions, as in the recent Schools' cases, which are more like
shrewd essays in sociology and political thought than clear interpretations of the positive law.[1] If political studies (and some day
politics, too) is to be a science, then, to be also a democratic science,
it must be sure what democracy is; so then we get the alarmingly
confident and coercive series of definitions offered by Merriam and
Lasswell, far more *a priori* and sweeping in content than any but the
most eccentric philosopher of history would dare. Lasswell, especially, has responded to criticism or to self-criticism by the greatest
generosity in baring his non-scientific assumptions. But neither
generosity nor innocence is a substitute for learning from experience.
For to learn from experience is to reject any such simple notion of
politics as a clear 'means-end' relationship.

The uniformity of individualism also conditions the simple appeal
to facts, so characteristic of American political argument—as if an
appeal to facts would settle everything. 'Facts' in political science

[1] I refer to the historic decision, *Brown v. Board of Education*, 74 S. Ct. 686 (1954).
I am not saying that the use of the Supreme Court as a third chamber of decision for
political issues too contentious for a Federally organized Congress is not an admirable
device; it is. But it is a *political* function, only *legal* in a sense so broad as to obliterate
any distinction whatsoever.

are still affected by having been originally simple 'muckraking' facts, facts to be laid before the people for the people to judge. The true education in social science, Lester Ward had said, 'should consist in furnishing the largest possible amount of the most important knowledge, letting the beliefs take care of themselves'. The image of the muckraker may now have given way to that of the psychiatrist, but it is still the therapeutic discovery of hidden information that is the goal. If we knew enough, there would be no problem of judgement in social and political matters; in any case, the facts should not be interpreted, but put before the people—'The People Shall Judge'.[1] The scholar and the politician are often content to take their judgements from the beliefs of the majority—'Democracy', as Mr. Justice Holmes once ironically remarked, 'is what the crowd wants'. The first element of paradox, then, in 'the atomistic social freedom' is that while for all those who believe in it, it is never less than the warmth of a passionately-shared belief, yet for some individuals this combined force is oppressive, and for all it is enervating, no stimulant to a genuine individuality.[2]

In this highly atomistic environment, the 'science of politics' contains two extremes of political doctrine that should be distinguished. One is ultra-democratic, and the other is élitist. The relationship between the science of politics and the spirit of Jacksonian democracy has already been made clear. But it can also be believed that the principles of American politics are more promises than actualities; therefore, a scientific intelligence is needed to guide society towards a full realization of democratic individualism. These two views flow from two types of belief in 'progress'. The former view sees progress as operating through a kind of self-adjusting mechanism in society (though there can be, within this view, considerable tension between the primacy of capitalism or of democracy). But the élitist view sees progress as an immanence, restrained by 'metaphysical' and 'traditional' patterns of thought, views which scientific intelligence must combat to achieve the potentially greater rationality. Ward spoke of 'the artificial means of accelerating the spontaneous processes of nature', whereas both a 'capitalist' like William Graham Sumner, and a 'democrat' like V. L. Parrington, could view an extension of popular democracy itself as a natural means of progress, needing, certainly, scientific information to be put before it, but not

---

[1] The phrase of Mr. Justice Brandeis, which is also the title of the anthology used in the introductory social sciences' course at Chicago.

[2] May I again point to the University of Chicago for a telling illustration of this? In their *Calendar* for 1952 is the announcement: 'The University encourages the student to seek self-sufficiency in solving his educational and social problems. To aid the student's attaining this objective several kinds of counselling service have been provided.'

238

needing the guardian rule of scientific statesmen: the practical argument of Ward in favour of the 'sociocrat', but also the vision of Edward Bellamy's *Looking Backward* (one of the best-intentioned hells in Utopian literature). These two views, however, have rarely excluded each other in particular political scientists: both Merriam and Lasswell, at different stages of their work, sometimes within the same book, swing towards, in Mannheim's sense, both ideology and Utopia, acceptance of the *status quo* or radical reform. More or less consistent examples can be found of the crudest rationalization of the mere arbitrary present in the name of social science,[1] and of the crudest pseudo-socialistic élitism;[2] but the consistency is never absolute. American social thought appears to oscillate between these two extremes of 'mere opinion' and of *'scientific* knowledge'. The vast intermediate ground, in which somewhere lies the genuinely good and practical tradition of American politics, this only inspires conviction out of the practical impossibility of either extreme, and out of the largely uninterpretive writings of the historians.

The doctrine of inevitable progress still pervades nearly all American social thought, linking, at least psychologically, the historic individualism to the anti-traditionalism, and rendering more difficult any historical self-understanding. Hobhouse, as well as Bury, had formally distinguished 'progress' from 'evolution', seeing evolution as *any* coherent change, and progress as that change which we value. But though formally they recognized 'devolution', and thus that progress was not inevitable, yet clearly both Hobhouse and Bury, and the American social scientists more so, in fact treated moral progress as if it were necessarily cumulative, like technological progress. Now, if there is nothing 'inevitable' about progress, there seems only an emotional reason for using the concept. If the possibility of devolution is admitted, then 'progress' becomes merely an acknowledgement after the event that we are in a preferred position than we were before it. It is a form of psychological guarantee, but a dangerous form of guarantee, for a nation as for an individual. An individual, by insuring his property or his liability in motor accidents at too high a rate, can encourage a weakening of his own responsibility. For a nation to believe that the most important things are

[1] See Marshal E. Dimock, *Free Enterprise and the Administrative State* (University of Alabama: 1951). Trying to have everything at once, he speaks of his using:

'. . . the pragmatic, the realistic approach. The free-enterprise system then becomes a subject of scientific enquiry, the product of cause-and-effect relationships growing out of human and institutional activities as well as a system of goal values. Such a combination makes it more meaningful and more readily defended and improved because when problems arise in its functioning, it is possible to discover how they arose and what, if anything, can be done to correct them (p. v)

[2] See the interpretation that Harry Elmer Barnes put upon Lester Ward, above, pp. 65–6.

inevitably covered and secure is to delay the task of rationally clarifying the hard from the soft assets of a political heritage. The enterprise of ideas is then limited to the mortgaging and remortgaging of an existing practice, although the anxiety that leads to this for quest for assurance in fact points to a vagueness and a weakness in the underlying assumptions, and the practice itself all too often degenerates into mere activity, activity for the sake of activity.

The metaphor of insurance can be pressed a little further. For insurance, to meet its potential liabilities, depends upon the assumption of a closed system, that is to say, the refusal of those risks whose incidence are not statistically calculable: flood, famine and disaster, acts of War and 'acts of God'. And it is this kind of incalculable risk in politics, mass poverty and the class and dynastic wars of Europe, which Americans believed, despite the Civil War, that they had successfully evaded. *Within* a political community those accidents that are not insurable may be met by private charity and by government action. But the conduct of politics itself must be based on an understanding that is not helpless or meaningless in face of *external* contingencies; indeed, at the best, upon an understanding that can mediate and compromise with, anticipate and comprehend, external forces, even though they are not measurable. It is no accident that the first signs of an intelligent doubt as to the possibility of a science of society, among many ordinary American social scientists, markedly occurs after the Second World War.

The uniqueness and unanimity of American liberalism, her very domestic strengths, have made it hard for most Americans to understand the outside world and all those illiberal convictions and differences of temperament that are not merely due to unhappy homes. The weakness of American self-understanding plagues her in international politics, although equally the objective strength of her domestic political and economic practices calls down on her head a mixture of incredulity and jealousy in the common opinion of her allies. The general ideals of democracy as articulated the most in America, and the particular interests of America as a nation, these are somehow felt by both sides to involve a contradiction, although few other nations would agree to judge even themselves by such high initial standards. But the ending of the closed system of American expectations has engendered thought as well as confusion, a thought that is thrown back into trying to understand the nature of her own achievement, and what it can mean still to say 'these truths we hold to be self-evident', when palpably so much of the world does not. We are here face to face with the full difficulty of the second paradox in ordinary American thought: the traditional anti-traditionalism. Certainly a nostalgia for the past has not been unmarked in common

American literature—Mr. Auden's 'Enormous novels by Coeds' that 'reign down on our defenceless heads' are mostly 'historical'. But this has nothing in common with a genuine historical understanding. The past, because it is irrelevant, can be turned to for diversion.

However, the so-called 'new conservatism' while it shares something of this nostalgia, has also a more serious element, at least it is argued by more serious people.[1] But at the moment these writers are a polemical symptom of American unrest, more than contributors to a reinterpretation of American history and political thought. Francis Wilson seems to fall into the American 'New Deal liberal' use of the word conservative and to attempt the dispiriting task of giving the great publicists of business enterprise a Burkean flavour. Russell Kirk is a latter-day United Empire Loyalist whose love of Burke, and romantic nostalgia for Burke's adopted homeland, drives him into ignoring or distorting the actual American liberal political tradition and, further, into a kind of aristocratic transcendentalism that loses touch with the conservative virtue of historical understanding.[2] Whereas Clinton Rossiter gives an eloquent, if far from novel, account of the traditionalism inherent in the American Revolution, and he blandly calls the substantive doctrine 'conservatism', not liberalism or Whiggery. The 'new conservatives' are an interesting sign of thought, but it is thought that merely repeats the error of the old Progressive historians in attempting to explain American history by a consistent 'left-right' dialectic, only it now takes its stand on the ground that was once made, almost by definition, untenable. From Kirk's almost rationalistic attempt *to create* an American conservatism there does come, however, a criticism of contemporary American liberalism, such as could only come, we may fairly say, from at least a conservative temperament. Kirk, like Walter Lippmann too of late,[3] still regards the problem and perception of legitimate *authority* as being central to any politics. Amid his irritating 'conceit of culture', as a friend has called it, there is the solid sense that a constitutional politics is a blending of authority and consent; in Lippmann there is the attempt to establish a broader context for American thought, by showing that the exclusive stress on the *consent* aspect of politics would, in modern democratic theory, be entirely illiberal if removed from the restraining bounds of Parliamentary institutions that are, fundamentally, Medieval, not

[1] I am thinking mainly of Francis Wilson, *The Case for Conservatism* (Seattle: 1951); Russell Kirk, *The Conservative Mind, from Burke to Santayana* (Chicago: 1953); and Clinton Rossiter, *Conservatism in America* (New York: 1953).

[2] There is a challenging review of Kirk's doctrines in Gordon Lewis, 'The Metaphysics of Conservatism, *Western Political Quarterly*, VI (Dec. 1953), 728–41: see also my 'The Strange Quest for an American Conservatism', *Review of Politics*, XVII (July 1955), 359–76.

[3] See Walter Lippmann's *The Public Philosophy* (Boston: 1954).

modern. 'Authority' and the institutionalized expression of 'community', although concepts that far antedate conservatism as a political doctrine, yet are concepts viewed by modern American liberal theorists with a particular and a symptomatic dislike, indeed with a revulsion by the social scientist as scientist.

If there were a simple dichotomy between conservatives and progressives in actual American politics, there would be little difficulty. But the very recurrence in 'theoretical writings' of such an unAmerican protagonist as the conservative is a sign of how eager certain American liberals are to invent him, rather than of his political reality. Without a clear opposition that can be branded as 'conservative', 'authoritarian' and 'against the people', the American academic liberal would be forced into the task, far more difficult than polemical rhetoric, of understanding how much he himself does or should exercise authority.[1] It is a complete misunderstanding, for instance, though a typically American misunderstanding, to see the work of the late Junior Senator from Wisconsin as that of an 'authoritarian personality'. He may be so, according to the Adorno scales, but his tactics and support were fundamentally democratic, just as much as that of his predecessor in Wisconsin, the late 'wise and good' Robert La Folette. McCarthy's following was not a semi-Fascist rabble, but ordinary, decent Americans who could not but believe that a threatening outside world must be a result of an internal American mistake or treason—control of their habitual environment has always seemed so much a matter of American will; who exhibited in the uniformity of their liberalism an almost complete forgetfulness of that notion of tolerance of opinion which has been such a prized and hard-raised fruit of Anglo-American experience.

The only possible internal danger to democracy in America could come, as De Tocqueville clearly saw, through the 'tyranny of majority opinion', not through the tyranny of a minority. It is precisely this acceptance of majority opinion as the standard of right that we have observed as so strong among believers in a science of politics. And it is precisely in this clear perception of the tension between democracy and liberty that De Tocqueville's analysis is still fruitful. In his understanding of the need for both moral and institutional limitations upon democracy, there is an analysis that should form the starting point for any reconstruction of American political

[1] Two clear cases that come to mind of academic good-behaving liberals branding as 'conservatives' some bad-behaving liberals are Robert McCloskey's *American Conservatism in the Age of Enterprise: a study of William Graham Sumner, Stephen J. Field and Andrew Carnegie* (Cambridge, Mass.: 1951); and Chapter XXV, 'The Conservative Defence' of Merle Curti's *The Growth of American Thought* (1st ed., New York: 1943).

thought, particularly as it must now place itself, as De Tocqueville sought to do, in the wider context of the whole Western world. Unlike the 'new conservatives', De Tocqueville accepted egalitarian democracy as a *fait accompli* in America, so that his concern to temper the democratic principle with an 'aristocracy of talent' was merely to argue that democracy also would be weak, like France of the *Ancien Régime*, if it could not use its best talent in politics, could not draw some of its energy away from economic enterprise. This was not to recreate conservative England, but was to fulfil the already expressed hopes even of Jefferson, and more strongly of the more bourgeois Adams, that a 'natural aristocracy' could be drawn from a democratic environment, in contrast to the 'artificial aristocracy' of a class-structured nation. Neither of these men doubted that the policy had both difficulties and dangers, but its possibility lay in the ability and willingness of the right sort of men to try to play the role. The founding generation that created the Constitution was also the generation of the greatest and best leadership. Liberty consisted not in the average conduct of the average elector, but in the vitality and differences of the political leaders. There followed in Jacksonian times a revulsion of such men from personal involvement in democratic politics, almost a failure of nerve; and they gave an exaggerated trust to the formal institutions of the Constitution. The armies of the Civil War did not appear to suffer from the lack of an officer class to fill the middle ranks; the common sense, easy initiative, and talent for improvisation of American officers impressed even the Prussian and Austrian military observers, despite the Americans' terrible ignorance of drill. But this type of ability has all too rarely been willing to accept political responsibility. They are interested in politics as it touches their particular 'interest'; the member of the 'Third Chamber' of State Legislatures is often a man of greater ability than any in the elected Houses. All this is no new plaint. But it is important to see, firstly, that the theoretical problem is closely allied to the sociological one. The best men may enter politics again when there is an intellectual way of appreciating the importance and the nature of American politics. And, secondly, that men and measures both suffer when those who claim to inform the political thought and knowledge of a nation's education are also concerned, for the sake of the consistency of false theories, to reduce politics to a technique—and a 'scientific' technique at that, the student of politics trying to learn from the experience of the industrialist, not really from the natural scientist (who could teach him little, but an example of caution and humility), and scarcely at all from the politics of America's great statesmen.

The very weaknesses discussed, the uniformity of individualism and the traditional anti-traditionalism, spring from a high achievement, an achievement of a degree of liberty and relative equality so high as constantly to take away the need for understanding the specific and the universal in American political experience, however pressing the need for understanding the outside world now makes this self-understanding. The material abundance and ease of most American life are, cruelly, among the very things that hinder both the impetus and the ability to achieve self-understanding, and also make 'American liberalism', in the eyes of so much of the outside world, not a doctrine hard-proved through time, but an indulgent luxury of economic power. It is ironic that America, after having been misunderstood in the early nineteenth century as a universal prophet of liberalism and democracy, instead of as a peculiarly fit environment to nourish liberalism, once people came to her, is now, after having closed her doors to mass immigration, trying to recapture such a universal appeal for purposes of foreign policy. Britain, after exciting envy but rarely emulation, because of the obvious uniqueness of her politics, is similarly searching, or dreaming, of being the Athens of example, now that she is no longer the Rome of power. America seeks to recapture the image that she had before the days of her world power. Both, from the exigencies of foreign policy, are seeking to capture an element of universal truth in their political heritage. This is not an entirely mistaken or a necessarily dangerous enterprise. The particular motives may hinder such an enterprise, but to create thought at all is often to find soon a changed perspective on the problem. For the problem is not one of the art of drafting programmes or of public relations, but of maintaining the art of historical and philosophical discourse which is not the extravagance but the necessity of political freedom.

So this not to argue that the task of American political thinkers is to furnish an ideology for the Free World that can be stamped as slogans on tubes of penicillin, sacks of grain and the handles of tools to be distributed to the underdeveloped areas of the world. There are enough of these already. Wilsonian democratic idealism failed precisely because of the practical specificity of its content; it was at once a failure of self-understanding and a concession to a European misunderstanding that construed the example of a unique and legitimate nationalism into a dogma of national self-determination, which in fact meant (though never in America) racial self-determination. I am suggesting that something closer to the practical import of the 'national self-interest' view is needed, which is associated with the recent writings of Hans Morgenthau and George Kennan, their plea for a realistic and political approach to international diplomacy. But their theory of politics is itself a *plea*, masking an ideal: the ideal

244

of politics as a limited activity, not as an omnicompetent approach to conflicts of interest, whether the pseudo-competence of democratic ideology or of social science. As suggested earlier, the main task of modern political theory is to achieve a theoretical understanding of the difference between the traditional concept of politics and the modern concept of ideology.

Modern political theory, then, in its highest form, is concerned with the historical grounding and the internal logic of what is most clearly called 'Constitutional-Democracy'—'polity' is archaic, though 'mixed-government' is more expressive; but not with the absolute justification of democracy as such, as a political, social and educational principle. 'Democracy' is only one principle in a Constitutional politics, as liberal American publicists of all hues are now too apt to forget, unlike, for instance, Mason of Virginia when he argued at the Philadelphia Convention 'that we had been too democratic, but [he] was afraid we should incautiously run into the opposite extreme'; or like Wilson of Pennsylvania who supported Mason's plea for a direct election of the lower house by saying that he: ' . . . was for raising the federal pyramid to a considerable altitude, *and for that reason* wished to give it as broad a basis as possible'.[1] To these men 'democracy' was espoused not a catch-all concept of both organization and morality, but was a particular principle of —or within—*government*. 'No government', said Wilson, 'could subsist long without the confidence of the people.' But he did not mean that responsible *Government* as an executive authority is thereby eliminated or is even specifically enlightened as to what is its responsibility for the 'people' as an historical community, not merely as an aggregate of particular contemporary votes. 'We do not adopt the popular polity because it is perfect,' wrote Fenimore Cooper in his neglected tract, *The American Democrat*, 'but because it is less imperfect than any other.'

Constitutional politics is a procedure and an activity of creative conciliation because there exist many operative ideals and interests for personal and social life, not because none should exist (as a nuisance to rational calculation) or because any one alone should exist (as the absence of politics in Utopia or Heaven). Politics cannot make men good, but they can make it easier or harder for us to be good. And politics depends for its limitations, in part, upon a conviction that there is a realm of things worth doing for their own sake, as well as pragmatic activities—the distinction that Aristotle drew between leisure (*scholē*—to Hobbes, 'the Mother of Philosophy') and occupation (*ascholia*). It is not that politics can make

---

[1] From the debates of 31st of May, quoted in S. E. Morison, ed., *Sources and Documents Illustrating the American Revolution* (Oxford: 1929), pp. 239–40, my italics.

men good, but that only the existence of good men can ensure a secure and worthy polity. When a habit of disinterested moral speculation is no longer of a piece with an understanding of a national history, a political culture loses any ability both to be itself and to be a wider example.

The obvious danger of the awakening distrust of social science is that the motives for a criticism of scientism in many may be a purely pragmatic realization that the science of politics has not and cannot 'deliver the goods' amid the frustrations of world politics. There are some who reject it because they wish to find, in the phrase of the day, 'a fighting faith for democracy', or some such self-debasing nostrum. Mr. Whittaker Chambers in his too much maligned book, *Witness*, showed an understanding of Communism far more profound and subtle than any American political scientist had done. He showed how immeasurably stronger is the Communist purpose, faith and plan to anything in the free world. But he argued that the free world is doomed unless it overcomes its 'total crisis' by discovering 'a power of faith which will provide man's mind, at the same intensity, with the same two certainties: a reason to live and a reason to die'. Such a solution is only to create the disease more strongly in our own midst. Using social science as the faith instead of religion, Harold Lasswell clearly wishes to do just this: to study the techniques of propaganda and the 'science of communications' so as to inflict a ready file of short democratic definitions upon the outside world. But the primary task is understanding, not action (and an understanding that will show the worthlessness of such definitions for 'goals for research' or guides for politics).

As a small part of such an understanding, I think that it is not irrelevant to have tried to show how the idea of a science of politics should appear so plausible amid the unity of American liberalism and the specific faith in progress. For from within the substantial unity of American politics and thought, a better understanding must come. It cannot come from re-inventing a 'left-right' dialectic that has no relevance to distinctively American political thought, only a marginal relevance to some aspects of American politics, and even a rapidly declining relevance in the outside world. Because American political parties are so non-doctrinal, it is not the primary task of the political theorist to find their inner coherence, or to try to sharpen their outward appearance. The attempt to trace a theoretical coherence in party policies and allegiance is primarily the task of the historian, not of the political theorist. I say this because it is evident that too many fine minds, now in reaction to the aims of a science of politics, have studied insignificant or ephemeral Agrarian movements just because these movements had a doctrine and an ideological programme; but they have not come to terms with the main common tradition.

American political theory will, indeed, start and finish with the unity of American expression, but it will seek to deepen it and to steady it. It will seek to show that the element of liberty in the Lockean settlement is greater than the element of community power. It will seek to show that within the broad community of America subsidiary communities should not be distrusted merely to prove a national uniformity. It will seek to show that the very tension between democracy and liberty is a reason why the political institution is better than a nuisance even if it is incapable of rationally reflecting the precise structure of society. It will seek to show that the native political ability is hindered, more than sustained, by a belief in inevitable progress. Lastly, it will seek to show the wider historical and philosophical context that gives meaning to the notion of a sacred area of personal privacy. If political theorists in America can help to do these things, they will in fact have transcended the limitations of the Lockean settlement while enjoying its benefits; or, rather, they will have shown that in the long run its plausibilities are outweighed by its ambiguities, both philosophically, in the arbitrariness of its idea of natural right, and sociologically, in the changing of the Lockean-Jeffersonian garden of a village into the suburb of a city.

'The world will never be safe for democracy, it is a dangerous trade we practise.' The 'givenness' of American life can no longer be taken for granted, and neither can it be rescued by an intellectually empty citizenship training, nor by the attempted reduction of liberalism to scientism. If the idea of a science of politics could develop in the United States more fully than elsewhere, it was by reason of an existing high achievement in practical politics that could allow so much to be taken for granted, and could, when the first consequences of a lack of clarity appeared, make the turning to analogies with the industrial triumph seem more reasonable than a reploughing of the hallowed furrows, which might be ruts, of speculative political literature. The dangers of liberal-democracy, in other words, are in proportion to its possibilities. The American experiment can still lead the world into the greatest degradation of mediocrity imaginable, or into the widest imaginable extension of her general example as the country of the common man, which rightly treasures the image of Lincoln as a genuine criticism of the traditions of both Burke and Robespierre. To redeem recent American political thought from the sterility and narrowness of the idea of a science of politics, there is needed, not any direct change in political and social structure, but only an indirect change in the understanding of that structure.

For it is no longer plausible to view the American civilization either as a closed or happily isolated society—and thus a wholely predictable system—or as *the* society where a fixed system of natural rights had first been established and could then be generalized universally. The 'science of politics' has been a political doctrine and an intellectual movement passionately concerned to regain that original American sense of uniqueness and completeness which has been frustrated by the incalculable politics of an undeniable reinvolvement in a complicated and changing outside world. Such a movement could only succeed in the sense of forsaking actual politics for the abstract safety and certainty of pseudo-science.

'The world is largely ruled by ideas,' wrote Charles Beard in introduction to the first American edition of Bury's *The Idea of Progress*, 'true and false.' Constitutional-democracy is not weak and insecure until such time as a science of politics can render it perfect; it is fairly strong and fairly secure while we do not take such beliefs, and the class of such beliefs, too seriously.

INDEX

Adams, Charles Kendall, 24–5
Adams, Henry, 29–30, 228
Adams, Herbert B., 16, 24
Adams, John, 4, 6, 15, 234
Adorno, Jacob, 206–7
American History, *see* History and Political Science
    Literature, *see* Literature
    Political Science, *see* Political Science
    Political Science Association, founding of, 101
    Political Thought, 3–11, 133–4, 141, 233 ff.; *see also* Democracy; Progress
    Legalism of, 13, 237
    in Progressive Era, 73 ff.
    Unity of, 5–8, 9–11, 235, 247
    Revolution, *see* War of Independence.
Amherst College, 26
Anglo-Saxon Racial theories, 30, 97–9
Atomism, *see* Individualism
Authority, *see* Power

Bagehot, Walter, 25, 103
Bancroft, George, 29
Barnes, Harry Elmer, 39, 49–50, 65–6, 157
Beard, Charles, 75, 80, 83, 101, 111–12, 141
Behavioural Sciences, methods of, xiii–xiv
Benthamism in America, 9
Bentley, Arthur Fisher, 92, 118 ff.
Bernard, L. L., 156, 159
Biological theory, 37 ff., 56 ff., 89–90, 125; *see also* Darwinism; Spencer; Sumner; Ward
Boorstin, Daniel, 13
Bradley, F. H., on pragmatism, 89
Bryce, James, 100–1, 113–17, 171
Burgess, John W., 26–9, 97–9, 166
Bury, J. B., *Idea of Progress*, 39

Catlin, G. E. G., 143, 170, 189, 199n.
Chicago, 108, 135–6
    School, xiv
    'Trinity', 92, 159
    University of, 238
Citizenship, Literature of, 8–9; *see also* Politics, Participation in urged
    Teaching, in early Republic, 3–5, 13–15; in post-Civil period, 23–5, 32–6
Civil Service Reform, 32–3, 76
Civil War, influence on social thought, 37–43
Cohen, Morris, 217–18
Columbia University, 16–17, 21
Commons, John R., 40, 83n.
Comte, Auguste, 169
Conant, James B., 218–19
Conservatism, 6–7, 51, 98–9, 234–5; *see also* 'New Conservatism'
Content Analysis, 186–9
Cook, Thomas I., 111–12
Cornell University, 21
Croker, 'Boss' Richard, 33
Croly, Herbert, 77 ff.
Curti, Merle, 9n.

Darwinism, 43–8, 117, 125
Democracy, Constitutional, 245 ff.
    'Direct', 76, 166–8, 238, 242
    and Science, *see* Science and Democracy
Dewey, John, 74, 88 ff.
Dimock, Marshal E., 239
Dunning, William A., 135–7

Easton, David, 129, 177, 192
Eaton, Dorman B., 32–3, 105n.
Ebenstein, William, xii
École Libre des Sciences Politiques, 27
Economic Theory, 178; *see also* Political Economy
Education, expansion after Civil War, 19–20; *see also* Citizenship

249

Index

Eliot, Charles W., 19
Élites, *see* Political Science and Élites
Elliott, W. Y., 147, 170, 173
Evolution, *see* Progress

Fabianism, 110
Fainsod, Merle, 118, 123
Fiske, John, 30
'Formalists', *see* Institutional School
Freedom, 200
French Influences, 27
Freud, Sigmund, 110–11, 183, 201n., 202
Friedrich, C. J., 150n., 192n.
Frontier theory, *see* Turner

German influences, 19, 22, 24, 27–8
Gilman, Daniel Coit, 19
'Givenness' of American beliefs, 13
Godkin, Edwin L., 33
Goodnow, Frank, 101
Gosnell, Harold D., 138, 160, 171n.

Haddow, Anna, *Political Science in American Colleges*, 13–15, 23, 25
Hamilton, Alexander, 3–4
Hart, Albert Bushnell, 96–7
Hartz, Louis, 80, 235
Harvard University, political studies at, 5, 104–5
Haven, Joseph, 12–13
Hegelianism, 30, 59–9, 89, 114n.
Herring, Pendleton, xi
Historical Knowledge, 125, 128–9, 228, 240–4
History and Political Science, 30–1, 34
Hofstadter, Richard, 39n.
Holmes, Oliver Wendell, Jr., 37, 46, 127–8
Huxley, T. H., 43

Ideology, science of politics as, 189, 223, 245
Individualism, 40–3, 54–5, 74–6, 173, 193, 222–3, 228, 235–8
Institutional School, 95 ff., 112, 228–9
International Law, 22
International Relations, vii, 232, 244
Isolationism and Political Science, 112, 139–42, 228, 232, 240, 248

Jefferson, Thomas, 4, 7
and Teaching of Politics, 13–15, 236
Johns Hopkins University, 21–2

Key, V. O., 229
Knight, Frank, 170

Laissez-Faire, 9, 40–3, 50–6, 193, 239
Laski, Harold, 146–7
Lasswell, Harold D., xi–xiii, 100–1, 105n., 141, 149, 159, 176 ff., 213–214, 222, 225
Law and Political Science, 13; *see also* American Political Thought, Legalism of
Lemonade, 149
Lerner, Max, 175, 229
Lieber, Francis, 15–18
Lippmann, Walter, 84, 109–11, 123, 241
Literature, realism in, 85–7
Lloyd, Henry Demarest, 85–6
Locke, John, and American thought, 10–11, 247
Logical positivism, 189
Lowell, A. Lawrence, 102–5
Lynd, Robert, 175n.

Madison, James, 14, 64, 206
Malthusianism, 47–8, 56–7
Manifest Destiny, 20–1, 30, 38
Mannheim, Karl, 172–3
Marxism, 140–1, 161, 179
Merriam, Charles E., xiii–xv, 104, 105n., 108–9, 133 ff., 159, 177, 181
Michigan, University of, 21
Money-Kyrle, Roger, 203–5
Morganthau, Hans, 156, 232–3, 244
Munro, William B., 173
Myths, 182

Naturalism, 85–6
'New Conservatism', 241

Pennsylvania, University of, 21
Policy Sciences, 191 ff.
Political Economy, 22
Political Philosophy, nature of, 7–8, 36, 48, 68, 146, 174–5, 220–7
Political Science, as American Nationalism 29, 140
early Definitions of term, 3–8, 23
and Élites, 180–5
Founding of, 13–17, 21, 27; *see also* names of universities
and Group theory, 92, 118 ff.
and History, 21, 125, 241
Methods of, xi–xv, 101–17, 120–2,

250

Index

Whewell, William, 12
White, Andrew D., 19, 21–4
Willoughby, W. W., 58, 99–100
Wilson, Francis, 135n., 241
Wilson, Woodrow, as Politician, 76, 81, 134

Wilson, Woodrow, as Political Scientist, 25n., 26, 104, 106–7
Woolsey, Theodore, 96–7
Wright, Carroll D., 34

Yale University, 21